EVENTS THAT CHANGED THE WORLD

PETER MURRAY

EVENTS THAT CHANGED THE WORLD

**OVER 100 MAJOR EVENTS
THAT HAVE CHANGED THE WORLD
IN THE PAST 100 YEARS**

NEW HOLLAND

First published in Australia in 2004 by
New Holland Publishers (Australia) Pty Ltd
Sydney • Auckland • London • Cape Town

14 Aquatic Drive Frenchs Forest NSW 2086 Australia
218 Lake Road Northcote Auckland New Zealand
86 Edgware Road London W2 2EA United Kingdom
80 McKenzie Street Cape Town 8001 South Africa

National Library of Australia Cataloguing-in-Publication Data:

Murray, Peter A. (Peter Allan)
Events That Changed The World

ISBN 1 74110 149 2
ISBN 1 74110 251 0 (South African edition)

1. History, Modern - 20th century.
2. World History.
3. World politics - 20th century
I. Title.

909.82

All images: Getty Images; the Australian War Memorial (page 259)

The author and publisher have made every effort to ensure the information contained in this book was correct at the time
of going to press and accept no responsibility for any loss, injury or inconvenience sustained by any person using this book.

Editorial research assistant – United States: Jacqueline Horney

Contents

Introduction

It was August 2001, early evening, and I was on a Virgin Airlines flight between Sydney and Adelaide. The flight attendants placed me in row one as I was running late. On my left was a businessman returning from a hard day of sales in Sydney and on my right was a trainee pilot from Saudi Arabia. This was my first time in the front row and as the flight attendants casually visited and chatted to the pilots with the cabin door open, it struck me as unusual. But, Virgin was a new airline in Australia and their approach to customer service was different. I chatted to my Saudi Arabian neighbour who was dressed in traditional Arab garb and he informed me that he was training in Adelaide to become an airline pilot for Emirates. He had a strong accent and it was difficult to understand him. I recall thinking how unkempt he was, but put it down to his long journey back to Adelaide from Dubai. He asked, and was granted permission, to visit the pilot's cabin where he stayed for over 30 minutes, by which time we were due to land in Adelaide. Nothing strange at the time and just another business visit for me to the east coast.

Just four weeks later, I was doing my usual thing with the remote and flicked my way into the Foxtel news channels to be witness to the events of 9/11. CNN had gone live with the first images of fire in the North Tower of the World Trade Center, later to be followed by the actual collision of Flight 175 from Boston into the South Tower. Like millions of others I watched in amazement and horror. It was a fateful night. As the time passed, I watched people jumping off the roof of the buildings and wondered how many thousands had lost their lives. It was like a bad Hollywood movie. Hours later, the events of 9/11 were declared acts of terrorism and what unfolded was even more horrifying.

What would happen now had my Saudi Arabian friend asked to visit the captain's cabin? Would he even be allowed on a flight today?

Over the past 50 years, I have been witness to many of the events that have changed the world. Growing up in a country that was at war with its neighbour, my early years were filled with the sound of air raid sirens warning of possible bombing attacks. My father was an army officer so we lived in areas of high security and there was always potential danger. Stories of war were always told and my father was permanently drafted to dangerous areas. I grew up in a world that was reliant on newspapers, radio and newsreels. There was no television and we were hungry for news from any part of the world.

My interest in the history of the world has become a passion. The past 50 years have been an exciting time for our planet yet wars, famine, terrorism and natural disasters have played a major role in our development.

When considering the contents for this book, I decided that it was impossible to include every event that has made a difference. The period between 1900 and 2004 could be considered as an exciting era of development for our planet. Television, space travel, flight, motor vehicles, the computer, mobile phones, fashion and many inventions have altered the way we live forever. Exciting developments in areas of health and medicine have also made us a stronger population.

Events that Changed the World is a compilation of the most memorable events and developments that have occurred since the year 1900. Explorers take us to the top of Mount Everest, the North and South Poles, inside tombs and to distant reaches of our planet. Scientists reveal new developments including the structure of the atom, DNA and the polio vaccine. Inventors introduce us to flight, air-conditioning, the computer, the transistor radio, the microwave and television.

Over the past 100 years, war and terrorism have dominated the world's affairs. This book includes the events of recent times including 9/11 and the Madrid bombings, the Bali bombings and the new plague of suicide bombings. World War II was been pivotal in shaping the world. The events of the war including the dropping of the atomic bomb on Hiroshima, the Nuremberg Trials, Auschwitz and the attack on Pearl Harbor are documented in detail. There are also chapters on the Korean War, the Six-Day War in the Middle East and Operation Desert Storm.

We have lost many great world leaders including John F. Kennedy, Martin Luther King and Indira Gandhi to assassins. Suddenly and unexpectedly we have also lost celebrities and movie greats including Elvis Presley, Marilyn Monroe and Princess Diana.

We have witnessed many disasters including the sinking of the *Titanic*, the *Exxon Valdez* oil catastrophe, deaths in space, nuclear accidents and the introduction of SARS, AIDS and the Ebola virus.

The collapse of the Soviet Union, the end of apartheid in South Africa and the fall of the Berlin Wall have signalled the end of an era for many countries and a victory for freedom.

On the lighter side, *Events that Changed the World* includes a summary of fashion through the ages, the first McDonald's restaurant and the world's obsession to create the tallest building.

These are just some of the chapters that are included in *Events that Changed the World*—a memorable experience that will change the way you view our world.

PETER MURRAY

2004 Madrid Train Bombing

The devastating terror attacks in Madrid killed over 180 people and wounded 1800 others when bombs exploded on four trains during the busy morning rush hour of 11 March 2004. The attack left the whole world in shock and was the worst act of terrorism in Spanish history. The trains were full of commuter office workers, students and many young school children. Three of the trains set off from Alcalá de Henares station, 12 kilometres to the east of Madrid, and the fourth originated from Guadalajara, but passed through the station en route for the city. Later, the police discovered a stolen van containing seven detonators and an Arabic language tape near the Alcalá de Henares station. After further investigation it was discovered that the bombers had loaded rucksacks containing about 10 kilograms of explosives on board each train as they passed through the station.

At 6.40 a.m., as the first train drew to a halt inside Atocha station, three bombs exploded in the third, fourth and sixth carriages. At least 34 people were killed instantly and hundreds were wounded. Almost simultaneously, four more bombs detonated in the second train about 500 metres outside the station, killing 59 others. This train was running two minutes behind schedule and it is believed that the bombers intended the detonations to occur at the same location, maximising their power and causing further damage. Emergency hospital services were set up near the Atocha station to deal with the hundreds of injured passengers. Police found a further three unexploded devices at the station. As the third train pulled through the nearby El Pozo station, two more bombs exploded leaving at least 70 people dead. As the fourth train pulled through another nearby station, Santa Eugenia, the last bomb exploded killing a further 17. It is believed that each of the detonations was set off using mobile phones and highly sophisticated explosive devices. Thirteen such devices were reported to have been used, 10 of which exploded.

The casualties in this attack far surpassed Spain's previous worst bomb attack at a Hipercolor chain supermarket in Barcelona, which happened in 1987, killing 21 and wounding 40. The previous attack was carried out by the Basque armed terrorist group Euskadi Ta Askatasuna, meaning 'Basque Fatherland and Liberty'. The group was also known as ETA. However, the authorship of the Madrid attacks remains unknown. Early official statements identified ETA as the prime suspects, but the group, which usually claims responsibility for its attacks, denied any involvement. Later evidence would strongly suggest that Islamic extremist groups may have organised and carried out the attacks.

Chronology of Events

6.40 a.m. A train pulls into Atocha station. Three bombs explode.

6.45 a.m. Train 17305 leaves Guadalajara, en route to Chamartín carrying many school children and commuters travelling to work.

7.00 a.m. The second train, commuter number 21431, leaves Alcalá de Henares, en route to Alcobendas.

7.10 a.m. The third, 21435, leaves following the same route as the second from Alcalá de Henares en route to Alcobendas.

7.15 a.m. Train 21713, the fourth train, leaves Alcalá de Henares, en route to Príncipe Pío station.

7.39 a.m. Three bombs explode on the first train 17305 by Téllez Street, 500 metres short of entering Atocha station, killing 34 people. Seconds later, four bombs explode on the second train 21431 on track 2 inside Atocha station killing a further 59.

7.41 a.m. Seventy more people are killed instantly when two bombs explode on train 21435 at El Pozo station.

7.42 a.m. The last bomb explodes on train 21713 at the Santa Eugenia station; 17 people die.

8.40 a.m. The Spanish Red Cross puts out an emergency appeal for blood as supplies dwindle.

9.27 a.m. All incoming trains to Madrid are stopped due to fears of further explosions.

Opposite: Forensic experts look for clues around the damaged train near Atocha station.

2004 Suicide Bombers

Asymmetric warfare, where one side lacks the resources of the other, has led to those lacking turning to guerrilla warfare. One form of this kind of warfare is suicide bombing, which can kill hundreds of people, including the deliverer. The bombs range in size from a pack worn around the waist to the fully fuelled planes utilised by terrorists on 11 September 2001. Perhaps the most infamous suicide bombers in World War II were the Kamikazes. These Japanese pilots drove their bomb-laden planes directly into enemy warships. As the war became more desperate for the Japanese, the Kamikazes became more daring and their attacks more frequent. A lesser known group, the Viet Minh, also operated during World War II, using suicide bombing techniques in their battle against the French and Japanese. With the Vietnam conflict many of these surfaced again as Viet Cong.

In the last few decades suicide bombings have become prominent in the Middle East. This tactic has been carried out primarily by Arab men and boys, but recently bombers have included women and adolescent children encouraged by their parents. Much of their motivation is religious. Rewards in their 'afterlife' spur them towards becoming a martyr. There is also the lure of their families receiving prestige or financial compensation. None of these motivations is new. For centuries fallen soldiers have been hailed as heroes, honoured for their sacrifice. However, there are no moral lines drawn in the terrorist bombings—the more vulnerable the victim the better. Targets are undefended and innocent civilians, including women and children.

In 2000, during the Al-Aqsa Intifada, the second wave of violence and political conflict between Israel and the Palestinians, suicide bombings occurred almost daily, with Palestinians using the bombs against the Israelis. These bombings were crafted with maximum casualties in mind. Because the bomber is ready to die in the act, deterrence is extremely difficult. The only hindrance for the bombings has been in the form of reprisals towards the bomber's family, this undermines their motivation. These bombings are not limited to the Middle East. More than 20 countries have endured suicide bombings. In Sri Lanka, a guerrilla group called the Tamil Tigers has been responsible for more than 75 bombings since 1980. In Turkey the Kurds, or Kurdistan Workers Party, has utilised suicide bombers. After Iraq was occupied by the United States in 2003 suicide bombings became frequent. The main target, though others have also suffered, has been the US military. Although the bombings have been effective in engendering fear, the tactic has been less than effective in furthering each cause. The outrage by such action has generated a call to arms by all those impacted. There is a backlash to the brutality. Hopefully, the lesson will someday be learned that these actions, void of morality, will not go unanswered.

Facts and Figures

- The first recorded Palestinian suicide attack was a young man who killed himself and eight others in Afula in April 1994. 120 Israelis died in attacks between 1994 and September 2000.

- 440 Israelis were killed and 3000 injured in attacks from September 2000 to December 2003. Islam faith states that martyrs go straight to paradise—they do not die.

- From mid-2003 to April 2004 there have been at least 24 suicide bombings in Iraq, including four where more than one attacker has been involved.

- Suicide bombers are characteristically non-violent, quiet types. On 29 March 2003 an Iraqi attacker pretending to be a taxi driver needing help killed four US soldiers when his car exploded at a checkpoint. This was the first suicide bombing attack against US forces in Iraq.

- February 2003 marked the highest number of suicide bombers in Iraqi history. One of these bombings included twin suicide bombers who killed 109 people in two Kurdish party offices in a northern city of Iraq.

- In October 2003, four suicide bombers targeted the international Red Cross headquarters and three Iraqi police stations in Baghdad, killing 40 people.

Opposite: In recent years, outrage over terrorism and the subsequent repercussions have initiated protests and riots around the globe.

2003 Overthrow of Saddam Hussein

Ruling Iraq for over 20 years through fear and violence, the world watched as Saddam Hussein's reign came to an end on 13 December 2003. The dictator was captured after an eight-month hunt while hiding in a specially prepared underground bunker near the town of Tikrit. During Saddam's merciless dictatorship, beginning in 1978, he led his nation into wars with Iran in the 1980s, then with the United States and its allies in 1991.

In 2003, by his refusal to give up his power, he entered a month-long war with the United States, Britain and other coalition forces including Australia. After years of cruelty and dominance in Iraq, the totalitarian leader was overthrown during Operation Iraqi Freedom in April 2003, but he went into hiding soon afterwards. The Operation was initiated after the United Nations claimed that Iraq was failing to cooperate with UN weapons inspectors. US President George W. Bush pushed the UN Security Council for months to take a tougher stance with Baghdad. Coalition leaders including Bush, British Prime Minister Tony Blair and Australian Prime Minister John Howard, decided to act on their own. Bush gave Saddam a 48-hour deadline to leave Iraq and when he refused, the President ordered a military strike intended to demolish the Iraqi leadership. A massive air bombing campaign and land invasion followed, and US forces rapidly advanced towards Baghdad.

Less than three weeks later, the Iraqi regime collapsed, though sporadic fighting continued in the capital and other cities. After a few unconfirmed sightings, Saddam went into hiding and even after massive searches was nowhere to be found. Then, on 13 December, US military officials received information from a family with close personal ties to Saddam Hussein that he may be hiding near the town of Adwar, about 15 kilometres south of Tikrit. Six hundred US soldiers along with coalition Special Forces were instructed to kill or capture Saddam Hussein when found. Only hours later, Saddam was found hiding underneath a carpet at the bottom of a small 'spider hole' measuring 2 metres deep and wide enough for a person to lie down inside. Saddam, described by US commanders as bewildered and disoriented, was captured without resistance.

Chronology of Events

28 April 1937 Saddam Hussein is born in the village of Al-Awja near Tikrit, Iraq, north of Baghdad.

1958 Saddam marries Sajida. He is arrested for killing his brother-in-law and spends six months in prison.

4 September 1980 Saddam initiates a war with Iran, seeking to obtain Iranian oil reserves.

28 March 1988 Saddam gases the Kurdish town of Halabaja. Over 5000 people are killed and 10 000 injured.

8 August 1988 Saddam agrees to a cease-fire with Iran. Iraq wins the conflict.

2 August 1990 Saddam seizes Kuwait.

16 January 1991 The United States begins bombing Baghdad in response to Saddam not handing over Kuwait. In February 1991 the Gulf War ends.

January 1993 Saddam breaks the peace terms from the end of the Gulf War. The United States bombs Iraq as a result.

8 November 2002 UN Security Council resolution threatens 'serious consequences' if Iraq refuses to disarm.

7 December 2002 Iraq delivers to the United Nations a declaration denying it has weapons of mass destruction.

17 March 2003 US President George W. Bush gives Saddam an ultimatum. Either he leaves Iraq within 48 hours or the United States will pursue military action.

18 March 2003 Iraqi leadership rejects US ultimatum.

19 March 2003 The United States and other coalition forces start Operation Iraqi Freedom in an effort to remove Saddam Hussein and his regime from power.

24 March 2003 Saddam delivers a defiant speech on Iraqi television trying to rally his troops and unite his people in the war against the United States.

9 April 2003 Jubilant crowds greet US troops in Baghdad, then topple a large statue of Saddam.

Opposite: Saddam Hussein is dragged from his hiding hole by US troops.

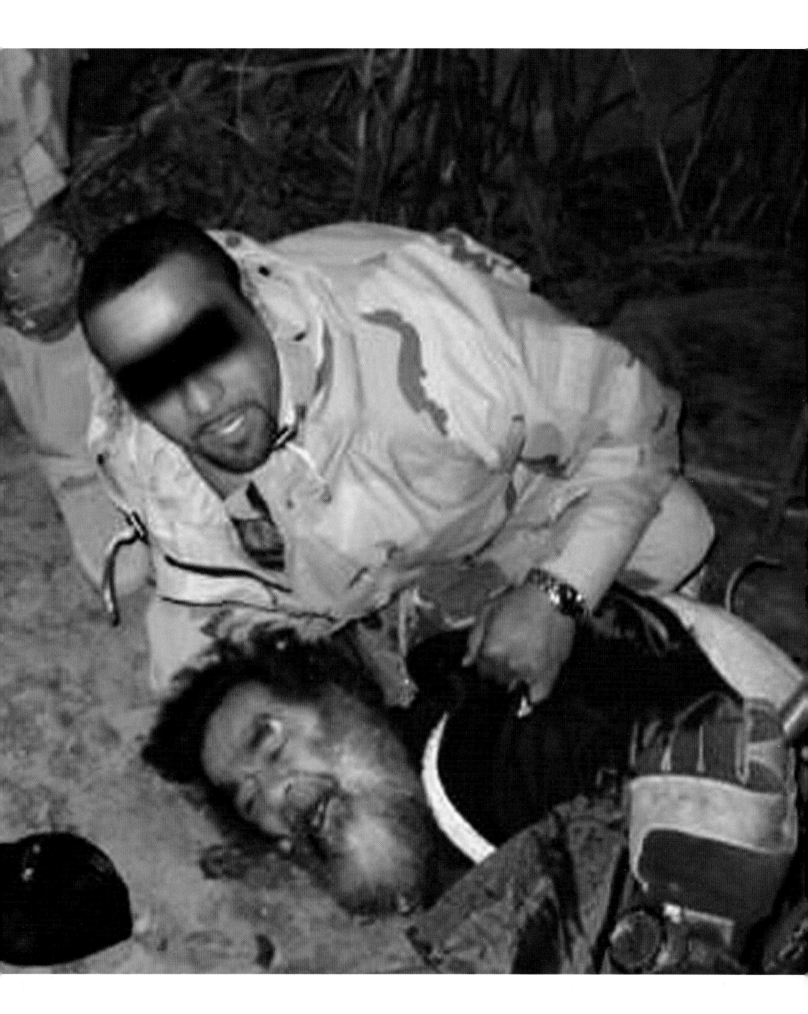

2003 Tallest Skyscraper

The introduction of skyscrapers has made the world a very interesting place and they have allowed us to use the sky as well as the earth for living and working space. In the late 1800s, builders realised they could utilise steel beams as skeletons for buildings. The outside walls were no longer part of the structure but rather a thin skin, designed only to protect the building from the elements. No longer bound by bricks, buildings began to stretch toward the sky. The quest to build the world's tallest building quickly took on the flavour of a race.

In the 1930s New York became the focal point as two builders, former partners, competed to see who could reach the highest. The Bank of Manhattan, rising 283 metres from the street level, looked like it would take the prize. Then, just one week after the Bank of Manhattan was completed, the Chrysler Building, which appeared shorter, was topped by a spire. The Chrysler Building enjoyed its status as the world's tallest building for one year. Then the Empire State Building took its place at the top, at 384 metres. It was not dethroned for more than 40 years. In 1973, the World Trade Center rose to number one, at 417 metres. One year later the Sears Tower in Chicago opened, at 442 metres tall.

Malaysia claimed the number one position when the Petronas Towers, in Kuala Lumpur, officially opened in August 1999. The elegant, slender, twin towers joined by a bridge at the 41st floor, rise 452 metres above the city. A new structure opened its doors in early 2004. Taipei 101, built in Taiwan, is laying claim as the world's tallest building. The 508-metre building has yet to be completed and the Council on Tall Buildings and Urban Habitants stated that the status cannot be claimed until the building is occupied and in use. Taiwan's President, Chen Shuibian, believes that the building will help bring Taiwan into the world's spotlight. Another building was set to open in 2004 in China. It originally would have been shorter than Taipei 101, at 460+ metres, but that has changed. The Shanghai World Financial Centre will now not be completed until 2007 and it is promised that when it does open it will be taller than Taipei 101. The skyscraper has become a unique form of art in our world, a study of structure, style, strength, function and height.

Facts and Figures

Building heights and rankings for the world's tallest buildings are often disputed. They are measured to the height of the structural top and are all inhabitable as measured by the Council on Tall Buildings and Urban Habitants. Other tall structures are not included.

1. Taipei 101 in Taipei is yet to be completed but will stand 508 metres high with 101 storeys.
2. Petronas Towers, built in 1998 in Malaysia; the twin towers are 452 metres high and have 88 storeys.
3. The Sears Tower in Chicago, constructed in 1974, has 110 storeys and stands 442 metres tall.
4. Jin Mao Building in Shanghai, built in 1999, has 88 storeys and stands 421 metres high.
5. The World Trade Center was destroyed by terrorists in 2001, but was built in 1973 and had 110 storeys and stood 417 metres.
6. Two International Financial Centre in Hong Kong, built in 2003, has 88 storeys and is 415 metres tall.
7. The Sky Central Plaza in Guanghou, China, was erected in 1997, has 80 storeys and is over 391 metres tall.
8. Chun Hing Square in China was built in 1996, and although it only has 69 floors it stands at 384 metres.
9. The Empire State Building, built in 1931, has 102 storeys and is 384 metres tall.
10. Central Plaza in Hong Kong, built in 1992, has 78 storeys and is 374 metres tall.
11. Also in Hong Kong, the Bank of China Tower, built in 1989, has 70 storeys and is 369 metres high.
12. The T&C Tower in Taiwan, constructed in 1997, has 85 storeys and stands at 348 metres.
13. Amoco Building in Chicago is next, built in 1973, it is 80 storeys high and is over 346 metres high.
14. Central Station in Hong Kong, built in 1998, is also 346 metres tall and has 79 storeys.
15. John Hancock Center in Chicago, built in 1969, is 100 storeys and stands at 344 metres.
16. The Critic Plaza, also known as the Sky Central Plaza is also in China, built in 1997, it has 80 storeys and stands 322 metres tall.

Opposite: The Petronas twin towers in Malaysia were officially opened in 1998 and became the world's tallest building.

2003 Exploring Our Solar System

From our small world we have gazed upon the cosmic ocean for untold thousands of years, but it was not until the 21st century that we were able to gain a deeper understanding of our solar system. The space exploration revolution changed the way we view our world and altered the understanding we have of our universe. At the same time, we were able to achieve what was once thought impossible—space travel. Ancient astronomers observed points of light that appeared to move among the stars. They called these objects planets, meaning wanderers, and named them after Roman deities such as Jupiter, Mars, Venus, Mercury and Saturn. The star gazers also observed comets with sparkling tails, and meteors or shooting stars apparently falling from the sky.

Science flourished during the European Renaissance. Fundamental physical laws governing planetary motion were discovered, and the orbits of the planets around the Sun were calculated. In the 17th century, astronomers pointed a new device called the telescope at the heavens and made startling discoveries. But it has been the years since 1959 that have amounted to a golden age of solar system exploration. Advancements in rocketry after World War II enabled our machines to break the grip of Earth's gravity and travel to the Moon and to other planets. This period has been deemed 'the Space Race' as Russia and the United States competed to achieve world firsts such as the first human in space and the first landing on the Moon.

Since the race started, much has been accomplished, starting with automated spacecraft then human-crewed expeditions to explore the Moon. Machines have orbited and landed on Venus and Mars, explored the Sun's environment, observed comets and asteroids, and made close-range surveys while flying past Mercury, Jupiter, Saturn, Uranus and Neptune. These travellers brought a quantum leap in our knowledge and understanding of the solar system and dozens of previously unknown objects have been discovered. Future historians will likely view these pioneering flights through the solar system as some of the most remarkable achievements of the 21st century.

Chronology of Events

Our solar system consists of a star we call the Sun, the planets Mercury, Venus, Earth, Mars, Jupiter, Saturn, Uranus, Neptune and Pluto. It includes the satellites of the planets; numerous comets, asteroids, and meteoroids; and the interplanetary medium. The Sun is the richest source of electromagnetic energy (mostly in the form of heat and light) in the solar system. The Sun's nearest known stellar neighbour is a red dwarf star called Proxima Centauri, at a distance of 4.3 light years away. The whole solar system, together with the local stars visible on a clear night, orbits the centre of our home galaxy, a spiral disc of 200 billion stars we call the Milky Way. The Milky Way has two small galaxies orbiting it nearby, which are visible from the Southern Hemisphere. They are called the Large Magellanic Cloud and the Small Magellanic Cloud. The nearest large galaxy is the Andromeda Galaxy—a spiral galaxy like the Milky Way but four times as massive and 2 million light years away. Our galaxy, one of billions of galaxies known, is travelling through intergalactic space.

Opposite: The Rosette Nebula lies in our galaxy approximately 5000 light years away and spans 90 light years across our solar system.

2003 Space Shuttle Disaster

The exploration of space has led to many great achievements for the whole of humankind and has revolutionised the way we see our world. However, there have also been great tragedies throughout the race to space and many lives have been lost. Over 20 cosmonauts and astronauts from the Soviet Union and the United States of America have perished in accidents related to space travel since 1967. The first tragedy was during a pre-flight test of *Apollo I* at America's Kennedy Space Center. On 27 January 1967, astronauts Virgil Grissom, Ed White and Roger Chaffee lost their lives when a fire swept through their Command Module.

The next disaster took place on a Soviet mission when Vladimir Komarov was killed as his spacecraft crashed to Earth only a few months after the *Apollo I* catastrophe. On 23 April 1967, Komarov's parachute failed to open due to problems with a pressure sensor, making the spacecraft fall to Earth almost undamaged. This accident delayed further missions, dooming the Soviet's plan to land the first man on the Moon. Another devastating accident occurred in a later *Soyuz* mission. *Soyuz 11* successfully carried cosmonauts Georgi Dobrovolski, Viktor Patsayev and Vladislav Volkov to live on the world's first space station in 1971. After a normal re-entry to Earth, the recovery team opened the capsule to find the crew dead. It was later determined that the crew had died of asphyxiation due to a faulty valve. In 1986, seven American astronauts died when the space shuttle *Challenger* exploded during take-off. The shuttle was carrying five men and two women, including the first civilian in space. Only 73 seconds into the flight the shuttle blew up as the world watched the disaster live on their televisions. Danger from falling debris prevented rescue boats from reaching the scene for over an hour. On 1 February 2003, the space shuttle *Columbia* broke apart in flames about 60 000 metres over Texas, 16 minutes before it was supposed to touch down in Florida. All seven on board were killed. The shuttle's 16–day science mission was over and as it was heading toward Earth, system failure occurred causing the shuttle to explode. These deaths were tragic sacrifices in the development of space travel. Many safety precautions were taken after each accident, making future missions safer.

Chronology of Events

1 February 2003 It is a perfect day to land the shuttle. There are no weather issues to complicate the orbiter's final approach to the Kennedy Space Center in Florida and the touchdown is set for 9.16 a.m.

8.15 a.m. Space shuttle *Columbia* fires its braking rockets and streaks toward touchdown.

8.53 a.m. Ground controllers lose data from four temperature indicators on the inboard and outboard hydraulic systems on the left side of the spacecraft. The shuttle is functioning normally otherwise, so the crew is not alerted. The shuttle is currently over California.

8:56 a.m. As *Columbia* moves over Nevada, sensors detect a rise in temperature and pressure in the tyres on the shuttle's left-side landing gear.

8.58 a.m. Data is lost from three temperature sensors embedded in the shuttle's left wing.

8.59 a.m. Data is lost from tyre temperature and pressure sensors on the shuttle's left side. One of the sensors alerts the crew, when communication is lost.

9.00 a.m. All vehicle data is lost. The shuttle is 207 135 feet over north-central Texas and is travelling about Mach 18.3, 18 times the speed of sound. NASA officials try to re-establish communication for several minutes. Texas and Louisiana residents report a loud noise and bright balls—shuttle debris—in the sky.

9.29 a.m. NASA declares an emergency.

1 p.m. NASA administrators officially announce the loss of the shuttle and all on board.

2 p.m. The President addresses the nation from the Cabinet Room at the White House. 'Columbia is lost,' he says. 'There are no survivors.'

3.20 p.m. NASA suspends shuttle flights for the length of the investigation. The Texas public safety department reported more than 2000 debris fields, scattered from the small town of Nacogdoches, about 270 kilometres south-east of Dallas, to the Louisiana border.

Opposite: The space shuttle Challenger *explodes 73 seconds after take-off from the Kennedy Space Center, Florida, claiming the lives of all seven on board.*

2002 The SARS Virus

In November 2002 in Guangdong province, a Chinese farmer in Foshan county was admitted to hospital and diagnosed with severe pneumonia. However it was not until mid-February the following year that the People's Republic of China shook the world with an announcement that an apparent outbreak of an unknown virus had left 305 people infected and resulted in five deaths in Southern China. The disease was eventually identified as SARS, Severe Acute Respiratory Syndrome, which soon became a global epidemic infecting thousands. Symptoms of the illness begin with a high fever accompanied by chills, headaches and body aches. After a few days a dry cough develops, which often progresses to pneumonia.

At the onset, the Chinese government tried to cover up the outbreak but soon lost control of the situation. Finally, in February 2003, the outbreak was reported in Asia. The World Health Organisation (WHO) was alarmed and issued a global alert in March. The WHO recommended postponing non-essential travel and travel to and from the affected areas came to a standstill, but the disease continued to spread rapidly. Vietnam, Hong Kong, Singapore and Canada began to report cases of SARS. Eventually the disease impacted two dozen countries in North and South America, Europe and Asia. Soon the whole world was in a state of panic. In the United States, the University of California at Berkeley refused to accept students from China and other regions of Asia affected by SARS for the summer season.

By May, European health ministers met in an emergency session intended to standardise measures to combat SARS across the continent. Laboratories from countries across the globe joined together to battle the disease. Extraordinary progress was made because of the mutual cooperation and collaboration. By May, the outbreak started to slow in momentum and the WHO began to lift travel restrictions. Although some patients unexpectedly suffered relapses, June saw great success in overcoming the epidemic. By July, the last restriction was lifted and the epidemic was declared over. More than 8000 people were infected by SARS during the epidemic, resulting in 774 deaths. Only the worldwide effort kept the situation from growing into a greater tragedy.

Chronology of Events

16 November 2002 An outbreak of what is first suspected as severe pneumonia, but actually SARS (Severe Acute Respiratory Syndrome) begins in the Guangdong province of China.

10 February 2003 The People's Republic of China finally notifies the WHO about the sudden outbreak, reporting 305 cases including five deaths. Later the Chinese government apologises for delays in reporting the epidemic.

21 February 2003 A Chinese doctor who had treated cases in Guangdong checks in at a Hong Kong hotel and infects up to 12 other guests. He later dies, but it is estimated that up to 80 per cent of the cases in Hong Kong derived from the doctor.

25 March 2003 Nine tourists in Hong Kong are diagnosed with the disease when a Chinese man infects them during a flight to Beijing. The Singapore government enforces compulsory quarantine of any infected person.

30 March 2003 Hong Kong authorities quarantine Block E of the Amoy Garden Apartments due to more than 200 cases in the building.

4 April 2003 Chinese Health Minister announces the disease is under control in mainland China and releases the names of drugs claimed to be effective in curing the syndrome.

8 April 2003 Hong Kong health officials warn that SARS has spread so far domestically and internationally that it could be here to stay. The WHO remains optimistic.

16 April 2003 The virus is officially named SARS after the Director of the Michael Smith Genome Sciences Centre announces that they have broken the genetic code of the virus suspected of causing the disease.

4 May 2003 The newly infected number of people in Hong Kong drops to a single digit.

23 May 2003 After a re-count of the number of SARS patients in hospital, WHO lifts the tourism warning from Hong Kong and Guangdong.

Opposite: A Chinese medical worker puts on her mask as she prepares to enter a hospital in Beijing.

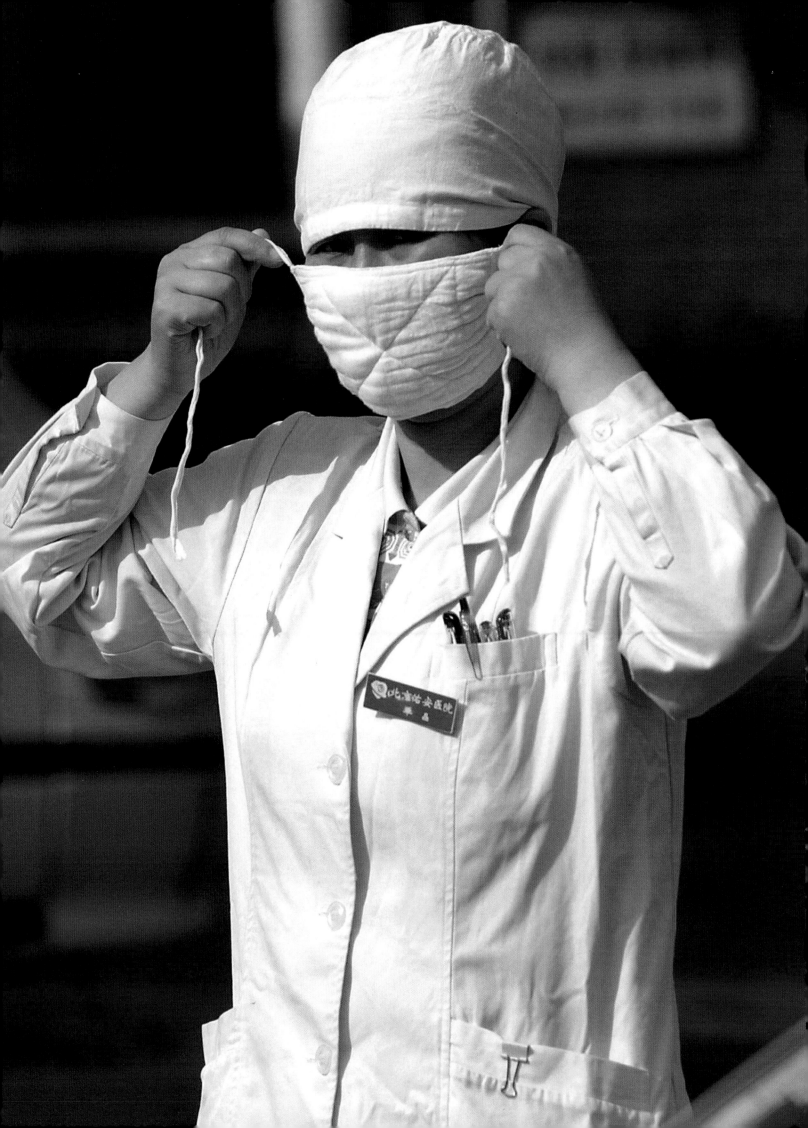

2002 The Bali Bombing

Thousands of tourists are drawn to Bali each year to experience its beautiful beaches, many markets and relaxing atmosphere. The international playground Bali offers is set in Indonesia, which happens to have the world's largest population of Muslims. Though it is a predominantly Buddhist island, Bali was chosen as the location where terrorist group Jemaah Islamiyah would strike on 12 October 2002, killing almost 200 people, most of them tourists.

Saturday 12 October was sunny and beautiful. Once night fell, festivities moved indoors and many tourists packed the local nightclubs in the Kuta Beach district. On Saturday night just after 11.00 p.m. the otherwise perfect day was shattered by the worst act of terrorism in Indonesia's history. Three bombs had been strategically placed and timed to cause the largest loss of lives. Two of the bombs, smaller in size, were planted outside two popular night spots—Paddy's Irish Bar and the Sari Club. They went off first and were designed to move people into the streets. The last bomb, in a Mitsubishi L-300 minivan, was designed for maximum destruction and detonated after the streets were filled. The block where the explosion occurred was destroyed by the blast and subsequent fire. Hundreds of tourists found themselves in a burning nightmare. People fled the area, some on fire and most tripping over what moments before had been fellow revellers, now dead.

During the next several hours many showed themselves as heroes. Rescue workers and volunteers risked their lives to rescue the blast victims from burning buildings. The wounded filled nearby hospitals and clinics, with more volunteers rushing to assist. Early Sunday morning the task became grimmer as the focus turned to those who had died. In all, 190 died in the tragedy and more than 100 were wounded. The following days were filled with some rejoicing as friends and families were reunited, but more tears flowed as the death toll rose. Many of the victims were from Australia, but 24 countries in all suffered casualties. The investigation and manhunt for the bombers followed. Less than a month later the first suspect was arrested and by the spring, trials began. Several of those responsible were brought to justice, but the fight against terrorism continues.

Chronology of Events

April 2002 Jemaah Islamiyah member, Muklas, returns to his home town of Tenggulun to plan an attack. He meets his brother Amrozi and they decide to target Bali.

September 2002 Chlorate and other chemicals bought by Amrozi are packed up in cigarette boxes and taken to the bus depot in Surabaya where they begin their journey to Denpasar, Bali.

5 October 2002 Amrozi, Idris, Ali Imron and Dulmatin arrive in Bali and check into the Hotel Harum in Denpasar. They hold a meeting with other terrorists.

12 October 2002 At 11.00 p.m., a car packed with bombs is driven to Kuta and parked outside the Sari Club. Soon after, a mobile phone detonator is called and the bomb explodes, killing 190 people and wounding a further 100.

October 2002 The United Nations lists Jemaah Islamiyah as a terrorist organisation.

5 November 2002 Amrozi is arrested in Tenggulun, East Java. He confesses to owning the minivan used in the Sari Club attack and names others, including his two brothers. He also confesses to buying the explosives.

21 November 2002 Imam Samudra, a Jemaah Islamiyah member, is captured. Samudra's confession reveals that a suicide bomber named Iqbal had died in the attack on Paddy's Bar.

24 November 2002 Indonesian police find books and video discs of speeches by Osama Bin Laden in the house rented by Samudra, near Solo.

12 May 2003 Amrozi's trial begins in Bali. He is charged with planning and carrying out an act of terrorism, an act punishable by death.

2 June 2003 Imam Samudra's trial begins. He faces the same charges as Amrozi.

7 August 2003 A panel of five judges finds Amrozi guilty and sentences him to death. Amrozi smiles and raises his arms in the air as dozens of mostly Australian survivors and relatives of the victims cheer.

Opposite: A body is removed from the site of the blast.

2001 September 11

At approximately 8.50 a.m. on the morning of 11 September 2001 the first pictures of the burning World Trade Center were broadcast live on television. The news anchors, reporters, and viewers had little idea of what was happening in lower Manhattan, but soon the world was set in a state of shock. Terrorist attacks have plagued the world for decades but none of such massive consequence had taken place on American soil until 9/11. Thousands were killed as planes crashed into the World Trade Center and the Pentagon—and the world watched every minute in horror.

As the day began the attack was already in motion. Four separate commercial aeroplanes started to head west from the east coast. Each flight had terrorists on board, committed and trained to use the planes, which carried up to 90000 litres of jet fuel, as flying bombs. At 9.30 a.m. US President George W. Bush made a statement condemning the terrorist acts. Less than 15 minutes later Flight 77, with five terrorists in control, was driven into the Pentagon building. The last of the planes, United Airlines Flight 93, was delayed 41 minutes before take-off. Because of the delay, passengers became aware of the tragedies in New York and Washington and knew that planes were involved. After noticing suspicious behaviour during the flight, the 41 passengers and crew were determined not to let the terrorists have their way, and paid with their lives. Many called their loved ones from mobile phones minutes before the plane crashed in rural Pennsylvania, killing all 45 people on board.

The damage at the World Trade Center continued to spread with many trapped occupants diving 100 storeys to their death. At 9.50 a.m., about an hour after being hit, the South Tower of the World Trade Center collapsed. Forty minutes later the North Tower did the same. The forces unleashed by the disintegration of the towers caused 23 additional nearby buildings to be damaged beyond repair. Very few survivors, and a surprisingly small number of bodies, were ever found in the remaining rubble. The intense heat of the fires had caused the bodies to be completely incinerated. Emergency services responded quickly. In Manhattan, firefighters, police officers and rescue teams rushed to save lives, hundreds dying in the effort. The tragedy caused the loss of nearly 3000 lives, including 343 firefighters.

Chronology of Events

7.58 a.m. United Airlines Flight 175 departs Boston for Los Angeles, carrying 56 passengers, two pilots, and seven flight attendants. The Boeing 767 is hijacked after take-off and diverted to New York.

7.59 a.m. American Airlines Flight 11 departs Boston for Los Angeles, carrying 81 passengers, two pilots, and nine flight attendants. This Boeing 767 is also hijacked and diverted to New York.

8.01 a.m. United Airlines Flight 93, a Boeing 757 carrying 38 passengers, two pilots, and five flight attendants, leaves Newark, New Jersey, for San Francisco.

8.10 a.m. American Airlines Flight 77 departs Washington's Dulles International Airport for Los Angeles, carrying 58 passengers, two pilots, and four flight attendants. The Boeing 757 is hijacked after take-off.

8.46 a.m. American Flight 11 from Boston crashes into the North Tower at the World Trade Center.

9.03 a.m. United Flight 175 from Boston crashes into the South Tower at the World Trade Center.

9.25 a.m. All domestic flights are grounded by US Federal Aviation Administration.

9.45 a.m. American Flight 77 crashes into the Pentagon.

10.05 a.m. The South Tower at the World Trade Center collapses. The White House is evacuated.

10.10 a.m. A large section of one side of the Pentagon collapses. United Flight 93 crashes in a wooded area in Pennsylvania, after passengers confront the hijackers.

10.28 a.m. The North Tower at the World Trade Center collapses.

Opposite: One of the World Trade Center's twin towers collapses.

2000 Disintegration of Yugoslavia

At the end of World War I the Versailles peace treaty set a boundary in the Balkans, forming a single country. In 1929 the country was officially named Yugoslavia, the land of the southern Slavs. Consisting of a multi-ethnic mix of Serbs, Croats and Slovenes, the country was stricken with a long history of conflict. Their moral, political and social differences were vast, with mutual hatred deeply ingrained. The unrest that had marked the area for decades was not settled by a common country or a common name. The region suffered further changes and atrocities during World War II.

At the end of the war, in 1945, Josip Tito took control of the country declaring it 'Socialist Yugoslavia', a communist country. The nation was divided into six republics—Croatia, Montenegro, Serbia, Slovenia, Bosnia-Herzegovina and Macedonia. Serbia was further divided into two provinces, Kosovo and Vojvodina. The communist rule discouraged nationalism and worked surprisingly well. The area became relatively stable and living standards increased, however, the underlying tensions increased as well. Frictions between regions and national debt combined with the deep animosity that each ethnic group held for the other. Tito had all he could manage to just hold the country together. When Tito died in 1980 Yugoslavia initially stayed together but remained extremely strained.

In 1986 Slobodan Milosevic became head of Yugoslavia, his vision for a 'Greater Serbia' had an anti-Albanian slant, bringing fear to the residents of Slovenia and Croatia. The two regions declared themselves independent in June 1991, and the lesser regions were caught in the middle of the strife. Yugoslavia began to crumble and full-scale civil war threatened. Fighting broke out in Croatia and thousands died before a cease-fire was declared in January 1992. Bosnia declared independence later the same year and conflict quickly erupted. Muslims were driven from their homes in operations known as 'ethnic cleansing'. The UN peacekeepers sent into the area could not contain the situation. By the end of 1996 a peace treaty was finally signed and Bosnia, devastated by the fierce fighting and with tens of thousands dead, was divided between the Serbs and Croat-Muslims. In March 1998, violence erupted in Kosovo, the poorest and most volatile of the regions.

Terrorist attacks were rampant as Albanian and Serbian forces clashed. UN resolutions and sanctions went unheeded and NATO finally resorted to air strikes against Yugoslavia in March 1999. Three months later a peace deal was arranged between Yugoslavia and NATO. The next year, Milosevic was voted out of office and handed over to the authorities for investigation into his involvement in war crimes. Vojislav Kostunica became the new president. By 2003, the country of Yugoslavia was dissolved and replaced by a looser union, Serbia and Montenegro. The ethnic tension remains.

Chronology of Events

1945 Socialist Yugoslavia is formed after years of unrest; the federation is evidently multi-ethnic.

1980 The slow disintegration of Yugoslavia begins after Tito dies and individual republics assert their desire for independence.

1986 Slobodan Milosevic becomes the leader of Yugoslavia.

1990 The first free elections in Croatia for more than 50 years are held. The communists lose to the conservative, nationalist HDZ led by Franjo Tudjman.

1991 Break-up of former Yugoslavia, Slovenia and Croatia declare independence.

1992 War in Bosnia breaks out and results in diplomatic and economic sanctions being imposed on Yugoslavia.

1995 Dayton Peace Accords are signed, ending the war in Bosnia. Croat forces retake three of the four areas created by the UN. Croatian Serbs flee to Bosnia and Serbia.

1996 Croatia restores diplomatic relations with Yugoslavia.

1999 Serbian leader, Milosevic, rejects NATO ultimatum. Air raids occur for 78 days with NATO bombing Yugoslavia. In June, a UN resolution puts Kosovo under international rule.

2000 Parliamentary elections are held and Vojislav Kostunica wins over Milosevic, but the next day a second election is called.

Opposite: Belgrade residents celebrate in front of the parliament.

2000 The New Millennium

Many people held their breath on 31 December 1999, wondering what the new century would hold and if Y2K (the millennium bug) would change everything while others prepared to celebrate. It was thought computer programs may stop working or produce erroneous results when the clock ticked over to the new millennium because programs stored years with only two digits. The year 2000 would be represented by '00' and would be interpreted by software as the year 1900. This would cause date comparisons to produce incorrect results and potentially lead to disaster. Luckily, this was not the case and instead it was the parties welcoming the year 2000 that provided mass hysteria.

Although the new millennium officially started on 1 January 2001, the party started one year earlier and around the world people stopped what they were doing to take time and enjoy the moment. Many cities hosted huge events. Three million gathered in Berlin, crowds stretched from the west to the east side of the city and celebrated with the biggest party in Germany's history. In London two million people celebrated when Big Ben struck midnight. There was no mistaking the moment as it was accompanied by a 200-gun salute and 35 000 kilograms of fireworks set off from barges on the Thames River, making it the world's biggest and longest fireworks display ever. Paris held a party where two million people celebrated, the Eiffel Tower being the focal point for a spectacular fireworks display. New York City hosted a $7 million party, with 1.5 million partygoers in Times Square. When the ball dropped, so did 1500 kilograms of confetti. Sydney held its biggest fireworks display for the one million partygoers. Rio de Janeiro hosted the world's biggest beach bash, with three million swimsuit-clad participants, while in Moscow people crowded into public squares ankle deep in snow to celebrate.

There were many other events of note: Tokyo, the first of the world's mega-cities to enter the millennium hosted bayside events and rock concerts. In Los Angeles, the famous Hollywood sign was lit for the first time since the 1984 Olympics. 'A Celebration for the Nation', was hosted in Washington, DC, with the Washington Monument becoming a giant sparkler. In Cairo perhaps the most visual celebration occurred, as laser lights and fireworks were set off with the pyramids as a backdrop. Many events, while large, were not as big as expected due to a variety of obstacles.

In most of the large celebrations painstaking efforts were taken with security to make sure terrorists did not have opportunity with the huge potential targets. Due to specific threats, some cities chose to forgo large gatherings. Another consideration was the Y2K uncertainty, making travel more of a concern. Of course there was always the potential of the weather dampening scattered festivities. Perhaps the most controversial attempt to bring in the new millennium occurred in the place that defines time for the world, Greenwich, England. The Millennium Dome, a $1 billion structure built for the occasion, was not well received. Only 10 000 partygoers joined Queen Elizabeth II under the Dome. When 1 January finally arrived, the world woke up to just another new day and all the fears of the Y2K bug disappeared.

Opposite: Times Square in New York at the stroke of midnight beginning the new year, new century and new millennium.

2000 Brazil's Rainforest Depletion

The world's tropical rainforests make up 14 per cent of Earth's surface, contribute to almost a quarter of our oxygen and dramatically affect global weather patterns. They also are home to 10 million species of plants, animals and insects. Many medicines are derived from plants found solely in the rainforests, including successful anti-cancer drugs. However, humans have continued to abuse rainforests, leaving us with less than half of what we had in the 1950s. Typically, rainforests are located in a 4800-kilometre band around the Equator, between the Tropic of Cancer and the Tropic of Capricorn.

Brazil is home to the third largest rainforest in the world, located in the Amazon River Basin. It is the largest country in South America and has a total area of 8.5 million square kilometres. Lavish 'frontier' forests make up 27 per cent of Brazil, which is 17 per cent of the world's total frontier forests. Because of this, in terms of the diversity of plant population, Brazil ranks number one. Other rainforests are located in the Congo River Basin in western Africa and much of South-East Asia. Smaller rainforests are scattered throughout Central America, Madagascar, Australia and India.

Brazil's population has increased tenfold since the 1960s, and by the 1970s Brazil had become Latin America's leading economic power. Much of Brazil's growth and industry has affected the rainforest. Because of grazing cattle, new crop land, commercial logging, mining and expanding roadways, the forest has been greatly reduced. As a result, Brazil has lost 570000 square kilometres of rainforest—an area the size of France. During 1994 and 1995, deforestation reached its peak and 29000 square kilometres were lost each year. The native tribes that live in the rainforests have been severely affected as well and many cultures have been lost.

Brazil is now trying to change the tide. Currently 29 per cent of the Brazilian forest is protected as a national or state forest, biological resource, extractive reserve or indigenous land. Privately owned land makes up 25 per cent and 46 per cent is untitled public land. The bulk of the timber harvesting comes from the untitled public land. From that reservoir more timber is harvested than from any other tropical forest. Although there is a regulatory system to govern the harvesting, 80 per cent of the wood taken is done illegally. The Brazilian government is working to better monitor timber activities, improve recovery programs and curb illegal forest practices. They are also working to establish new national forest lands, and are hoping to have an area about the size of Spain designated as national forest by the year 2010. Many international organisations have been formed to help in the fight to protect the Brazilian rainforests, as well as other rainforests throughout the world. The rate of deforestation, while still alarming, has decreased in recent years. The rich abundance of nuts, fruits and medicinal plants may substantiate the rainforest's survival. Harvesting the rainforest's bounty instead of destroying it could prove to be vastly more profitable than the practices that have led to its destruction.

Facts and Figures

Until 1970 Deforestation had amounted to approximately 100 000 square kilometres.

1970–88 Brazilian rainforest destruction dramatically increases, averaging 21 500 square kilometres a year.

1988 The destruction decreases by 27 per cent after Brazilian authorities adopt preservation policies.

1990 Brazil actively discourages illegal deforesting and enforces harsh penalties.

1991 The total of deforested areas is estimated at 415 215 square kilometres.

1991–92 Deforestation is reduced to 11 000 square kilometres a year.

1994–95 Deforestation rate climbs up and reaches an all-time high, destroying 29 000 square kilometres each year.

Opposite: The settlement of goldminers, ranchers and farmers in the Amazon Basin have made major impacts on the environment.

1999 NATO Attacks Serbia

The date 24 March 1999 marked the beginning of Operation Allied Force. This operation was launched by the North Atlantic Treaty Organisation (NATO), an alliance of 19 countries including Canada, Germany, Poland, Turkey, Britain and the United States. Utilising air strikes, the target was the southern providence of Yugoslavia, Kosovo. The objective was to degrade and damage the military and security structure that Yugoslav President Milosevic had used to depopulate and destroy the Albanian majority in Kosovo. Deep roots of cultural bitterness marked the relationship between the Kosovo Albanians and the Serbians of Yugoslavia.

In early 1998, large-scale fighting broke out and about 300 000 Kosovo Albanians were forcefully displaced and many killed by the Serbian military. In October 1998 a cease-fire was agreed upon. The situation erupted again in January 1999. By March, the Kosovar Albanian delegation signed an Interim Peace Agreement but the negotiations stalled when the Federal Republic of Yugoslavia's delegation would not comply. Thinking they could wipe out the Kosovar Liberation Army before being bound by an agreement, and counting on NATO to move slowly, the Serbians moved quickly. Violence in the Kosovo area increased. Serbian security forces drove large numbers of civilians from their homes. NATO took no time and once it was clear a political solution could not be reached, at 2.00 p.m. on 24 March, the air strike began. NATO cited five objectives to their action: the first was to stop violent military action in Kosovo; the second was to withdraw Serbian forces from Kosovo. They also wanted to place an international military presence in the area to ensure the safe return of refugees, and obtain the assurance of Serbian willingness to act according to a political framework for Yugoslavia that would conform to international law.

While the air strikes were going on another force began moving humanitarian aid. Hundreds of thousands of refugees continued to move out of Kosovo. Camps were set up in bordering countries and massive amounts of supplies were brought in. Also, steps were taken to make sure the instability did not spread into neighbouring countries. The air strikes continued, growing in intensity and scope as the weeks wore on. An agreement would not come until finally, on 3 June, Yugoslavian President Milosevic agreed with the peace plan. An agreement was signed on 9 June, and air strikes were suspended on 10 June. With the peace agreement a UN peacekeeping force moved in. Without the peacekeeping force in place, few of the more than 800 000 refugees would dare to return home. The task ahead would be one of rebuilding, with many countries pledging to help.

Chronology of Events

Week 1 NATO carries out its threat to bomb Serbia over Kosovo, attacking a sovereign European country for the first time in the alliance's history. After a few nights of endless bombing, NATO decides to move into the second phase of its military campaign against Yugoslavia, authorising its commanders to target tanks and other facilities. More than 500 000 Kosovo Albanians have been forced to flee their homes.

Week 2 NATO intensifies its bombing campaign, hitting government buildings in central Belgrade and key bridges. The appearance on Belgrade TV of three US soldiers captured by Serbia on the Macedonian border brings a new emphasis to the conflict for Americans.

Week 3 The cease-fire ends and NATO moves into the third week of its campaign with even heavier bombardments. Macedonia removes 30 000 refugees from its border camps and the UN expresses concerns for their safety. NATO forces destroy a passenger train in an attack and 10 civilians are killed. The week ends with an announcement that NATO is bringing in large-scale reinforcements.

Week 4 The week begins with an admission from the Alliance that it had accidentally bombed a refugee convoy, leaving Kosovo refugees dead. Yugoslav forces extend their 'ethnic cleansing operations' beyond Kosovo to smaller villages and British Prime Minister Tony Blair describes the continuing air strikes as a just cause.

Week 5 NATO moves into the second month of its bombing of Yugoslavia with strikes at targets in the heart of Belgrade closely associated with Slobodan Milosevic himself, including his residence and party headquarters.

Opposite: Ethnic Albanian children play and watch a US soldier in downtown Gnjillane, Kosovo.

1999 Introduction of the Euro

At the end of World War II, Europe began to work toward political and economic unity. With the idea that the closer the ties between individual countries the less likelihood there would be for war, the European Union was formed. This union consists of 15 separate countries all agreeing to work together. A shared currency was a major step in unification—an economic bond would make European war almost unthinkable.

By 1998, preparations for the upcoming monetary change were well in progress. The European Central Bank was established and negotiations with the candidate countries began. Each country in the European Union could voluntarily join the monetary union. Their country's currency would have a fixed exchange rate within the system, and all countries in the union would share a single interest rate and foreign exchange rate. Eleven countries in the European Union fulfilled the convergence criteria and officially began the union on 1 January 1999. The single currency was conveniently named the 'euro'. The countries involved were Austria, Belgium, Finland, France, Germany, Ireland, Italy, Luxembourg, Netherlands, Portugal and Spain, and a single currency was recognised in Europe for the first time since the Roman Empire ruled. Only three countries in Europe did not join initially—Denmark, Sweden and the United Kingdom—though the option to join remained open. The individual country's national currency notes and coins would not be done away with, in fact the euro notes and coins did not begin to circulate until January 2002. But in banking, the value of the euro was displayed alongside the value of each country's currency.

In the financial market, transactions were made exclusively in euros after the union began. All other transactions remained optional whether or not the euro would be used for a further three years. One great benefit to the merger was that the single currency eliminated the problems caused by multiple currencies. Transaction costs were reduced and exchange rates no longer fluctuated. Interest rates were standardised and price comparisons were no longer tedious. A stable business environment was fostered and corporate mergers within Europe became easier because multiple currencies were no longer a factor.

The change to the euro system did add pressure to the economies of the countries at the commencement, but ultimately added great strength. With the integration, the euro-zone became a huge market with 290 million residents, second only to the United States. Europe emerged as a formidable competitor on a global scale. The unification in Europe continues. Defence cooperation is being drafted and political, economic and security bonds are forming. Employment is at the front of European concerns and the Union has recently formed an 'Employment Pact'. As the individual countries fall in step with one another they are able to make great strides.

Chronology of Events

1957 Treaty of Rome is signed and creates the European Economic Community and the European Atomic Energy Community with a common European market as an objective.

1986 Single European Act is signed, revising the goals of the Treaty of Rome and committing to the creation of a single market by the end of 1992.

1988 The heads of state and governments of the European Economic Community ask the European Commission to develop a schedule for the implementation of a common currency.

1991 The Treaty on European Union is decided to enter into force in November 1993. It calls for economic and monetary union by 1999 as well as political union, including foreign and security policy.

1995 European Council adopts the name 'euro' for the single currency.

1998 Eleven European Economic Union member states qualify to be part of the Economic and Monetary Union when it begins on 1 January 1999. European Central Bank is inaugurated as responsible for managing the development and introduction of the euro.

September 2001 Euro notes and coins arrive in banks in the 12 euro-zone countries. Banks distribute notes and coins to retailers and other institutions in preparation for the changeover.

Opposite: One great benefit of the merger was that the new, single currency eliminated the problems caused by multiple currencies.

1999 Columbine High School Massacre

Two students, Eric Harris and Dylan Klebold, walked into the cafeteria at Columbine High School in Littleton, Colorado, just after 11.00 a.m. on 20 April 1999. They each placed a duffle bag on the floor, then returned to their cars. They had determined the cafeteria would be filled with the most students at 11.17 a.m., and they waited for the two bombs in the duffle bags to explode at that time.

When the bombs failed to detonate, they met at the highest point on campus—the top of the west exterior steps of the school. At 11.19 a.m. they began shooting with sawn-off shotguns. Students eating their lunches on the lawn and coming out the west doors were shot as they scrambled for cover. Klebold walked back down the stairs and shot two of the fallen students at close range. Only one survived. At 11.22 a.m., a custodian called a deputy at the high school for assistance. One minute later, confused emergency 911 calls were made. By this time Harris and Klebold had begun firing into the building through the west doors, inflicting more injuries. When the first deputy pulled into the parking lot, Harris shot at the officer. The officer returned fire. The two students turned and entered the school. Students began to flee the building and hide.

Harris and Klebold walked up and down the library hallway, throwing pipe bombs and randomly shooting. At 11.29 a.m. they entered the school library where 56 people were hiding—10 were killed and 12 more injured. They moved out of the library at 11.36 a.m. and began walking through the halls, again throwing pipe bombs. In the cafeteria they tried to detonate one of the bombs, but only succeeded in starting a fire. Outside, reinforcements from other police forces, paramedics, and the SWAT team converged on the school. Students continued to escape the building, fleeing to the cover of the police cars. About noon, paramedics moved in to care for the wounded students on the lawn. Two minutes later Harris and Klebold began shooting out the window. Deputies returned fire and paramedics continued to treat the wounded. Shortly after this, Harris and Klebold killed themselves. Twelve students and a teacher were killed before they committed suicide.

Harris and Klebold had planned their attack for quite a while. Far from being secretive, they had submitted a video essay for a class project alluding to the violence to come, and posted their plans on a website. They were both openly hostile, often alarming fellow students. Concerned parents had contacted the local authorities, but no action had been taken. Other shootings had occurred previously and more followed, but none matched the shock of Columbine.

Facts and Figures

6 December 1989 The École Polytechnique massacre took place in Canada. Marc Lépine entered the École Polytechnique, separated the men from the women and began to scream about how he hated feminists. He then killed 14 women before committing suicide.

13 March 1996 The Dunblane massacre occurred at a primary school in the small town of Dunblane in Scotland. The 43-year-old killer, Thomas Hamilton, walked in to the school armed with two pistols, two revolvers and 743 cartridges and opened fire. Sixteen children aged 5 to 6 years old and one teacher died. Hamilton then committed suicide.

March 1997 In Yemen, a man with an assault rifle attacked hundreds of pupils at two schools in Sanaa, killing six children and two adults.

26 April 2002 The Erfurt massacre took place in Germany where 13 teachers, two students and a police officer were shot dead by a 19-year-old expelled student, who then killed himself.

24 March 1998 Jonesboro massacre occurred in Arkansas, US, at a middle school. Four students and a teacher were killed by Mitchell Johnson, 13, and Andrew Golden, 11. They were both sentenced to confinement until they reached the age of 21, the maximum under Arkansas law.

20 April 1999 The Columbine High School massacre.

8 June 2001 The Osaka School massacre took place in a Japanese primary school when 37-year-old Mamora Takuma stabbed 18 children, killing eight.

Opposite: Columbine High School students mourn beside Rachel Scott's car at Clement Park near the high school.

1998 International Space Station

After the intense competition of the Space Race, a much friendlier project began. The International Space Station represents a global partnership of 16 nations lighting the pathway for peaceful cooperation between nations in the 21st century. This project is an engineering, scientific and technological marvel, ushering in a new era of human space exploration. With the Space Station, a permanent laboratory is being established in a realm where gravity, temperature and pressure can be manipulated to achieve a variety of scientific and engineering pursuits that are impossible in ground-based laboratories. The Space Station will be a test bed for the technologies of the future and a laboratory for research on new, advanced, industrial materials, communications technology, medical research and much more.

The date 29 January 1998 marked an important milestone for the International Space Station as senior government officials from 15 countries met in Washington and signed agreements. A representative from the United States signed the 1998 Intergovernmental Agreement on Space Station Cooperation, along with representatives of Russia, Japan, Canada and participating countries of the European Space Agency (Belgium, Denmark, France, Germany, Italy, the Netherlands, Norway, Spain, Sweden, Switzerland and the United Kingdom). Led by the United States of America, the International Space Station would be the largest, most complex international cooperative science and engineering program ever attempted. Taking advantage of the technical expertise from participating countries, the International Space Station brings together scientists, engineers and researchers from around the globe to assemble a premier research facility in orbit. The international partnership will ultimately assemble more than 100 components in low Earth orbit over a period of five years, using more than 40 assembly flights.

When completed, the station will provide access for researchers around the world to permanent, state-of-the-art laboratories in weightlessness. On-orbit assembly of the Space Station began on 20 November 1998, with the launch of the Russian-built *Zarya* (Sunrise) control module which will be completed in 2005–06. The space station orbits the Earth at an inclination of 51.6° to the Equator. It can be reached by the launch vehicles of all the international partners, providing a robust capability for the delivery of crews and supplies to the station. It also provides excellent Earth observation with coverage of 85 per cent of the globe and over flight of 95 per cent of the planet's population. When complete, the Space Station will be over 100 metres wide and 87 metres long. It will weigh almost half a million kilograms and will be able to house up to seven astronauts at one time.

Opposite: Space shuttle Atlantis *lifts off from Cape Canaveral, taking the crew of seven to the International Space Station.*

1997 The Death of Princess Diana

Princess Diana first captured the heart of a prince and then the world when she married Prince Charles in 1981. In a story that read like a fairytale, the English kindergarten teacher with a shy smile became a princess. Warm and kind, she was immediately popular. Diana utilised her popularity to bring causes and charities to light. Later, as she faced disappointment and a failed marriage, her resolve to move ahead won her even more respect. Her untimely death in August 1997 shook the world.

The marriage was difficult from the start. She was young and ill prepared to take on the demands of public life. Her warmness was in contrast to her husband's cool demeanour and by the end of the 1980s she was heading in a different direction to her husband. By 1992 the couple had separated and in February 1996, Diana and Charles were officially divorced. Almost a year after her divorce she was invited along with her boys to vacation with a long-time friend of her father, Mohammed Al Fayed, in St Tropez. His son, Dodi Al Fayed, was also there on vacation. Dodi and Diana renewed an old friendship and after that vacation the two were together several times. The last time they were together was the night both died in the fatal car crash.

Dodi and Diana left the Ritz Hotel in Paris early Sunday morning on 31 August, in a black Mercedes. A few minutes later, while being chased by motorcycles and paparazzi, their car crashed into a pillar of a tunnel underneath the Point d'Alma. The driver, Henri Paul, was immediately killed. Dodi Al Fayed was pronounced dead at 1.30 a.m. After rescue workers cut through the roof and doors of the car, the two survivors, Diana and her bodyguard Trevor Rees-Jones, were taken to hospital. The bodyguard survived. Princess Diana, just 36 years old, was pronounced dead at 4.00 a.m., having suffered massive wounds and blood loss. The morning papers read, 'Death by Paparazzi'. Diana's brother, Charles Spencer, stated, 'Every proprietor and editor of every publication that has paid for intrusive and exploitative photographs of her has blood on his hands today.' Nine photographers and one press motorcyclist were part of a two-year investigation on charges of manslaughter and failure to assist persons in danger. At the end of the two years all charges were dropped, as information surfaced that the driver of the Mercedes was legally drunk and had been taking medication for depression when the accident occurred.

There were many unanswered questions and whispers of conspiracy regarding the accident. Questions about a white Fiat, other vehicles, Diana's lengthened trip to the hospital, and who was in the tunnel have been raised by Dodi's father and others. Concerns about who could benefit from Diana's death and the end of a possible controversial relationship with the Muslim Egyptian, Al Fayed, gave way to international ramifications. Whatever the cause, the beloved princess's death was mourned around the world. On 6 September 1997, more than a million people lined the five-kilometre funeral route to Westminster Abbey and billions watched her funeral across the world. The princess was buried in sanctified ground on an island in the centre of an ornamental lake on her family's estate where she will no longer be disturbed.

Chronology of Events

31 August 1997 The world reels from news of Princess Diana's death.

3 September Paparazzi are called in for questioning.

5 September Princes William and Harry meet crowds of mourners outside St James's Palace. The Queen makes her first radio and TV speech since the tragedy.

6 September Hundreds of thousands of mourners line the streets of London for Diana's funeral at Westminster Abbey. The procession and ceremony are watched on television in 60 countries around the world. Her body is taken to an island on the Althorp estate for burial.

11 September Londoners face the huge task of flower removal; the princes return to school; the toxicology report says Henri Paul, the driver of the Mercedes, ingested both alcohol and prescription drugs on the night of the accident.

30 September Earl Spencer announces plans to build a museum in Diana's honour.

Opposite: The beloved princess's death was mourned around the world.

1997 *Pathfinder* Lands on Mars

The mission to Mars by the *Pathfinder* was an undeniable success. Launched in December 1996, the *Pathfinder* consisted of a parachute, rocket braking system and air bag system to land less than one second from its projected arrival time on Friday 4 July 1997, at 12.57 p.m. The *Pathfinder* contained a robot rover, named the Sojourner, designed to collect data for the NASA scientists. The 60-centimetre, 13-kilogram, six-wheeled rover was expected to operate for only one week but instead kept going until 27 September, 11 times longer than planned. The *Pathfinder* landed in an area called the Ares Vallis, a rocky flood plain 50 kilometres from the centre of the zone chosen for the mission.

One of the great successes in the mission was that the scientists were able to predict successfully the landing location's terrain, even though the detail they had to work with was the size of a football field. This helped build confidence that this success could be repeated in the future. The first objective was to get the Sojourner off the *Pathfinder* lander. A wayward airbag, blocking the manoeuvre, had to be dealt with. Once accomplished, the scientists encountered another problem. The information transfer from the rover to the lander was not working properly. After working all day on the suspect software problem, Mission Control began receiving a stream of data sent from the rover to the lander to the centre. Cheers went up and someone said, 'We're alive, we're alive.' Early Sunday morning the Sojourner began to search the red planet armed with various scientific tools, including a spectrometer and camera. The rover performed analyses of rocks and soil and sent back a variety of readings on winds and other weather factors. During the 30 days of the mission more than 16 500 images from the lander and 550 from the rover were sent back to Earth, and 2.3 billion bytes of information were communicated. The data received was twice what had been expected. As the weeks went by, scientists were able to gain an accurate understanding of the surface of the planet.

The project's scientist manager stated, 'We finally have a feeling of what it would be like to be on the surface of Mars now standing there. The dust would kick up. We would feel these temperature changes.' Scientists discovered that temperature on Mars fluctuated greatly, as much as 20°C in just a few seconds. One of the primary purposes of the mission was to demonstrate a simple, low-cost system. The total cost of this mission was $280 million. Designated as one of the first NASA Discovery class missions, it was declared a complete success, fulfilling all of its scientific, engineering and technological goals. The mission paved the way for future missions and opened a new era of space exploration.

Chronology of Events

12.57 p.m. 4 July 1997 The *Pathfinder* lands on Mars.

4.50 p.m. The transmitter is turned on and the Sun rises at the landing site.

4.55 p.m. A carrier signal is received on Earth.

7.13–8.00 p.m. Troubles occur as an airbag blocks the way of rover.

9.00 p.m. Rover ramp is deployed.

11.58 p.m. Rover is finally deployed from the lander.

1.30 a.m. 5 July The Sun sets at landing site; images are sent back to Earth.

3.00–4.00 a.m. Rover is on Mars and panned images are available to Earth.

5.00 a.m. Mission is deemed a complete success as images continue to return to Earth showing Mars from every angle seen by the rover.

Opposite: This NASA Mars Global Surveyor shows the Charitum Montes, south of Argyre Planitia, in early June 2003.

1997 Scientists Clone Sheep

Cloning is the production of genetically identical offspring from a single-parent living organism. It has existed in horticulture for years, happening spontaneously as trees produce offshoots, and widely conducted with a purpose by gardeners. In single-celled organisms, reproduction occurs by division; this is a form of cloning. By the 1960s, scientists were successfully cloning lower vertebrates such as frogs. But the cloning of higher mammals was considered not only impossible but evil. In 1997, scientists from the Roslin Institute in Scotland announced that they had done the impossible. They announced that they had successfully cloned an adult mammal a year before. As photographers from around the world snapped their pictures, the scientists introduced Dolly to the world.

Dolly was the result of experimentation—a genetically engineered, exact replica of a six-year-old sheep. She behaved just like a sheep, bleating and wandering around her pen. Her very existence proved the sceptics wrong and aroused international excitement—and fear. One year earlier the institute made the news by cloning a sheep embryo producing five identical lambs. That was impressive but most scientists still did not believe it was possible to make a clone of an adult animal. The institute set out to prove them wrong. Four hundred and thirty eggs were taken from 40 sheep and the nucleus of each was removed to be replaced by the nucleus from a mammary cell out of an adult sheep. By this method the scientists reconstructed 277 eggs. The eggs resulted in 29 embryos which were implanted into the wombs of 13 surrogate mother lambs. Only one successfully developed—Dolly. One big question was would she be her 'mother's' age or her age? Although she was young and healthy, her DNA structure mirrored the older sheep's. All chromosomes are capped with telomers, tiny strands of DNA that shorten each time a cell divides, eroding as an animal ages. Dolly had old telomers. She eventually became the mother, by natural means, of four lambs that had normal telomers. Dolly died when she was just six years old, having suffered from arthritis and finally a lung disease. Most sheep live to be at least thirteen.

With the relative success of cloning the sheep, questions arose about cloning humans. In theory, the same technique could be used to produce human clones. Dr Ian Wilmut, the scientist who pioneered the cloning technique, stated that while human cloning is theoretically possible, it was ethically completely unacceptable. Critics have said that in cloning humans, scientists are tampering with the very essence of humanity. Regardless, the cloning of animals continues to make advances as other animals have been successfully cloned. The cloning of humans, however, has remained strictly taboo.

Chronology of Events

1952 The first clone to be created is from a tadpole. Robert Briggs and Thomas King used cells from a tadpole embryo to create identical tadpoles.

1976 Transgenic mice are produced by Rudolf Jaenisch of the Salk Institute. The process involves the injection of human DNA into newly fertilised mouse eggs to produce mice that carry human genes. The offspring of the mice also contain these human genes. Different human diseases can be studied by creating mice with the appropriate genetic composition.

1978 The world's first test-tube baby is conceived through in vitro fertilisation. Using the husband's sperm, British doctors fertilise an egg in a Petri dish and then implant the embryo in the uterus of the healthy woman.

1987 Sheep and cows are cloned from embryonic cells.

1997 Dolly the sheep, the world's first mammal cloned from a cell of an adult animal, was born in 1996, but her existence isn't revealed to the world until 24 February 1997. Polly, the first sheep to contain a human gene was born during the same year.

2001 US fertility specialist Panayiotis Zavos and a team of international scientists announce that couples had volunteered for an experiment to create cloned children. The team said it was poised to help infertile couples bear clones as early as 2003.

Opposite: Dolly, the world's first cloned sheep.

1996 Carl Lewis Wins Four Gold Medals

Frederick Carlton Lewis was the runt of his family. Born on 1 July 1961 in Birmingham, Alabama, Lewis did not excel in athletics like his brother and sister. To make matters worse, his entire family was athletically inclined. Both his parents were high school track coaches. Carl stayed involved in sports nonetheless. When he was eight years old, while running with his parents' track club, Lewis was introduced to Jesse Owens. Lewis did not know then that one day he would beat Owens' record. As Lewis grew so did his abilities and by the time he graduated from high school in 1979 he was named the top-ranking high school track athlete in the United States. Three years later, Lewis joined the Santa Monica Track Club. There he began competing in international competitions. He secured a place on the 1984 Olympic team and competed in Los Angeles. He matched Jesse Owens' record by winning an amazing four gold medals in track and field.

Four years later Lewis was back, competing in the Olympics once more. Again, he won the gold and brought home two more medals. Many thought that would be it for Lewis. The majority of athletes at the time would compete in one or occasionally two Olympic Games. Then they would retire, moving on to other endeavours. But in 1992 a now familiar face was back in the Olympic arena. Lewis proved that he still had it in him by winning two more gold medals and surprising the world. The Olympics were no longer the realm of the very young. Retiring from competition was still not an option for Lewis, although little was seen of him over the next several years. Lewis was saving himself.

At 36, the track star once again made the US Olympic team. Lewis not only competed but won another gold medal in the long jump. While winning the gold, Lewis broke Mike Powell's long jump record. After 16 years of competing in the Olympics, Carl Lewis had nine gold medals to his credit. He also set numerous records. Mark Spitz, Olympic swimmer, was the only other American athlete to ever bring home nine gold medals. Lewis was only the second track and field athlete ever to win the gold in the same event in four consecutive Olympics; discus thrower

Al Oerter was the other. Carl Lewis stuck with athletics as a young underdog. Later in life, he remained a champion year after year. The charismatic athlete made a career out of competing and set the pace for others to do the same.

Carl Lewis is now a strict vegan. In 1990, he changed his diet and has since released the Carl Lewis Diet. According to Carl, 'Your body is your temple. If you nourish it properly, it will be good to you and you will increase its longevity.'

Chronology of Events

1 July 1961 Frederick Carlton Lewis is born in Alabama.

1974 Lewis starts to compete in long jump and sprint racing.

1980 Lewis is selected for the US Olympic team, but the American boycott of the Games delays his debut.

1983 He wins his first major title at the World Championships, achieving victory in the 100 metre sprint, long jump and relay event.

1984 Lewis is a favourite at the Olympic Games in Los Angeles and wins the 100 metre, 200 metre, long jump and relay, equalling Jesse Owens' performance in 1936.

1987 He repeats the victory at the World Championships in Rome.

1988 Lewis wins Olympic gold for the 100 metres when Ben Johnson is disqualified for doping. He also wins the long jump title.

1991 Lewis is beaten by compatriot Mike Powell at the World Championships in Tokyo.

1992 At the Barcelona Olympics Lewis wins his third consecutive Olympic long jump title.

1996 At 36, Lewis wins the long jump title with remarkable ease, taking his fourth consecutive Olympic title at the Atlantic Olympics. He retires afterwards.

Opposite: Carl Lewis celebrates on the podium after receiving the gold medal in the long jump at the 1992 Barcelona Olympic Games.

1996 Mad Cow Disease

Bovine Spongiform Excephalopathy (BSE) is now known around the world as Mad Cow Disease. The disease was first found in the United Kingdom in 1986. It attacks the central nervous systems of cattle in a progressive and lethal manner making vacuoles, clear holes in the brain, which give it the appearance of a sponge. Before 1986 the disease had been present in sheep for at least 200 years. The disease then made an unexpected jump from sheep to cattle, with deadly repercussions. The infection was due to the use of sheep parts in the production of protein supplements fed to cattle. Adding to the dilemma, initially when cattle died, their carcasses were also included in the feed mixture. Soon British farmers were facing an epidemic in their herds. By 1993 more than 1000 cases of BSE were reported each week. Due to the long incubation period, the rate of infection did not start dropping until late 1993. More than 160000 animals were infected, amounting to half the dairy herds in the United Kingdom.

Soon questions were raised about the possible effects on humans. The British government assured the public there was no reason for concern. On 20 March 1996, this assurances were shattered by the announcement that 10 cases of Creutzfeldt-Jakob Disease (CJD) were reported in people who were not considered 'at risk'. CJD is the human equivalent to mad cow disease and historically has struck about one in a million people worldwide with symptoms similar to Alzheimer's disease. In Britain, during the following years 43 cases of CJD occurred with a high concentration of people who worked among cattle on farms or in slaughter houses. Finally the government took notice after 10 victims were diagnosed with a new type of CJD. All were young, the eldest being 42, and all could trace their exposure to consuming infected beef. This prompted the 20 March announcement. Overnight beef prices dropped dramatically. A main staple of the English diet, it was taken off the menu by thousands in Britain. The European Union and several other countries banned all exports of British beef on 24 March. All cattle over 30 months of age were banned for sale in Britain. Three months later the process of selection became wider and by June 1998, Britain announced that all cattle known to be exposed to mad cow disease would be eliminated.

Eventually 3.7 million cattle were destroyed. The government tried to help the farmers by compensating their losses, but many still faced bankruptcy. There was no market and no means for income. By 2003, 139 cases of CJD were reported with 100 deaths in Europe. Believed to have an incubation period of 14 to 16 years in humans, the numbers are expected to rise.

Chronology of Events

November 1986 Britain makes first diagnosis of Bovine Spongiform Excephalopathy (BSE), a new disease in cattle.

July 1988 Britain announces that all cows known to be infected with BSE will be destroyed as a precautionary measure. Eventually 3.7 million cattle are destroyed.

1989 Britain bans human consumption of certain offal, including brain, spinal cord, thymus, spleen and tonsils. The United States prohibits the import of live ruminants, including cattle, sheep, bison and goats, from countries where BSE is known to exist in native cattle.

1990 The European Commission bans imports to the Continent from Britain of cattle over six months old.

1996 The British government admits that BSE could be transmitted to humans in a variant form of Creutzfeldt-Jakob Disease (CJD). The classical form is a slow degenerative disease in humans seen in about one person in a million worldwide each year; the new one is much faster.

27 March 1997 Europe bans British beef and beef products.

3 December 1997 Britain bans the sale of unboned beef as a precautionary move to prevent the risk of BSE.

1 August 1999 Export ban on British beef is lifted.

Currently Smaller outbreaks continue to occur throughout the world. It is believed that any people who may have contracted the disease will not have symptoms for many years.

Opposite: By June 1998, Britain announced that all cattle known to be exposed to mad cow disease would be eliminated.

1995 Ebola Outbreak in Zaire

The Ebola virus has been an elusive killer in our world for over 30 years, causing horrific deaths for up to 90 per cent of those infected. Surfacing all over the globe, it has predominantly affected Africa, killing almost 800 people in the period since it was discovered. The results are dramatic and usually fatal, affecting both humans and other primates. The reservoir of the virus remains unknown and a treatment has not yet been discovered. The best practice the medical profession can offer is the prevention of spreading the disease once it emerges.

The first possible death caused by the Ebola virus happened in 1972. A medical student in Africa died suddenly after displaying what would be later considered classic symptoms. In 1976 a large outbreak occurred in Sudan and Zaire. Over 300 fatalities occurred in Zaire alone, a further 141 in Sudan. This is when the virus was first officially recognised and gained its name, Ebola haemorrhagic fever. The virus was named after a river in Zaire, now the Democratic Republic of the Congo, where the outbreak occurred. The rest of the name describes the effects of the disease—severe haemorrhaging.

Another smaller outbreak followed in Sudan three years later. For the next 19 years little was seen of the disease. Then, on 6 January 1995, Ebola struck again. A 42-year-old man was admitted to Kikwit General Hospital suffering severe fever. Soon, three members of his immediate family were infected and died, 10 members of his extended family becoming ill over a nine-week period. The infection impacted Kikwit and three surrounding villages. At least one person went to the Kikwit II Maternity Hospital for help and there a lab technician was infected. The lab technician was admitted to the Kikwit General Hospital on 9 April with a fever and bloody diarrhoea. The doctors suspected his bowels were perforated due to typhoid fever and performed surgery. He died on 14 April. The epidemic was about to explode. Medical personnel involved in the operating theatre started feeling ill several days later. Each experienced a fever, headache, back, joint and muscle aches and extreme fatigue. In some cases they began to haemorrhage. One of the workers was transferred to a hospital in Mosango, almost 120 kilometres west of Kikwit. They still did not know what they were dealing with and the disease rapidly spread from person to person. Families and friends of those infected began feeling ill.

Because of the lab technician's unusual death and the illness that followed, the South African government became concerned and formed a committee to investigate. One committee member had been involved in the follow-up of the 1976 outbreak and suggested Ebola as a possibility. Zaire quickly appealed to the World Health Organisation on 10 May about the epidemic. Samples were sent and it was quickly confirmed that Ebola was the killer. Help soon came, attempting to stop the spread of the disease. Four hospitals were the hub of infection and spread the virus. Many patients and staff contracted the disease because of low hygiene levels; disposable gloves were rarely used, and needles were re-used. Although nothing could be done to treat those already infected, aid was given to quell the spread of the disease. By the time the epidemic ended, 316 cases were reported and 245 people had died.

Chronology of Events

1976 In Yambuku, Zaire, 318 cases of Ebola are diagnosed, 280 of which are fatal.

1976 More people are diagnosed in Nzara, Maridi, Tembura and Juba in Sudan totalling 284 cases, 141 resulting in death.

1977 A single fatal case is diagnosed in Tandala, Zaire.

1979 A smaller outbreak of 34 cases erupts, killing 22 people in Sudan between 31 July and 6 October.

1995 316 are diagnosed with Ebola in Kikwit, Zaire. In total, 245 die.

1996 There is a single non-fatal case in Plibo, Liberia.

1996–97 In Gaban, 37 cases are diagnosed, 21 die.

Currently Minor outbreaks continue to occur. A cure is yet to be found.

Opposite: A woman who survived the deadly Ebola virus with her baby daughter at their home in the village of Pabbo, Uganda.

1995 Rugby Puts South Africa On World Stage

South Africa was affected by apartheid in many ways. One consequence was that South Africa's sports teams were banned from participating in international competitions. The ban hit especially hard in the sport of rugby. The nation viewed rugby with a fervour that bordered on religion, but the team, in their black and green jerseys, was a symbol of the separation of races. Rugby was a sport available only to the white elite.

When South Africa banished apartheid in 1991 and embraced democracy the world sports community welcomed them back. South Africa was asked to sponsor the third Rugby World Cup in 1995, one of the world's leading sports competitions. The newly reformed country accepted the privilege and the nation became determined to make up for the time they had lost. However, South Africa's team had missed out on 15 years of playing in the international arena.

Even though the Springboks were once one of the great rugby superpowers in the world, South Africa had little chance of winning. As the competition drew to a close South Africa, embittered after a long struggle, drew together. Francois Piennar, the captain of the Springboks, fostered the 'rainbow nation' concept, embracing people of all colours and races. The team that had once been a symbol of segregation now united the players and the spectators. For one month all differences were forgotten.

As the contest grew close the pressure mounted and the Springboks had good reason to be nervous. The first team they were scheduled to play was Australia, the defending World Cup Champions and Australia was heavily favoured to win. As the Springboks took the field their nerves melted and they were unstoppable, winning 27–18. The game against France was almost cancelled due to stormy weather. If the game had been played the South Africans would have been eliminated, based on their disciplinary record. As France's record was better, the South African team anxiously watched the weather and held their breath. The weather broke and the teams took to the soggy Johannesburg stadium field. Again, the Springboks prevailed. The championship round was played against New Zealand's All Blacks. In the rounds before, New Zealand's team had demolished all comers. In a titanic clash, the two teams held each other in a death grip and the match went into extra-time. South Africa triumphed, 15–12. What followed was a uniquely significant moment, not only in sports history but in the history of a nation emerging from a great struggle.

The World Cup trophy was presented to Nelson Mandela, the black president of South Africa. He then presented the trophy to Francois Piennar, the Springboks' white captain. The Springboks, with a team that could never have played together during the period of apartheid, were World Cup Champions. The games were marked as the Rainbow World Cup, and the streets of South Africa had a rainbow of people, regardless of colour or religion, rejoicing together over the remarkable victory.

Opposite: Nelson Mandela congratulates the Springbok rugby team on winning the Rugby World Cup.

1994 Genocide in Rwanda

The beautiful country of Rwanda, only 26 000 square kilometres in size, is the location of one of the greatest crimes against humanity during the second half of the 20th century. With continual strife stemming from religion, a deep rift grew and festered between the Hutu and the Tutsi factions. In 1990 the Rwandese Patriotic Front, made up of Tutsi exiles, invaded the country and a civil war erupted.

Over the next two years assassinations and massacres became common. Thousands died but the hatred was not quelled. Instead, it ultimately exploded. International leaders were warned of the slaughter that was to come, but no one believed the report and no measures were taken to prevent the killing. On 6 April 1994, Rwanda was plunged into a well-planned bloodbath. Rwandan President Habyarimana and the Burundian President were killed when Habyarimana's plane was shot down. That night the 'final solution' began to roll and for the next 100 days the country overflowed in blood. Although 2500 soldiers from the UN peacekeeping force were present, they were forbidden to intervene. In fact, as the killings increased, the force withdrew, abandoning Tutsi refugees to be slaughtered and leaving behind only a small force. Citizens from France, America and Belgium were evacuated from the country by their governments, but again, even those Rwandans working for the Western countries were not assisted. The UN Secretary-General and the US President were unwilling to commit their assistance.

Within a week, tens of thousands of Rwandans were killed. By the end of April the number of dead had risen to hundreds of thousands. Many more fled the country as refugees. Still, internationally, governments hesitated to call the killing genocide. To use that term would have meant committing to action, bound by international treaty. By mid-May half a million Rwandans had been killed, and the United Nations finally agreed to send 5500 troops to Rwanda, stating that, 'acts of genocide may have been committed'. But the UN forces were delayed due to questions of who would fit the bill. Finally, on 3 July the Rwandan government collapsed and, when the Rwandese Patriotic Front took power on 9 July, the killing stopped. During the 100 days of slaughter, 800 000 were killed and two million refugees fled the country. Only afterwards did international help come to the aid of the survivors. UN Secretary-General Kofi Annan apologised to the parliament of Rwanda: 'Rwanda's tragedy was the world's tragedy…in their greatest hour of need, the world failed the people of Rwanda.' But the reality that the world stood by while so many died cannot be forgotten.

Chronology of Events

6 April 1994 President Habyarimana and Burundian President Cyprien Ntaryamira are killed when the Rwandan leader's plane is shot down at Kigali airport.

7 April The Rwandan armed forces and Interahamwe militia begin the systematic killing of Tutsis and moderate Hutus. Even though 10 Belgian UN peacekeepers are killed, the UN forces do not intervene as they are unwilling to breach their mandate.

9–10 April International civilians from France, Belgium and America are rescued by their governments.

11 April The International Red Cross estimates that tens of thousands have been slaughtered. UN soldiers protecting 2000 Tutsis at a school are ordered to withdraw to Kigali airport. Most are killed after their departure.

14 April Belgium completely withdraws its troops from the UN peacekeeping force in Rwanda.

15 April Thousands of Tutsis are slaughtered after gathering at Nyarubuye Church seeking protection.

21 April The United Nations cuts the level of its forces in Rwanda by 90 per cent to just 270 troops. The International Red Cross estimates the dead could now number over 100 000.

Mid-May The IRC estimates that 500 000 Rwandans have been killed.

22 June Finally, the United Nations authorises an emergency force of 2500 French troops under Operation Turquoise to create a 'safe' area in the government-controlled part of Rwanda. The killing of Tutsis continues.

18 July It is announced that the war is over and Pastor Bizimungu is named president. Over 800 000 Rwandans have been murdered.

Opposite: Abandoned bodies lie decaying during the invasion.

1991 End of Apartheid

Though South Africa is extremely rich in natural resources and boasts a wonderful climate, it is best known for apartheid. Apartheid, meaning 'apartness', was started by the white minority in South Africa to maintain domination and further racial separation from the black (African) majority in order to control the government and the economy. After being in place for more than 40 years, apartheid came to an end in the early 1990s.

In 1948, racial discrimination was not only legalised in South Africa, but actually set in place. Laws were passed that separated 'whites' from 'non-whites'. By 1950 the Population Registration Act was passed, requiring all South Africans to be racially classified. Three categories were designated: white, black (African), or coloured (of mixed descent, including Indians and Asians). The non-whites were forced to move from the newly designated 'white areas'. Other restrictions made marriage between whites and non-whites illegal and better jobs were classified as 'white-only'.

Non-compliance with the laws was dealt with harshly. To aid in monitoring and enforcing the laws all blacks were required to carry a 'pass book'. These books contained the individual's fingerprints, photo and vital information. 'Homelands' were established, assigning black people to specific reserves. Families were not taken into consideration and many times separated.

During the 1960s the South African government was under huge international pressure to stop apartheid. They chose to withdraw from the British Commonwealth of Nations rather than change. The movement for separation increased in fervency and violence. Laws continued to be issued, giving the government immense power to suppress the populace. By declaring a state of emergency, the government had virtually unlimited power to use force and imprison without cause.

By the 1970s South Africa was ready to explode. Pressure continued from outside the country and within its borders the 'non-whites' were beginning to fight back. Riots started in 1976 and continued for 14 years. Slowly the international pressure increased and foreign support vanished. The cost of necessities increased and several foreign investors chose to divest rather than be associated with South Africa's actions. The South African economy was severely affected. Apartheid began to crumble.

Finally, in 1990, President F.W. de Klerk obtained the repeal of the remaining apartheid laws. A new constitution was drafted. In 1993 a multi-racial, multi-party transitional government was approved. Free elections were held in 1994 and Nelson Mandela was elected as South Africa's first black president. The lingering traces of apartheid were outlawed. For their combined efforts in ending apartheid and making a peaceful transition into a non-racial democracy, Nelson Mandela and F.W. de Klerk shared the Nobel Peace Prize in 1993.

Chronology of Events

1948 The South African government begins to limit the freedom of black Africans even more when it launches a system of apartheid.

1959 The parliament passes new laws extending racial segregation by creating separate bantustans, or homelands, for South Africa's major black groups.

1960 Black protests against apartheid reach their peak when police kill 69 people in the Sharpeville massacre.

1962 Nelson Mandela is arrested for leaving South Africa illegally and for incitement to strike, and is sentenced to five years' imprisonment. He is later charged with sabotage and sentenced to life imprisonment.

1974 Because of apartheid the country is expelled from the United Nations.

1976 More than 600 students are killed by the South African government in the Soweto uprising. The leader of the protests, Steve Biko, is killed in police custody.

1990 De Klerk lifts the ban outlawing the African National Congress (ANC). He frees Mandela from prison.

1991 Nelson Mandela becomes President of the ANC. The IOC lifts a 21-year ban barring South African athletes from the Olympic Games.

1994 Nelson Mandela is inaugurated as President of South Africa.

Opposite: F.W. de Klerk addressing the Convention for a Democratic South Africa about constitutional reforms.

1991 Collapse of the Soviet Union

On 26 December 1991, over 70 years of communist authority crumbled. Although it changed the shape of the world, the collapse of the Soviet Union occurred with very little violence and led to the birth of 15 independent countries. The dissolution of the long communist rule was unexpected and happened relatively quickly and peacefully. The events that led to the collapse started in the mid-1980s. The Soviet Union or USSR, was a communist-ruled, one-party system consisting of 15 Soviet Republics—Russia being the largest and most powerful. After Mikhail Gorbachev became the leader of the Soviet Union in 1985, he launched the policies of glasnost and perestroika. Glasnost, meaning openness, relaxed political censorship and allowed freedom of speech and press; it also reduced the power of the KGB. Perestroika was restructuring and reducing the amount of money spent on defence. In 1987 Gorbachev's support was very high both inside and outside the USSR. His work effectively ended the Cold War but the measures set off an unforeseen chain of events.

The economic reforms Gorbachev instituted did not go as planned and conditions in the USSR worsened. The faltering economy strengthened the nationalistic movement. In 1989 Gorbachev shocked the world by announcing that the countries in the Warsaw Pact were now free to decide their own future. Borders began opening to the west and the Berlin Wall was torn down. The communist governments in the satellite states were overthrown one by one. Although proclaimed as an innovator across the West, the Soviet economy continued to weaken and Gorbachev was now not popular at home. By parliamentary vote, Gorbachev became president of the Soviet Union. The constituent republics began to resist Moscow's authority, no longer paying tax revenue to the main government or following legislation that conflicted with their local laws.

The final blows began in March as Lithuania declared independence and pulled out of the union. Boris Yeltsin, a critic of Gorbachev, began demanding Russian sovereignty from the union. He was elected, by the process Gorbachev set up, as president of Russia. Moscow now held a Soviet president in Gorbachev and a Russian President in Yeltsin. The Soviet Union was crumbling. Desperate to hold the union together, Gorbachev proposed a controversial new Union Treaty: a federation with a common president, foreign policy and military but a less centralised government, allowing for greater freedom within the republics. The USSR breathed its last breath. On 26 December 1991 the Supreme Council, comprising the highest legislative body in the Soviet Union, officially dissolved the USSR.

Chronology of Events

1985 Chernenko dies and is replaced by Mikhail Gorbachev as general secretary of the Communist Party; Andrei Gromyko becomes President. Gorbachev begins an anti-alcohol campaign and propagates the policies of openness, or glasnost, and restructuring, or perestroika.

1987 The Soviet Union and the United States of America agree to scrap intermediate-range nuclear missiles; Boris Yeltsin is dismissed as Moscow party chief for criticising Gorbachev's slow pace of reforms.

1988 Gorbachev replaces Gromyko as president; he challenges nationalists in Kazakhstan, and the Baltic republics, Armenia and Azerbaijan.

1989 Soviet troops leave Afghanistan and the Lithuanian Communist Party declares its independence from the Soviet Communist Party. The first elections for the new Congress of People's Deputies or parliament are held.

1990 The Communist Party votes to end one-party rule. Gorbachev opposes independence of the Baltic states and imposes sanctions on Lithuania. Yeltsin is elected president of the Russian Soviet Federative Socialist Republic by the latter's parliament and leaves the Soviet Communist Party.

August 1991 Senior officials, including the Defence Minister and Vice President as well as the KGB detain Gorbachev at his holiday villa in Crimea. Yeltsin bans the Soviet Communist Party in Russia and seizes its assets. Yeltsin recognises the independence of the Baltic republics and the Ukraine declares itself independent.

Opposite: President Bush and Mikhail Gorbachev at a peace summit in the United States.

1991 Operation Desert Storm

Saddam Hussein took control of Iraq in 1979 and in order to maintain control, immediately had 21 Iraqi cabinet members executed. These actions set the tone of his long ruling. After ruling as dictator for 11 years, Hussein decided to invade Kuwait, and on 2 August 1990 Iraqi troops invaded the country in less than four hours. Hussein now controlled Kuwait and 24 per cent of the world's oil supplies. On 8 August, Iraq claimed Kuwait as an annex. The next day the United Nations declared the annexation invalid.

Fearing they would be the next target, Saudi Arabia appealed to the United States for help. The United States as well as the United Nations imposed a number of economic sanctions against Iraq, which were not effective. A deadline of 15 January 1991 was set for Iraq to withdraw from Kuwait; to ignore this deadline would mean war. Desert Shield had already been implemented from 7 August 1990 until 16 January 1991. This was designed to shield the rest of the surrounding countries, Saudi Arabia in particular, from Iraqi aggression. It also involved the assembly of a very large multi-national force in Saudi Arabia; 35 nations were part of the military coalition. Other nations not involved in sending troops offered financial support for the operation.

Iraq did not comply with the UN ultimatum to withdraw troops from Kuwait by 15 January, 23.30 GMT. That same day US President Bush announced, 'Air attacks are under way against military targets in Iraq. Our troops will have the best possible support in the entire world, and they will not be asked to fight with one hand tied behind their back.' Bush promised it would not be another Vietnam; America would commit completely and prevail quickly.

On 17 January 1991, Operation Desert Storm commenced. It began with an Apache helicopter attack at 2.38 a.m., lighting up the Baghdad sky with fire. The intense air and naval campaign lasted for six weeks, targeting military and industrial locations within Iraq. The Iraqis also inflicted great damage in Kuwait by igniting almost 700 oil wells. A four-day ground offensive started on 24 February at 4.00 a.m. local time. With air and naval support, the war came to a quick conclusion and on 27 February, President Bush declared victory. Orders to cease fire were given, effective midnight Kuwaiti time. This was the first 'televised war',

with 24-hour coverage on a daily basis. Even forces in the conflict utilised CNN to stay updated with the latest action. In the end, Kuwait was liberated but Saddam Hussein was still in power in Iraq. For that reason, many called the Gulf War the unfinished war.

Chronology of Events

17 July 1990 Hussein accuses Kuwait of oil over production and theft from the Ramalla Oil Field.

25 July 1990 The United States responds by saying that it is an Arab matter, not one that affects the United States.

2 August 1990 Hussein invades Kuwait; President Bush freezes Iraqi and Kuwaiti assets. The United Nations asks Hussein to withdraw, but he refuses. Economic sanctions are authorised by the United Nations and the 82nd Airborne and several fighter squadrons are dispatched.

8 August 1990 Iraq annexes Kuwait. The next day the United Nations declares the annex invalid.

29 November 1990 The UN Security Council authorises force if Iraq does not withdraw from Kuwait by midnight EST 15 January.

16 January 1991 The first US government statement of Operation Desert Storm is made. White House Press Secretary Marlin Fitzwater announces, 'The liberation of Kuwait has begun.' The air war started on 17 January at 2.38 a.m. local time, with an Apache helicopter attack. US warplanes attack Baghdad, Kuwait and other military targets in Iraq.

17 January 1991 Iraq launches the first SCUD Missile attack.

13 February 1991 US bombers destroy a bunker complex in Baghdad with several hundred citizens inside; nearly 300 die.

23 February 1991 Ground war begins with marines, army and Arab forces moving into Iraq and Kuwait.

8 March 1991 The first US combat forces return home.

Opposite: Newly arrived marines are led through an encampment near an airfield during Operation Desert Storm.

1989 The *Exxon Valdez*

On the evening of 22 March 1989 the tanker *Exxon Valdez* reached the Alyeska Marine Terminal ready to take on cargo. Early the next morning a crew began loading crude oil into the huge tanker. The 295-metre vessel left the terminal that evening at 9.12 p.m. bound for Long Beach, California, with more than 200 million litres of North Slope crude oil in its hold. The ship had travelled the route more than 8700 times in 12 years with very few incidents, none of them serious. The *Exxon Valdez* navigated successfully through the Valdez Narrows, the most difficult part of the journey aided by an expert ship pilot, William Murphy. After the narrows, Murphy left the ship and the captain, Joe Hazelwood, radioed his plan to move the tanker out of the outbound shipping lane into the inbound lane to avoid icebergs. He began the manoeuvre then handed the control of the wheelhouse over to the third mate, Gregory Cousins. After giving precise instructions about when to turn the ship, Hazelwood retired to his quarters.

Throughout the incident several safety standards were not adhered to aboard the *Exxon Valdez*. There was not a second officer on hand in the wheelhouse while Hazelwood or Cousins worked, as required. Fatigue, operator error, and miscommunication worked together to create a disaster. The ship did not make the turn once in the inbound shipping lane. The *Exxon Valdez* crossed the shipping lane and then moved outside the lane completely and into dangerous waters. Cousins realised the ship was in danger when he saw warning lights for the Bligh Reef on the wrong side of the ship. They were so far off the course that the warning lights were between the ship and the open shipping lane. Quickly Cousins endeavoured to turn the tanker, but it was too late.

Early in the morning on 24 March the *Exxon Valdez* struck the Bligh Reef in Prince William Sound, Alaska. Eight of the 11 cargo tanks were punctured and crude oil began gushing from the tanker. At 12.26 a.m. Hazelwood radioed, 'evidently leaking some oil and we're gonna be here for a while'. His warning was a gross understatement as more than 41 million litres of crude oil, an amount that would fill 125 Olympic-size swimming pools, poured into the sound. The spill, though it has been pushed off the top 50 list for size, is still rated number one for the most damaging. Thousands of marine animals and waterfowl died as a result and about 2080 kilometres of shoreline were affected. A $2.1 billion Exxon-sponsored clean-up lasted four summers. The massive undertaking involved more than 10 000 workers at the peak of operations. The clean-up included 1000 boats, aeroplanes and helicopters. However, most of the work of the clean-up came from the winter storms in the area; still, some areas remain damaged. As a result of the *Exxon Valdez* incident, the US Congress instituted the *Oil Pollution Act 1990*. This act requires the Coast Guard to strengthen regulations on oil tankers, owners and operators. Also, hulls are now constructed with better protection against spillage.

Facts and Figures

Fifteen years after the *Exxon Valdez* oil spill, the environment of Prince William Sound region is still suffering from the devastating effects. The most recent survey of lingering oil was conducted in the summer of 2001 and covered roughly 8000 metres of shoreline.

The survey results indicated a total area of approximately 8 hectares of shoreline in Prince William Sound is still excessively contaminated with oil. Oil was found at 58 per cent of the 91 sites assessed and is estimated to have the linear equivalent of 5.8 kilometres of contaminated shoreline.

Results of the 2001 survey showed that the oil remaining on the surface of beaches in Prince William Sound is weathered and mostly hardened into an asphalt-like layer.

The survey revealed there are continuing low-level chronic effects of the oil spill, measurable in animal populations. These continuing effects are most likely to be restricted to populations residing or feeding in the isolated oil pockets. Sea otters and harlequin ducks fall into this category. Researchers have been monitoring these species and have found them to be recovering poorly since the spill. The area is not likely to completely recover for many decades.

Opposite: The oil spill from the Exxon Valdez *resulted in a $2.1 billion clean-up that took four years to complete.*

1989 Fall of the Berlin Wall

For most people the Berlin Wall represented more than just a physical barrier. It symbolised the separation between the communist countries and the rest of the world. After World War II, Berlin was split in half, forming East and West Berlin. East Berlin was governed by the communist Soviets and West Berlin was a 'Free City'. So many people fled from the East to West that measures were taken to keep people in. On Sunday 13 August 1961 East Berlin began to be blockaded. First, tanks and barbed wire blocked the way between the two sides, then streets were torn up and barricades erected. Homes next to the border were evacuated and subways interrupted. Citizens of East Berlin could no longer travel to West Berlin. They were locked behind the border. A more permanent wall soon replaced the barricades.

Twenty-five years later the political climate had changed. The Soviet Union began to lose power and the communist grip on its satellite states loosened. In May 1989 Mikhail Gorbachev visited West Germany. During his visit he stated that Moscow was not going to continue using force to prevent change in its satellite states. Quickly countries began to pull away from their Soviet overlords. Within six months more than 220 000 East Germans fled to the West while many stayed and worked to change East Germany from within. Non-violent demonstrations brought pressure upon the government. On 4 November, almost a million people gathered to demand their basic freedoms. Just before 7.00 p.m. on Thursday 9 November 1989, it was announced that East Germans would be allowed to move freely into West Germany; the measure would take effect immediately. News of the announcement spread quickly. Thousands of East Germans crossed into West Germany that evening. At the newly opened checkpoints excited West Berliners greeted the 'Trabi' cars from East Berlin. The East Berliners were offered flowers as a welcome, while reporters took pictures and interviewed bystanders, trying to capture the moment for the rest of the world. Celebrations took place at the Brandenburg Gate and the Kurfurstendamn in West Berlin.

With the borders open, the wall was no longer of use. The next day demolition of the wall began. The next few weeks were a unique time in Germany. Instead of closing at the normal 6.30 p.m., shops stayed open as long as they wanted. An East German passport was a free ticket on public transportation. November was not a time to think of future implications or logistics; it was a time to enjoy the moment—and the country did just that. The fall of the Berlin Wall, the symbol of division in Europe between the two contending blocs, heralded the end of the Cold War.

Chronology of Events

1949 Germany is divided into West and East. American, French and British zones become the Federal Republic of Germany. The Soviet zone in East Germany becomes communist German Democratic Republic.

1955 West Germany joins NATO. East Germany joins the Warsaw Pact.

1961 The Berlin Wall is constructed to prevent commuting between the two sides.

1968 It is announced in East Berlin that the city will not be united until the West becomes socialist.

1973 East and West Germany join the United Nations.

1989 Mass exodus of East Germans as Soviet-bloc countries relax travel restrictions. The Berlin Wall is torn down and many thousands celebrate.

1990 Chancellor Kohl leads a reunified Germany.

1991 Parliament names unified Berlin the new capital.

Opposite: Spectators watch as a man swings a hammer at the Berlin Wall.

1989 Tiananmen Square Massacre

Tiananmen Square is the biggest public square in the world, located in the heart of Beijing, China. The size of the square is overwhelming; at 40 hectares it could stage the Olympics with every event taking place at once. The name Tiananmen, meaning 'Gate of Heavenly Peace', does not reflect the location. As inhospitable as it is large, there are no benches, shade or water. Instead, swivel-mounted cameras tightly monitor all activity. The events that occurred in the square on 3 June 1989 shook the world to its core. A group of protesters, comprised mainly of university students, were killed by soldiers in Tiananmen Square while rallying for government reform. A report issued on 4 June by the Chinese government stated that 2600 were killed.

The crisis marked the growing conflict in the communist world, and Tiananmen became a symbol of change. Unrest started long before 3 June. In May 1986 a lone university student began the call of democracy. Although he was quickly silenced, his ideals were followed by other students. At protests in 1987, Hu Yaobang, a moderate communist official, intervened so the students did not get arrested. He was highly criticised by the government and then fired. When he died of a heart attack in April 1989, thousands of students gathered in Tiananmen Square in anticipation of his funeral. The next day a few students were let through the police line with papers listing their demands. The three demands from the students were: more democratic political representation, authority to organise student unions and an end to government corruption. Although they knelt for over an hour, no government official would receive them. The number of students in the square continued to escalate and on 26 April, Deng Xiaoping, the leader of China, warned the students to stop the demonstrations.

In May there was to be a summit between the Chinese and Russian leadership. More than 1000 foreign journalists gathered in Beijing for the event. Students, seizing the opportunity for worldwide coverage, converged on Tiananmen Square with white headbands, declaring that they were going on a hunger strike until the government met their demands. The tens of thousands of students were joined by workers, increasing the numbers into the millions. Five days into the hunger strike, on 18 May, the government invited the demonstration leaders to a meeting. The meeting quickly turned into a confrontation with neither side backing down. President Deng declared martial law the following day and the hunger strike was called off. On 3 July, troops made their way through the crowd into Tiananmen, ordered by the panicking government to clear the square. Protesters were beaten, arrested, and then the soldiers opened fire on the crowd. Most of the demonstrators scattered and the few remaining gathered in the middle of the square. The troops surrounded them and, early the next morning, killed them.

Chronology of Events

22 April 1989 Demanding to meet with Premier Li Peng, three student representatives carry a petition and kneel on the steps of the Great Hall in front of the 100 000 students who have gathered in the square the night before. Li Peng does not respond.

27 April Students from more than 40 universities march to Tiananmen in protest of the 26 April editorial, ignoring warnings of violent suppressions.

15 May On the third day of the hunger strike Gorbachev arrives in Beijing for the first Sino-Soviet summit since 1959. The government cancels plans to welcome Gorbachev at Tiananmen Square.

20 May The government formally declares martial law in Beijing, but the army's advance towards the city is blocked by large numbers of students and citizens.

3 June Troops receive orders to reclaim Tiananmen Square at all cost. Around 10.00 p.m., soldiers open fire on people who try to block the army's advance and those who are watching. Tanks and armoured personnel carriers move toward the centre of the city. Thousands of people in the streets are killed or wounded.

4 June Troops clear bodies surrounding Tiananmen Square and await further orders.

Opposite: Thousands of innocent people were injured or killed in the heart of Beijing.

1988 Lockerbie Disaster

Just four days before Christmas on the evening of 21 December 1988, Pan Am Flight 103 taxied out of the Heathrow Airport gate in London at 6.04 p.m. local time. It was behind schedule and didn't take off until 6.25, bound for New York. The 243 passengers and 16 crew members had all been checked through security as were their bags. However, no one checked the cargo hold before the luggage was loaded onto the plane. One item, not belonging to anyone on board, would cause the plane to explode just 38 minutes after take-off. At 6.56 p.m. the jumbo jet reached the cruising altitude of 9300 metres and at 7.03 p.m. the plane exploded.

The 259 people aboard the plane died in a terrifying flash, but for the residents of Lockerbie in Scotland the horror was just beginning. The sky lit up and there was a tremendous roar. What appeared to be meteors fell from the sky, but it was soon realised that the flying debris were parts of a plane and its passengers. Pieces landed in fields, backyards, rooftops and streets, causing a nightmarish rain in an 80 square kilometre area. The nose of the plane landed almost intact seven kilometres from the town in a field. Lockerbie did not go undamaged. Fuel from the plane was burning before it hit the ground and landed on many houses causing explosions. Twenty-one homes were completely destroyed and 11 residents of the small village died. Had the flight been on time, it would have blown up over the open sea.

Investigators began working to see what happened and who was responsible. Within a week it was apparent that a bomb on board the plane had caused the disaster. Each piece was gathered and placed together to solve the mystery. In February 1989 investigators were able to announce details about the bomb. It had been fashioned out of Semtex and activated by a timer. The bomb was hidden inside a radio-cassette player inside a brown suitcase. The suitcase was hidden in the plane's forward cargo compartment. Still, investigators did not know who placed the bomb or why. Finally two suspects emerged, both Libyans. The Libyan government refused to release the men upon initial request. It took 10 years of diplomatic talks and economic sanctions until the Libyan government finally allowed their release. In April 1999 the two suspects were sent to the Netherlands and a year later brought to trial. After a seven-month trial, Abdel Basset Ali al-Megrahi, a Libyan intelligence agent, was convicted and sentenced to life imprisonment. Al-Amin Khalifa Fahima was found not guilty and returned to a hero's welcome in Tripoli. There remain unanswered questions and many whispers of conspiracy. But there is no question that the 270 deaths had resulted in heartbreak from the tragedy.

Facts and Figures

- Air control had been issuing Flight 103's clearance to start its oceanic segment of the journey to New York, when Flight 103's signal went off their radar.

- Twenty-one of Lockerbie's houses were completely destroyed and 11 of its residents left dead, bringing the total death toll to 270. On board were passengers from 21 different countries and 189 of the 259 passengers were American.

- Investigators interviewed over 15000 people, examined 180000 pieces of evidence and researched in more than 40 countries trying to find out who was responsible for the bombing.

- Months after the bombing, a local Lockerbie man discovered vital evidence while walking his dog. He found a T-shirt, which turned out to have pieces of the timer embedded in it. Detectives were able to trace the T-shirt as well as the maker of the timer.

- In 1994, Libya agreed to a proposal that would have the trial held in a neutral country with international judges. The US and the UK refused the proposal.

- In 1998, the US and the UK offered a similar proposal but with Scottish judges rather than international ones. Libya accepted the new proposal in April 1999.

- After a seven-month trial Abdel Basset Ali al-Megrahi was sentenced to life imprisonment and Al-Amin Khalifa Fahima was found not guilty, returning home to Tripoli.

Opposite: What appeared to be meteors fell from the sky, but it was soon realised that the flying debris were parts of a plane and its passengers. Pieces landed in fields, backyards, rooftops and streets, causing a nightmarish rain in an 80 square kilometre area.

1987 Black Monday

The biggest Wall Street Stock Market crash in history was not the famous 1929 collapse, but almost 60 years later in the 'Black Monday' crash occurring on 19 October 1987. The drop in the Dow Jones Industrial Average in 1987 almost doubled the 1929 crash, though the effects were not nearly as devastating. Many factors led to Black Monday. The market had peaked in August of that year, but it only involved the largest stocks. Overall, the market was overvalued and inflated. Interest rates were high and the Federal Reserve pushed them even higher. In foreign currency markets, the value of the dollar was decreasing. Many investors moved their money from stocks to bonds because of the high 10 per cent interest rates the bonds were offering. The market began to slip. From the close of trading on Tuesday 13 October to the close of trading on 19 October, the Dow Jones Industrial Average dropped by almost one-third.

On the Friday before Black Monday the market closed at 2246.73, down 108.73. On Monday the bottom dropped out of the market. In one day the Dow Jones plummeted 508.32 points, the largest fall ever, with a 22.9 per cent loss. It closed at a record-breaking low of 1738.40 points. The total loss incurred during the week was almost $1 trillion. What was particularly astonishing about the day was the speed at which prices fell. Computerised trading had been introduced to the market just a year before and enabled billions of dollars of stock to be quickly moved. Many companies, instead of depending on the judgment of investors, depended upon their computers. If prices fell past the determined point, stocks were automatically sold.

The fall in the market on Monday triggered such a response and the computers began selling. The market became overwhelmed with orders, and the ticker fell behind. The system of the exchange could not keep up with the market action. There were too many investors selling stocks and not enough buying. The market quickly recovered and interest rates declined. Within the decade renewed trust in the market won back investors. Learning from this vivid crash, precautionary measures were taken. Circuit breakers were put into place in 1988. These measures were controversial then and still remain so. These circuit breakers restrict trading in times the market is unstable to prevent drastic changes—protecting investors and the market.

Below: Concerned traders on the floor of the New York Stock Exchange watch their monitors. Opposite: 19 October 1987 became known as Black Monday.

1986 Chernobyl Nuclear Accident

The fatally flawed design for a nuclear power plant resulted in the Chernobyl disaster in April 1986. Located in the Ukraine 130 kilometres northwest of Kiev, the power plant was an accident waiting to happen. Western engineers had warned of the poor design of the reactors, but the warnings were largely ignored. Compounding the problem was the quality of the reactors. Poor materials, substandard workmanship and tight production schedules combined with bad management multiplied the risks of disaster. Add to that poor maintenance and unqualified workers and the result was disastrous. The steam explosion and fire killed 30 workers, 28 from radiation exposure, and released radioactive material into the atmosphere. This was the worst nuclear accident in history.

The accident occurred on Saturday 26 April 1986 at 1.23 a.m. at the Chernobyl unit number 4 reactor. With the reactor shut down for routine maintenance, the operators decided to run a test to check if there would be sufficient electrical power to operate the emergency equipment and core cooling pumps in the case of a shutdown. Part way through the shutdown procedure, the process was stopped. The shutdown was again started, but the system was not in a proper condition. Errors multiplied as the operators tried to stabilise the system. Bad decisions met with the faulty design. A power surge that the operators could not control occurred at about 100 times the normal power. The temperature rose dramatically, causing the fuel to rupture. The fuel particles reacted with the water and caused a steam explosion, resulting in the destruction of the reactor core. The force of the explosion blew the cover plate off the reactor, releasing fission products into the atmosphere. Another explosion released fragments of burning fuel and graphite from the core, allowing air in and causing the moderator to begin burning. This burned for nine days.

The gradual meltdown released about a million times more radiation than the fallout from the 1979 Three Mile Island accident. Besides the 58 killed in the initial explosion, there would be no further deaths at the time. Much of Belarus, the Ukraine and Russia were exposed to the radiation. The radioactive cloud, boosted by winds, moved beyond the Soviet Union, spreading across most of Europe and setting off widespread alarm and criticism.

The Soviet reaction to the disaster was secretive and slow. The communication concerning the hazards was downplayed and the steps made to evacuate the area were criminally lacking. People living within 30 kilometres of the plant were still not informed of the danger a week later and continued as normal while being exposed to high doses of radiation. Although the area was eventually evacuated, hundreds of cases of thyroid cancer, especially in children, have resulted from the exposure. Many safety standards have been set in place as a result of the accident and much has been learned about nuclear energy.

Facts and Figures

Since the Chernobyl disaster, the surrounding area has suffered irreversible damage and many have died. The principal environmental effect of the accident has been the accumulation of radioactive fallout in the upper layers of soil in Chernobyl, destroying important farmland. The most severely impacted area has been the small country of Belarus, formerly a part of the USSR. It lost almost 20 per cent of its farmland during the years directly after Chernobyl and is still described as 'seriously contaminated' by international standards.

Other environmental effects include the threat to surface and ground water of the Ukraine area. Little can be done to reverse these impacts and the result is contaminated land surfaces, which will not recover for at least a further 50 years.

It is not only the farming and water that continue to suffer. At least one type of cancer can be directly attributed to the Chernobyl accident. Thyroid cancer among children is widespread in the areas with the highest radiation levels. From 1986 to 1990 there were 22 times more cases of thyroid cancer than in the five years previous to the disaster. Many other health problems such as birth deformities are also prevalent, not only from high radiation levels but also from malnutrition.

Opposite: The Chernobyl nuclear power plant reactor block 4, site of the catastrophic meltdown.

1986 United States Bombs Libya

The United States of America's relationships with Middle Eastern countries have always been tense, the country of Libya being no different. After years of tension between the two countries over control of oil supplies and the contentious rule of Libyan leader Moammar Gadhafi, conflict officially erupted in 1986. The United States took drastic action against the country after a series of attacks were carried out by Libyan terrorists killing many Americans,. The most provocative terrorist attack occurred around midnight on Saturday 5 April when a bomb exploded at La Belle Discotheque in West Berlin. Frequented by US servicemen, La Belle was destroyed after a two-kilogram bomb packed with plastic explosives and shrapnel exploded close to the dance floor. More than 200 people were injured and two US servicemen and one Turkish woman died as a result of the bombing.

Late in the evening on 15 April, under the code name El Dorado Canyon, the United States launched a series of military air strikes against ground targets in Libya. Five targets were selected: the Aziziyah barracks (the command and control headquarter for Libyan terrorism), Tripoli's main military facilities, the Side Bilal base, the Jamahiriyahan military barracks (a terrorist command post), and the Benina air base southeast of Benghazi. All but one of the targets had a direct connection with terrorist activities. The non-terrorist target was the Benina military airfield, the home of the Libyan fighter aircraft. This was hit to prevent air retaliation. While the attack aircraft were still in the air, US President Ronald Reagan made a public statement. In his address he said, 'Self-defense is not only our right, it is our duty. It is the purpose behind the mission.' He stated that the use of force was prompted by irrefutable proof that Libya had been behind the bombing of the West Berlin discotheque. American intelligence intercepted a message from Moammar Gadhafi, ordering the attack 'to cause maximum and indiscriminate casualties'.

The American attack was very large, with 100 aircraft employed. All five targets were hit simultaneously. Inadvertently, several residential buildings were also hit. Although the Libyans had expected retaliation for the bombing they were totally unprepared for the attack and offered no resistance. The main target, Gadhafi, escaped injury but his young adopted daughter was killed, along with 15 civilians. Many nations condemned the attack. Libyan acts of revenge occurred for years after the air raids, including the bombing of Pan Am Flight 103 in 1988.

Chronology of Events

7 January 1986 President Reagan invokes the International Emergency Economic Powers Act barring most exports and imports of goods, technology, services (except for humanitarian purposes) and all loans or credits to the Libyan government.

8 January President Reagan orders a freeze of Libyan government assets in US banks, including hundreds of millions of dollars of deposits held in foreign branches of American banks, as well as real property and other investments.

7 February The US revises sanctions to allow oil companies to continue operations in Libya temporarily to avoid 'abandonment of contracts or concessions, which would result in a substantial economic windfall to Libya'.

24 March The US Sixth Fleet challenges Gadhafi's claim to territorial waters in the Gulf of Sidra, and crosses into Libyan territory. This action provokes a Libyan attack during which two Libyan patrol boats are sunk and an onshore anti-aircraft missile site is destroyed.

15 April US bombers attack Gadhafi's headquarters, military airfields and suspected terrorist training camps around Tripoli and Benghazi in retaliation for Libyan role in the 5 April bombing and to deter future terrorist acts against US installations. The UK allows the United States to use British airfields for exercise, but France denies overflight rights for US planes.

17 April Gadhafi appears on Libyan television, ending speculation that he has been killed or injured in the US attack or subsequent shooting, and tells his countrymen to turn the lights back on in blacked-out Tripoli.

Opposite: Officials inspect the damage after the terrorist blast at Berlin's LaBelle discotheque.

1985 Hole in the Ozone Layer

The atmosphere of the Earth is made up of three main layers; the troposphere, the stratosphere and the tropopause. It is the events taking place in the stratosphere that have attracted international attention over the past 20 years. The stratosphere is home to our ozone layer and 'greenhouse gases'. Ozone gas is made up of three oxygen atoms. While ozone in the troposphere is a health hazard connected to air pollution, in the stratosphere it acts as an essential buffer, absorbing much of the sun's ultraviolet rays. It blankets the Earth in a layer which is thinnest at the Equator and thickest at the poles.

A British Antarctic Survey monitoring the atmosphere above the Antarctic in the early 1980s realised that there was a marked drop in the ozone level. The loss was reported in 1985, bringing the problem to global attention. They found the depletion mostly occurred over Antarctica in October, the springtime of that region. An international body for research was instigated and soon scientists conclusively determined the reason for the loss. Combined with the springtime weather in Antarctica, manmade products including halo carbons such as chlorofluorocarbons (CFCs), released into the air cause a breakdown of ozone atoms. Based on the scientific findings, the Montreal Protocol on Substances that Deplete the Ozone Layer was negotiated in 1987. Twenty-four countries and the European Economic Community signed the protocol.

Two revisions were made over the next five years as scientific understanding increased. This proved to be one of the most successful international agreements ever, aimed at cutting emissions in half by 2000. Scientists are hoping that the next 50 years will bring a turnaround of the problem. Global warming, or the greenhouse effect, is another concern voiced worldwide. Unlike the ozone problem, the scientific community is divided and the problem unclear. Scientists believe that the average global temperature has increased in the last 100 years, but the cause and impact of the increase have not been agreed upon. Many scientists do not believe that global warming is a result of human caused emissions, and others believe that industrial and auto emissions have acted like a greenhouse in the stratosphere, trapping sunlight. Most of the temperature change took place in the first part of the century, directly after the Industrial Revolution, however the gases emitted then would not be as much as they are currently. Oddly enough, in the 1970s when emissions were at their highest, the overall temperature dropped. The impact of a temperature change is also cause for disagreement. Adding to the uncertainty, no data before the 1900s is available.

The world has become more focused on environmental issues as a result of these studies and the United Nations Earth Summit met in 1992 and again in 1997, when the Kyoto Protocol was proposed. The ozone hole is a great example of a problem caused by man, which international legislation is effectively addressing. The global warming concern, on the other hand, is less clear and has caused major upheavals in the past 10 years.

Chronology of Events

1970s Scientists discover that chlorofluorocarbons (CFCs) could potentially harm the ozone layer.

1974 Chemists Sherwood Rowland and Mario Molina discover the ozone-depleting effects of CFCs, confirming earlier suspicions.

1976 NASA expands research to include the ozone layer.

1978 The United States is the first country to limit CFC use and ban CFC propellants. Other countries follow over the next few years.

1985 British scientists discover the ozone hole over Antarctica. Twenty-four different countries sign the Montreal Protocol in efforts to reduce the production and use of CFC and other damaging gases by 2000.

June 1990 The Montreal Protocol is revised to eliminate the use and production of CFCs by the year 2000 and fundraise $240 million to help developing countries find alternatives to using harmful chemicals.

22 October 1991 The UN Earth Summit releases studies showing ozone depletion has occurred worldwide, even over the populated Northern Hemisphere countries.

Opposite: Scientists at NASA located the largest ozone hole ever recorded over Antartica.

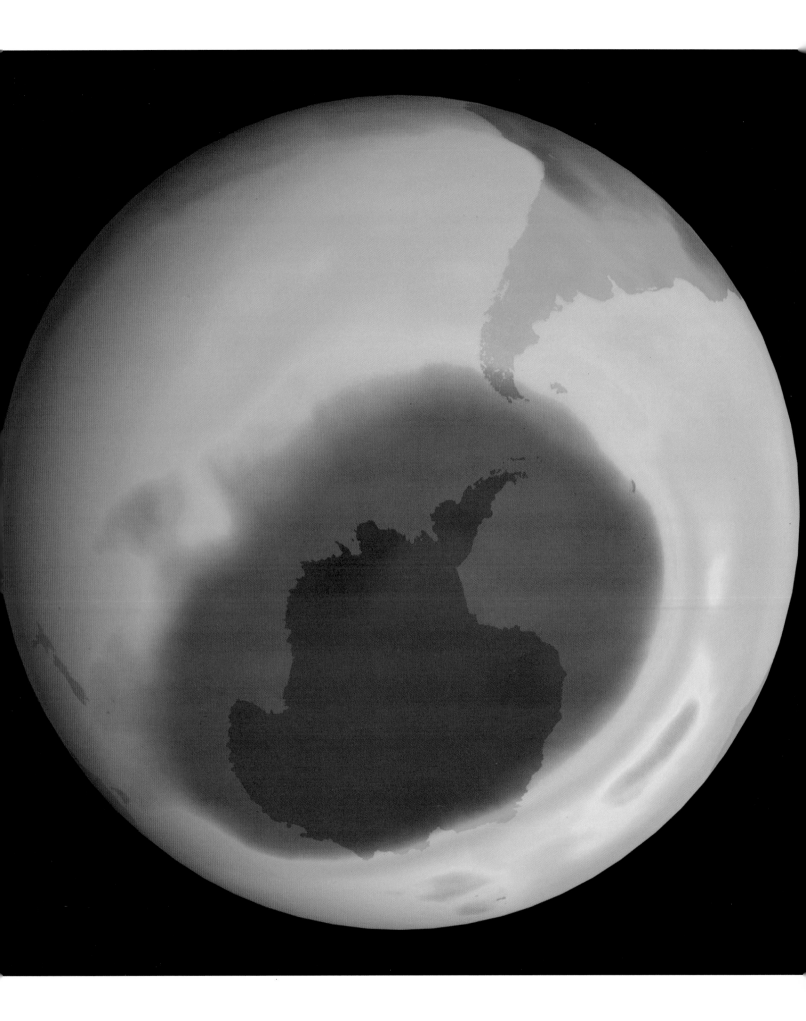

1985 Live Aid for Ethiopia

Irish singer and songwriter Bob Geldof proved that one man could make a difference to the world. In the autumn of 1984, during a time when he was working as lead singer for the punk rock band Boomtown Rats, he watched Michael Buerk's BBC documentary about the famine in Ethiopia. Deeply affected by the documentary, Geldof decided that something had to be done and began to devise a plan to help raise money. Geldof joined forces with Midge Ure, the lead singer and guitarist for Ultravox and together they wrote the song, 'Do They Know It's Christmas?'. Almost 40 of the United Kingdom and Ireland's most popular pop stars joined together and formed the group Band Aid. They recorded the song at their own expense, with studios donating time and resources as well. Released just before Christmas with the goal of raising money for famine relief, the song sold more than three million copies and became one of the best-selling singles in British history.

Bands around the world realised the potential good that they could generate. A single in America soon followed and Geldof was asked to help with production. Geldof had something bigger in mind. He wanted to have a large benefit concert to raise even more money for Ethiopia—Live Aid. He persuaded promoter Harvey Goldsmith to help. Geldof's concept was immense: 'We should try to have the most important rock artists of the last 25 years on one stage. It's going to be a global telethon because people are dying.' The end result exceeded his vision. Initially, acts were slow to commit, but as the concept caught on the event snowballed. The concert would be viewed by satellite with the largest satellite link-up and TV broadcast of all time. On 13 July 1985, the concert took place. The two main locations for the concert were Wembley Stadium in London and JFK Stadium in Philadelphia. Joining by satellite link for shorter sets were groups in Melbourne, Japan, Vienna, The Hague, Belgrade, Moscow and Cologne. Almost 60 performers and bands took to the stage. Phil Collins performed twice, first in the United Kingdom and then he climbed on board a Concorde, flew to the United States and performed again. Several bands that had not played together for years played for Live Aid, including The Who and Led Zeppelin. All the performers, from those who had not played for years to those on tour at the time, played their hearts out in the memorable 16-hour concert. While the fundraiser exceeded expectations in talent, it also exceeded expectations financially. Geldof had hoped to raise $1 million, but donations received were more than 60 times that amount. Many benefit concerts for various causes followed, inspired by Geldof's efforts.

Geldof continued in his efforts to raise money. His challenge to British Prime Minister Margaret Thatcher caused a change in British policy toward famine relief. In recognition of his work he was nominated for the Nobel Peace Prize and made an honorary knight by Queen Elizabeth II. Still, even today Ethiopia struggles with famine and the fight for relief continues.

Facts and Figures

- The concert, split between London and Philadelphia, brought together such stars as U2, Queen and Madonna.

- The 1985 Live Aid concert, one of the defining events in modern music, is to be released on DVD for the first time. Organisers will auction the rights to release the DVD after pirate copies were found for sale on the Internet. They are hoping to raise 'a few million pounds' for charity.

- Proceeds from the DVD release will go to the Band Aid Trust, which still exists to relieve poverty and hunger in Ethiopia and the surrounding area. Bob Geldof 'sees it as an asset of the people of Ethiopia' that was not being fully utilised, according to fellow founding Band Aid trustee John Kennedy. 'It's a surprise to all of us that we're still here 20 years on spending and receiving money. The successful bidder will have to get the permission of every artist—but we don't expect any of them to be anything other than cooperative.'

Opposite: Madonna performs at the Live Aid concert.

1984 Indira Gandhi Assassinated

Indira Priyadarshini Gandhi was the prime minister of India from 1966 to 1977 and again in 1980 until she was assassinated on 31 October 1984. As the first woman to ever lead a democracy she had remarkable ability as a political leader, forwarding India in several ways. Under her, relations with the Soviet Union improved. In 1971 India sent its first satellite into space and won a war with Pakistan. By the end of her life, India had one of the fastest growing economies in the world. When India won its independence in 1947, Indira Gandhi was close to the heart of the new government. Her father, Jawaharlal Nehru, became the first prime minister of India. Since he was a widower, Indira took on the responsibility of managing the official residence, acting as hostess and travelling extensively with her father. In these travels she was exposed to many of the top world leaders.

Not just her father's daughter, Indira Gandhi was very capable. In 1959 she became the fourth woman elected president of the Indian National Congress. Later she was appointed the Minister of Information, one of the highest ranking positions in the Cabinet. Many contended for the position of prime minister in 1966, when Lal Bahadur Shastri, the current prime minister, died of a heart attack just two years into his term. Indira Gandhi was chosen as a compromise, many thinking she could be easily manipulated. Serving as acting prime minister, she instead displayed extraordinary political skills and tenacity. She was officially elected in 1967.

In 1971 Indira was re-elected. Her second term was difficult and her popularity began to falter. The year 1973 was marked by public unrest. A weak economy, rampant inflation, poor living standards and government corruption resulted in many demonstrations. Add to this, in 1975 the High Court of Allahabad found her guilty of corruption in election practices and called for her to resign. She responded by declaring a state of emergency, nullifying the authority of her opposition and acquiring more power.

Nineteen months later an open election was allowed. Much to her surprise she was voted out of office. In 1980 Indira Gandhi was voted back into the office as prime minister. In June 1984 she authorised a military assault, Operation Bluestar, on the Golden Temple, the central Sikh

place of prayer. Many reasons for the attack were given, but the results were bloody and the Sikh considered the incident an unforgivable insult. As retaliation, two of her bodyguards, both Sikh, assassinated her. Indira Gandhi's son, Rajiv Gandhi, was her political successor and was sworn in just 12 hours after her death.

Chronology of Events

1917 Indira Priyadarshini Gandhi is born in Allahabad, India.

1930s While she was in school in Poona she often visited Mohandas Gandhi while he was in prison. She once commented that Gandhi 'was always present in my life; he played an enormous role in my development'.

1947 India is declared independent and Indira Gandhi's father becomes the nation's first prime minister.

1959 Indira is the President of the India National Congress.

1971 Gandhi wins the election by a substantial margin over conservative opponents. Under her ruling India begins to make great strides in the areas of food production and development of an industrial base.

1977 Her party is swept from power.

1978 Indira regains her parliamentary seat and two years later is re-elected to her fourth term as prime minister.

6 June 1984 India is faced with the problem of Sikh extremists in the Punjab using violence to assert their demands in an autonomous state. Gandhi orders the Indian army on 6 June 1984 to storm the Golden Temple at Amritsar, the Sikhs' holiest shrine. Hundreds of Sikhs die in the attack.

31 October 1984 Gandhi is assassinated by her own Sikh bodyguards as she walks to her office. Her only surviving son, Rajiv, succeeds her as prime minister.

1989 Rajiv's ruling ends, but he continues to campaign for re-election.

21 May 1991 Rajiv is also assassinated.

Opposite: Indira Gandhi was assassinated in 1984 by members of her Sikh bodyguard.

1982 Falkland Islands Invaded by Argentina

The Falkland Islands are a group of small islands in the South Atlantic that are located 480 kilometres off the Argentine coast. Although the British government has ruled the islands since the 1800s, in the early 1900s Argentina claimed sovereignty. In 1982, these clashes of control led to a brief undeclared war between Argentina and Great Britain fighting for control of the islands.

Early in 1982, Lieutenant General Leopoldo Galtieri of Argentina, quit long-standing negotiations with Britain and in a politically motivated effort, moved to invade the islands. The Argentine government was run by the military and under heavy criticism for economic mismanagement and human rights abuses. Galtieri believed that if he could 'recover' the islands Argentina would unite behind their military government with patriotic zeal.

Elite Argentine troops specially trained for the invasion landed in the Falklands on 2 April 1982. They quickly overwhelmed the small British garrison at the capital of Stanley. The next day the islands of South Georgia and the South Sandwich group were taken over by Argentine troops. The Argentine people reacted as Galtieri had hoped with large crowds gathering to show support and Galtieri became a hero. In the following weeks Argentine troops poured into the area and before the month ended Argentina had more than 10 000 troops stationed on the islands—most of them poorly trained. The British government declared a 300-kilometre war zone around the Falklands and sent a naval task force to re-take the islands. Europe united in support of Great Britain, and Latin America supported Argentina, with one important exception—Chile. Chile did not agree with their actions and moved their military to a state of alert. Argentina was forced to keep most of its best troops on the mainland. This, and the unexpected US support of Great Britain, did not fare well for Argentina. The British task force set out just three days after Argentina's invasion on its 12 000-kilometre journey to the islands.

On 25 April the British force re-took South Georgia Island. On 14 June, after 74 days of Argentine control, the main conflict ended when the large Argentine garrison surrendered. The South Sandwich Islands were back in British hands six days later. More than 1000 died in the conflict, three-quarters were Argentines. The defeat of Argentina in this conflict led to the fall of their military government, restoring civilian rule in 1983. In Great Britain, Prime Minister Margaret Thatcher garnered tremendous support and popularity because of the British win. The Falklands were back under British protection.

Chronology of Events

26 March 1982 Argentine president General Leopoldo Galtieri announces an invasion of the Falkland Islands will be launched in an attempt to divert public attention from the country's internal problems and restore the popularity and prestige of the dictatorship.

2 April The Argentine navy and thousands of troops land on the Falklands. A small detachment of Royal Marines on the islands put up a brave but futile resistance before the governor orders them to lay down their arms.

25 April Britain re-takes South Georgia Island.

2 May The President of Peru presents a peace proposal to Galtieri, who gives a preliminary acceptance with some proposed modifications.

7 May The United Nations enters peace negotiations.

11 May British Prime Minister Thatcher warns that peaceful settlement may not be possible. Special British forces night-raid on Pebble Island; 11 Argentine aircraft are destroyed on the ground.

18 May A peace proposal presented by the UN Secretary General is rejected by Britain.

28 May The longest and most devastating battle of the war kills 200 Argentine soldiers. About 1400 Argentines surrender and are taken prisoners. According to Argentine sources, only 400 of the 1400 recruits were in a condition to fight.

14 June After many die in continuing battles, the large Argentine garrison in Port Stanley is defeated, effectively ending the conflict.

20 June British re-occupy the South Sandwich Islands.

Opposite: Royal Marines from 40 Commando waiting to be transported by Westland Sea King helicopter to the Falkland Islands.

1981 The AIDS Virus

A new disease that would forever change the world surfaced quietly and subtly. A few scattered deaths occurred in Africa in the 1970s and by 1981 the disease showed up on both coasts of the United States. What was a few cases would soon lead to a fearsome epidemic. Kaposi's Sarcoma, a rare form of skin cancer, appeared in at least eight young homosexual men in New York.

Around the same time, cases of Pneumocystis carinii pneumonia, a pneumonia that did not affect healthy individuals normally, began to show up in both California and New York. Sandra Ford, a drug technician for the Center of Disease Control in Atlanta, noticed an unusual number of requests for the drug pentamine, used for the pneumonia. Then, much to her surprise, there were requests for refills—which had never happened before. The patients were not getting better. Tests indicated that their immune systems were destroyed. With no way to fight their illness, they began to die. The Center for Disease Control warned about the strange outbreak of a killer pneumonia. The announcement made in the bulletin, *Morbidity and Mortality Weekly Report*, on 5 June 1981, spoke of the mysterious disease without an identifiable cause. In the bulletin, five severe pneumonia cases in young homosexual men from Los Angeles were described. The report has been referred to as the 'beginning' of AIDS; in reality it was the beginning of awareness. A task force was formed by the Center of Disease Control to look into the cases of Sarcoma.

By the end of the year 152 cases had been reported and by June of the next year the number had climbed to 452. The disease was first named Gay Related Immune Disorder or GRID, because the victims were all homosexuals, but with the spread of the disease that name changed. First drug addicts using intravenous drugs became afflicted, then women, children and haemophiliacs. The disease spread outside the homosexual community earning a new name: AIDS—Acquired Immune Deficiency Syndrome—and it spread rapidly. A man referred to as 'Patient Zero' aided the spread of the disease. A French-Canadian airline steward, he was known in the homosexual community nationwide. Even after he was diagnosed with the disease and warned by doctors that his actions could quite possibly endanger others, he was not willing to give up his promiscuous ways.

Very possibly he infected hundreds, if not thousands. Others behaved similarly and the disease became common.

Little attention was paid to the disease at first and nothing was done about disease prevention. By 1985 the spread of AIDS had grown to such proportions that it could no longer be ignored. Over 12000 people in America alone were dead or infected and the disease was spreading around the world. Since that time much has been learned about the disease and treatments have been developed to prolong life, but a cure has not yet been discovered.

Chronology of Events

1930s HIV originated from rural areas in Central Africa where the virus may have been present for many years in isolated communities.

1960s Political upheaval, wars and drought forced the people from the small communities to migrate to cities, further spreading the disease.

1970 The HIV epidemic becomes prevalent in Africa, but is not correctly diagnosed.

1981 The first cases of AIDS are recognised in the United States in homosexual communities. Many are initially diagnosed with a form of pneumonia.

1982 The disease's name is changed from Gay Related Immune Disorder (GRID) to Acquired Immune Deficiency Syndrome (AIDS).

1985 The ELISA test to identify HIV in blood becomes available, followed by the development of the Western Blot test. These tests are first employed to screen blood for the presence of HIV before the blood is used in medical procedures.

1999 Scientists confirm that HIV spread from chimpanzees to humans on at least three separate occasions in Central Africa, probably beginning in the 1930s or 1940s.

Currently Although medical efforts continue, there is still no cure for the disease.

Opposite: About five million South Africans out of a popultaion of 44.8 million are infected with HIV or AIDS, the greatest number of any country in the world.

1981 The Personal Computer

A press conference on 12 August 1981 announced the launch of a new computer by IBM. The Personal Computer, or 'PC', would be the springboard for computers to come. The IBM Corporation was ready to introduce its smallest, lowest-priced computer system, the IBM Personal Computer. Designed for business, school and home, the system was easy to use but still quite expensive for the average family. However, the price was much lower than previous systems had been and by early August the machines were on the market. IBM thought 250 000 computers would sell in the first five years; instead, they sold more than three million.

The development of the personal computer began with the need for a fast computing machine, used to solve complex equations dealing with launches and bomb development, in World War II. By 1944 stored programming, or software, was developed. Two years later the first true computer, funded by the Pentagon, was made. It was a vacuum-tubed, room-sized mammoth and it was thought to be impossible for a computer to become any smaller. However, thanks to the invention of the silicon chip, the Altair 8899 became a complex version of the very first personal computer on the market, in 1975. This highly technical model was purchased in a kit and assembled at home. There was no monitor, just flashing lights and toggle switches and the applications were very limited. A select group of hobby enthusiasts began to tinker with them. They soon began designing their own versions and innovations, developed in their basements or garages.

Many companies began to spring up, including Apple. However, none of the new computers was overly popular in the general market. Big companies were the first to become interested in the development of this new concept. IBM, already in the market of machines with the typewriter and adding machine, began working on computer development by the late 1940s. In July 1980 IBM partnered with a young Bill Gates to discuss writing a highly top secret operating system for a new computer. The system developed was called MS-DOS. The development was kept under tight wraps and code words were used to discuss the project. The computer was called 'Acorn', and the secret plans, 'Chess'. Part of the process involved Intel engineers and IBM product developers working together, with a black curtain separating the two groups.

What emerged was the first popular computer, marking the beginning of the computer revolution. Within four months of being introduced, the personal computer was named 'Man of the Year' by *Time* magazine. Personal computers have dramatically altered the way people work, play, learn and communicate.

Chronology of Events

Mid-1940s Early computers are the size of houses and as expensive as battleships, yet have none of the computational power or ease of use common in modern PCs. They are originally used by the military to calculate large equations, but are extremely difficult to use. Only highly educated professionals are able to operate them.

1970s The miniaturisation of electronic circuitry and the invention of integrated circuits and microprocessors enables computer makers to combine the essential elements of a computer onto tiny silicon computer chips, thereby increasing computer performance and decreasing cost. The first microprocessor is originally designed to be the computing and logical processor of calculators and watches. From its simple design modern microprocessors evolved. In 1977 the Apple II was created. It was one of the first PCs to incorporate a colour video display and a keyboard, similar to the computers of today.

1980s In 1981 International Business Machines Corporation (IBM) introduces the IBM PC. It is designed with an open architecture that enables other computer manufacturers to create similar machines that could also run software designed for the IBM PC. Windows, an application program by Microsoft Corporation and the invention of the mouse made PCs even easier to use.

1990s–currently Since the early 1970s, computing power doubles about every 18 months due to the creation of faster microprocessors, the incorporation of multiple microprocessor designs and the development of new storage technologies. With the development of the Internet and the current capabilities of personal computers, almost every household has a PC. The future promises to make PCs even more powerful and useful.

Opposite: An IBM computer retail store displaying the latest products in 1981.

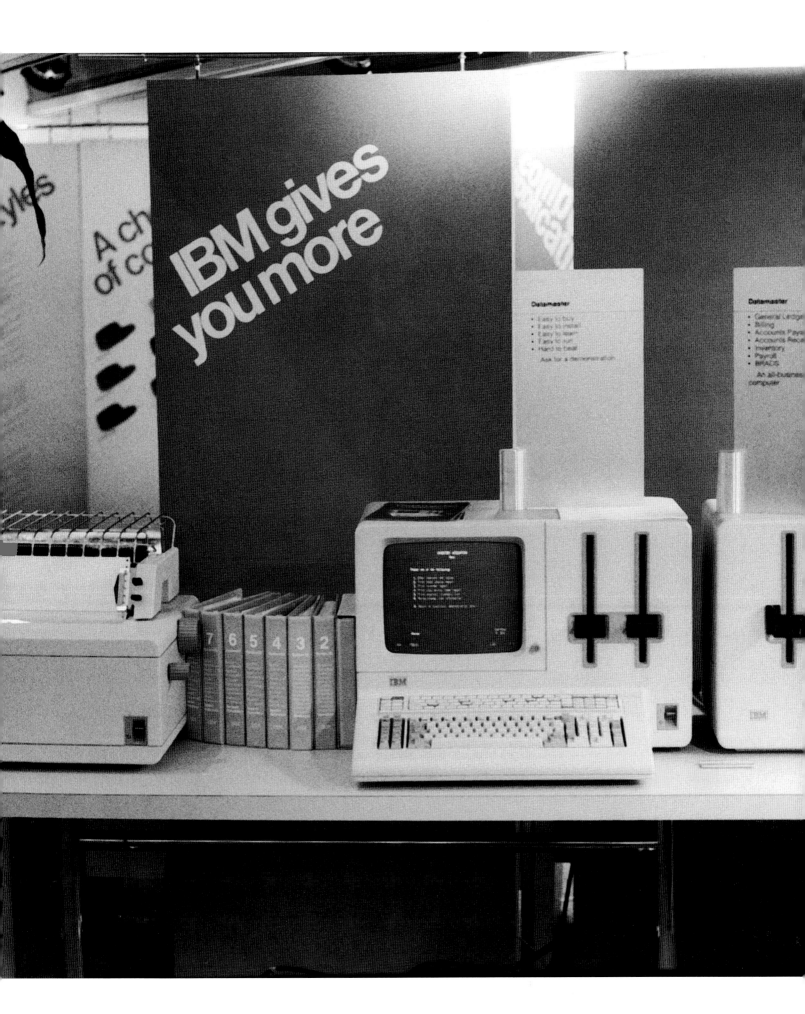

1979 Margaret Thatcher Becomes Prime Minister

Margaret Hilda Roberts, the daughter of a grocer, was born in 1925 in a small town north of London. Her father was active in local politics, serving on the town council and eventually becoming the mayor of the town of Grantham. His political activity sparked her interest and from an early age she had the desire to serve as a Member of Parliament. While in college she became the president of the Oxford University Conservative Association, the first woman to do so. After extensive schooling, she began work as a research chemist at a plastics manufacturing company in Essex in 1947. In her spare time she began studying law. Unsuccessfully, she stood for Parliament twice—in 1950 and 1951. She met Denis Thatcher in 1950 and soon the two were married. Two years later she gave birth to twins, Mark and Carol.

Though now a mother and wife, Thatcher did not forget her political passion. In 1954 she became a barrister and began practising. Finally, in 1959, she entered the House of Commons as a Member of Parliament for Finchley. Thatcher was the first woman to hold this position. She represented that seat for 15 years, until boundary changes made her the Member of Parliament for Barnet, Finchley. Thatcher worked tirelessly and was appointed as the Parliamentary Secretary to the Ministry of Pensions and National Insurance in 1961. She continued receiving appointments and her responsibilities grew.

Eventually, in 1974, she was elected as Leader of the Conservative Party, thus Leader of the Opposition. In 1979 the success of the Conservative Party in the general elections led to her appointment as Prime Minister, First Lord of the Treasury and Minister of the Civil Service. Thatcher was the first woman to hold the British position of Prime Minister. Upon being appointed, Thatcher stated her desire to bring harmony where there was discourse. Soon she had to deal with many conflicts including the Falkland Islands dispute with Argentina and disagreements with many powerful men. As the Prime Minister, Thatcher began her campaign to reverse Britain's economic decline. She worked to break the trade union power and demolish socialism. Her efforts at first had the opposite effect.

Unemployment skyrocketed and it looked like her plan was a failure. Three years after she began serving as Prime Minister, she was victorious in the fight to save the Falklands from Argentine takeover. This helped boost English confidence and the economy, and her popularity increased.

Thatcher was elected to three consecutive terms in the general election, the first British Prime Minister this century to achieve such long-standing popularity. She was succeeded by John Major in 1990.

Chronology of Events

Margaret Thatcher ruled during turbulent times. Here is a snapshot of her third term in office: 1987–90.

19 October 1987 'Black Monday': Dow Jones falls 23 per cent.

8 February 1988 Gorbachev announces Soviet withdrawal from Afghanistan.

15 March 1988 Budget: highest rate of income tax cut to 40 per cent.

17 May 1988 Interest rates cut to 7.5 per cent.

3 June 1989 China: Tiananmen Square massacre.

26 October 1989 Lawson resigns as Chancellor of the Exchequer; Major replaces him.

22 December 1989 Romania: dictator Ceausescu is overthrown and killed.

11 March 1990 Lithuania declares independence of USSR.

2 August 1990 Iraq invades Kuwait.

9 August 1990 United Kingdom announces commitment of forces to the Gulf.

3 October 1990 German reunification.

27 November 1990 Conservative leadership election second ballot; Major becomes leader.

28 November 1990 Margaret Thatcher resigns as Prime Minister; John Major succeeds her.

Opposite: Margaret Thatcher with her husband Denis outside No. 10 Downing Street after her general election success.

1979 Three Mile Island Nuclear Accident

When the Three Mile Island nuclear reactor plant was opened in Harrisburg, Pennsylvania, in September 1978, dedication ceremonies were held in celebration. The nuclear-generating station sat on a 330-hectare island in the middle of the Susquehanna River and housed four reactors. Excitement was high as the new plant was to be the energy solution for the future. The plant was considered too well-designed to have any serious problems. The Secretary of Energy, present at the dedication, called the plant a 'scintillating success', stating that 'nuclear power is a bright and shining option for this country'.

Just six months later an accident occurred at that very plant, which halted nuclear power growth for many years. Due to a malfunction in the cooling system, equipment failure and human error, the worst commercial nuclear accident in US history occurred. At 4.00 a.m. on 28 March 1979 the disastrous chain of events began. During routine maintenance on reactor Unit Two, an air hose was hooked up to the wrong valve and water was introduced into the incorrect part of the reactor system. This triggered a widespread shutdown of valves. A combination of mechanical errors, design error and human error quickly pushed the situation out of control. The reactor core was shut down, but still needed to be cooled. The water supply to the system shut off, preventing cooling, and operators worked furiously to get water back into the system. This was accomplished briefly, but another series of mistakes led to a dangerous loss of water, resulting in the reactor core becoming partially exposed. Radioactive gases escaped into the reactor building's containment section.

At this point the reactor was dangerously close to an irreversible meltdown. An official was able to restore enough coolant to the reactor core to prevent a complete meltdown. The number two reactor was shut down permanently with more than 90 per cent of damage to the reactor core. A 52 per cent meltdown was unable to be stopped.

The building where the reactor was located and several surrounding buildings were contaminated. The number one reactor was also shut down and was out of operation until 1985. Reporters on the scene the next day met with mass confusion. Sirens were going off, warning residents that radiation was being released. More than 100 000 people fled from the area. The press, unfamiliar with and intimidated by nuclear technology, painted a bleak picture of the incident. Panic spread, as there were many similar reactors across the country. Five days after the accident, with assurances of safety, President Carter visited the facility. This calmed the American public, but the damage was done to the nuclear industry.

It took more than a decade to complete the clean-up at Three Mile Island and even longer for nuclear power's reputation to recover. The Institute of Nuclear Power Operations was formed to address issues of safety and regulate performance.

Facts and Figures

The Federal Radiological Emergency Response Plan was not yet in place when the accident at Three Mile Island nuclear power plant occurred. During the initial response, the US Environmental Protection Agency (EPA) deployed offsite radiation monitoring and assessment teams from its labs, and provided onsite and headquarters assistance to the Nuclear Regulatory Commission—the lead federal agency for the response. These actions formed the genesis for today's Federal Radiological Monitoring and Assessment Center and the FRERP.

For eight years after the incident, the EPA maintained a continuous environmental radiation monitoring network in the area surrounding the plant. The state of Pennsylvania took over the responsibility of maintaining the radiation monitoring network in January 1988.

Opposite: A 52 per cent meltdown was unable to be prevented. The building where the reactor was located and several surrounding buildings were contaminated.

1978 Jonestown Suicides

Among the most shocking events of the 20th century was the tragedy that transpired in Jonestown, Guyana, on 18 November 1978. The Jonestown mass suicide, led by cult leader Jim Jones, was the largest ever recorded in South America and devastated the world.

In 1951 Jim Jones began attending communist meetings, quickly warming to the doctrine. Concerned about persecution, Jones decided to use the church as a cover to spread his communist 'gospel'. He worked within the Methodist and then the Pentecostal churches and found that by staging healings he could attract people and financial support. His social gospel did not reflect his true colours until the late 1960s. Jones became preoccupied with the notion he was being persecuted by racists and the government. This paranoia prompted several moves as he tried to find a utopia safe from the 'evil capitalistic society'. He proclaimed himself as the messiah and his followers as the chosen few. He stated that he alone had the truth. Among other things, he said that he had been Moses in a previous life, that he was really a black man in a white body and also that he was an alien.

By the 1970s his church had grown to over 8000 members. His group, The People's Temple, contributed to several charities and he backed several left-wing political candidates. But in 1977, a magazine article detailing his misconduct prompted Jones and 1000 of his followers to move to the Guyanese jungle of South America, later called Jonestown. Jones planned to create an egalitarian agricultural paradise. Hard labour was the reality, and his followers subsisted on rice, learning not to disagree with Jones. Dissent was met with severe punishment. Some of his people slipped away, much to his distress, and pressure from the outside grew as people brought back stories of suicide drills and Jones's ravings. US representative Leo Ryan, who had been contacted by many concerned individuals, decided to lead a group of relatives and reporters to Jonestown. Their visit on 17 November was relatively uneventful but several members quietly asked to leave with them.

The next day, 18 November, Ryan's group, with the defecting members, was ambushed when they tried to leave from a nearby airstrip. Ryan and four others were killed and 10 wounded. That night Jones told his followers, 'the time has come for us to meet in another place', and the Jonestown physician and nurses prepared a mixture of tranquillisers and cyanide. The vast majority of the group were convinced that they were committing 'an act of revolutionary suicide protesting the conditions of an inhumane world', and voluntarily took the poison. Over 900 people died including 294 children under the age of 18. Only 85 members of the group survived, many hiding in the jungle. The incident left the world in complete shock.

Chronology of Events

September 1954 James Warren Jones is given an invitation to preach at an Assemblies of God Pentecostal Church.

April 1955 His religious group the 'Wings of Deliverance' is formed, one of the few inter-racial congregations of the time.

1960 The group changes its name to the People's Temple to more adequately describe their assembly. It is officially made a member of the Disciples of Christ Churches. Jones is ordained as a minister.

1965 After many threats are directed at Jones and his followers from racists disapproving of their inter-racial church, the People's Temple is moved to Ukiah, California.

Early 1977 After receiving bad press and being investigated by the Internal Revenue Service, Jones moves to Guyana and the People's Temple Agricultural Mission is founded. It grows slowly, at first only housing approximately 50 people.

17 November 1978 US representative Leo Ryan arrives in Jonestown to investigate several reports made about the congregation. A few members ask to leave with him.

18 November 1978 Jones's followers kill Ryan and defecting members as they board a plane to the US. Later that night, Jones tells the group it is time to leave this world. He and over 900 followers commit mass suicide.

Opposite: Bodies lie in the compound of the People's Temple after 900 members of the cult participated in mass suicide.

1978 The First Test-tube Baby

A perfectly healthy baby girl was born on 25 July 1978 at 11.47 p.m. in Oldham General Hospital in Manchester, England. Louise Joy Brown, with blue eyes and blonde hair, looked just like any other newborn infant. But she was the world's first test-tube baby. Her birth marked the beginning of new hope for many couples. Over 20 per cent of women unable to conceive have blocked fallopian tubes, closing the route of the egg from the ovaries to the uterus. Dr Patrick Steptoe, a gynaecologist, and Dr Robert Edwards, a specialist in reproductive physiology from Cambridge University, began working together in 1966 to find a remedy for the problem. They had progressed to the point of successfully fertilising an egg outside a woman's body. However, they were having trouble successfully replacing the egg.

In 1977 about 80 attempts were made at implantation. Of these, many women never showed signs of pregnancy. The women who did become pregnant suffered miscarriages in the first few weeks. This was frustrating and heartbreaking for the couples and the doctors. The two doctors began to wonder if their procedure would ever succeed.

A young couple from Bristol, John and Lesley Brown, had tried for nine years to start a family, but failed due to blocked fallopian tubes. Finally, in 1976 they were referred to Dr Steptoe. On 10 November 1977, Dr Steptoe performed a procedure on Lesley Brown, removing an egg from her ovary with a long, slender probe. The egg was passed to Dr Edwards, who mixed it with sperm from John Brown. After the egg was fertilised, it was placed in a special nurturing solution designed to support the egg as it began to divide. They called this process in vitro fertilisation, since it was performed outside the body, in a laboratory vessel. (*Vitro* is the Latin word for 'glass'.) On previous attempts the egg was reintroduced after having divided into 64 cells, a four- to five-day process. This time the doctors agreed to alter the procedure and wait only two and a half days to implant the egg.

Within a short time Lesley showed signs of pregnancy. The weeks moved on and the pregnancy moved ahead normally. The world began to take note. With Lesley's rise in blood pressure, a short time before the baby was due, Dr Steptoe decided to perform a caesarean section to deliver the baby. Having scheduled the operation for the next day, Dr Steptoe sidestepped the press. He drove home as usual and the press assumed he was home for the night—but then he came back. That night in a small, very crowded operating room, Louise Joy entered the world. Her birth was greeted with mixed reactions.

The procedure, while considered a breakthrough for medicine and science, brought up ethical concerns. Top of the list were the health consequences for the child. Concerns for possible misuse in the future were voiced. However, for the Browns it was a simple question of family, and they finally had one. Five years later they had a second daughter, Natalie, using the same procedure. Later, Natalie became the first test-tube baby to become a mother herself. Today thousands of couples have followed in the Browns' steps to start a family using IVF.

Chronology of Events

1899 The first artificial insemination of an egg is performed with a sea urchin.

1907 Scientists are able to grow cells outside an organism, or in vitro.

1966 Doctors Steptoe and Brown begin study on in vitro fertilisation. None of the attempts over the next few years succeed.

1967 Scientists C.B. Jacobson and R.H. Barter use amniocentesis, a procedure in which DNA is taken from the womb for prenatal diagnosis of a genetic disorder.

1977 Artificial insemination (the procedure in which sperm is placed into the womb using a probe) becomes available. The world's first sperm bank opens, selling sperm of 'intellectually superior' donors, including Nobel Prize winners.

1978 The birth of Louise Brown, the first 'test-tube baby' conceived through in vitro fertilisation.

Opposite: Louise Brown, the first 'test-tube baby' born through in vitro fertilisation (IVF).

1977 Elvis Presley Dies

Elvis Presley, the 'King' of rock'n'roll, was born on 8 January 1935. He was to become one of the world's greatest superstars. His parents, Vernon and Gladys Presley, lived in Tupelo, Mississippi, but often moved in search of work. In 1953 Elvis graduated from high school in Memphis, Tennessee. After graduating, he began working as a truck driver. One day he passed a recording studio sign that read, 'Make your own records—$2 for four songs'. Elvis went to the Sun Records studio and recorded two singles, and that was where his singing career began. His unique sound was a combination of gospel and rhythm and blues, both of which were ingrained in Elvis's background, which mixed together to form rock'n'roll. After a year Elvis's new manager put together a deal with RCA records. Two days before his 21st birthday he entered the RCA studio and in January 1956 had his first hit, 'Heartbreak Hotel'. A new era of American music and culture began. Elvis quickly became an international star and appeared on several television shows, most notably, the *Ed Sullivan Show*. Before an audience of 56 million he sang and gyrated, causing such a stir the show was compelled to only film him from the waist up. Adults considered him a scandalous rebel, so naturally the teenage crowds loved him.

Soon movies entered the mix and Elvis quickly starred in four, but his career halted temporarily in 1958 when he was drafted. He enlisted in the US army and spent the next two years in Germany, a model soldier. When he returned to America his career continued. Although he worked hard to regain his popularity, his rebel stature was gone and he was soon replaced by the Beatles and other rising stars. However, he still had a huge following and in the next several years made 21 movies, all box office hits.

Elvis's private life began to suffer from his extreme fame. His most faithful followers sheltered him from the outside world and by the late 1960s he was almost a total recluse. He began overeating and abusing prescription drugs. In 1967, Elvis married Priscilla Beaulieu and they had a daughter, Lisa-Marie. Working in Las Vegas, he began sleeping days and working nights, continually eating too much and abusing drugs. He became unstable and paranoid. Priscilla divorced him in 1973. Elvis began to fall apart but he kept on performing. On 16 August 1977 Elvis was found dead in his bathroom at Graceland, his heart finally giving out. He left a large legacy behind. Over 400 million copies of his albums were sold, he made 33 movies and he was known worldwide simply as the King. Fans are still devoted and his Graceland mansion, now run by his daughter, receives over half a million visitors a year—some still refusing to believe that Elvis has left the building.

Chronology of Events

1935 Elvis Presley is born with stillborn twin brother, Jesse, in Tupelo, Mississippi.

1953 Elvis graduates from LC Humes High School in Memphis, Tennessee. He becomes a truck driver.

1954 Elvis pays $2 to a Memphis studio and records his first two songs. A few months later he releases his debut single 'That's Alright'.

1955 Elvis makes his first television appearance on *Louisiana Hayride*. He performs in his first major concert in Texas. Local kid Buddy Holly opens for him.

1956 The 'Hound Dog' single goes to number one and stays there for a record-breaking 11 weeks. Later that year, 54 million viewers turn their TV dials to CBS as Ed Sullivan introduces 21-year-old singer Elvis 'The Pelvis' Presley. *Love Me Tender*, Elvis's first film, premieres.

1957 The movie *Jailhouse Rock* opens in US theatres. It is still considered to be Elvis's best film.

1958 Elvis is drafted into the US army. Though he served his duty, America lost an estimated $500000 in taxes each year that Private Presley was in the army.

1960 US army promotes Elvis Presley to sergeant. He returns to civilian life after two years.

1967 Elvis Presley and Priscilla Beaulieu marry in Las Vegas, Nevada. A year later their daughter Lisa-Marie is born.

1977 Elvis Presley dies of a heart attack.

Opposite: A 1955 portrait of Elvis Presley.

1976 The Concorde

Supersonic commercial transportation was being talked about as early as the 1950s. In the summer of 1961, discussions began in earnest in England and France. Over a year later the French President, Charles de Gaulle, asked Britain to join with France in a cooperative effort to build an aircraft that would fly at supersonic speeds. The project was too big for either country to tackle alone; both countries' aircraft industries and financial backing would be needed for the task. On 29 November 1962, the two countries signed an agreement to undertake the project. The project was publicly named on 13 January 1963, when de Gaulle described the plane as 'the Concorde'. The project received international interest.

In 1964 US President Kennedy announced his desire for the United States to back the development of an American supersonic airline. Russia also began development of their own supersonic plane. Airlines too showed interest with Pan American Airlines signing an option to buy a number of the aircraft once they were developed. Other airlines followed suit. French and British journalists were shown an experimental model of the Concorde in Bristol, England, in October 1964. The first piece of metal was cut the following spring, marking the beginning of the prototype's production. During the next two and a half years great effort and extensive testing were expended to make the prototypes.

On 11 December 1967, the first French prototype was rolled out in Toulouse, France, with 1100 excited onlookers. It was called the Concorde 001, the 'e' added at the end due to French spelling. The British technology minister announced that the British prototype would also be called the Concorde, the 'e' standing for excellence, England, and Europe. The Concorde was proclaimed a generation ahead of any other public transportation in all categories. When the British Concorde 002 rolled out it was fully painted and already had modifications incorporated into the design. Meanwhile the Russians unveiled their supersonic craft, nicknamed the 'Concordski' because of its similarity to the Concorde.

Captained by test pilot Andre Turcat, the Concorde finally took off at 3.40 p.m. on 2 March 1969. Twenty minutes later it performed a perfect landing. The Concorde did not fly at supersonic speeds that day or during the next several test flights. It was not until the 45th test flight that the aeroplane exceeded Mach 1—the speed of sound. Much more needed to be accomplished before certification, but in 1976 the aircraft was finally available to airlines.

On 21 January 1976, Air France Concorde and British Airways Concorde took off at the same time in the inaugural flight of the commercial supersonic Concorde. Because the commercial aircraft was able to cross the Atlantic in three hours, passengers leaving from Europe beat the time difference and landed in New York before their local departure time. Though very time efficient, the Concorde proved to be very expensive to run.

Facts and Figures

- To fly across the ocean at nearly twice the speed of sound, the Concorde uses a tonne of fuel for every passenger seat. Usually seating 100 passengers, the plane costs over $400 000 to fuel. A Boeing 747 uses about $450 000 but the subsonic plane has room for 400 passengers.

- Maintenance costs were also high as for every hour in the air, the jet had to spend 12 on the ground for maintenance. The planes began to degrade with age and many blame technical faults for the Concorde crash in 2000, near Paris. The crash also caused fear among passengers, many not willing to pay the $13 000 for a round-trip plane ticket, and business slowed immensely.

- On 24 October 2003 the Concorde made its last commercial flight after 27 years of commercial flying. It was phased out due to expensive maintenance fees and decreasing passenger numbers.

- Though there are no more immediate plans to develop a new commercial concorde airline, it is said that a cheaper one will inevitably be developed. More than 250 000 people gathered at Heathrow Airport to watch the Concorde's last landing.

Opposite: The cover of Newsweek *features an exclusive photograph of the Concorde take-off that clearly captures the fire on the inboard engine of the flight.*

Newsweek

THE INTERNATIONAL NEWSMAGAZINE

August 7, 2000

After the Crash

The Concorde: What Went Wrong

The Future of Supersonic Travel

July 25, 2000: AF 4590 shortly after takeoff

1976 VHS Videotape

Many technological changes occurred in the 20th century that revolutionised the way we spend our time and the way we see the world. With the invention of VHS, home videos were introduced and eventually, Digital Video Discs (DVDs) took over the market. Over the past 50 years, these inventions have allowed us to essentially be able to control what we view at home. The compact VHS tapes were the first in a string of home entertainment inventions. The tapes are a result of a great deal of perseverance and dedication.

Before World War II the problem of how to record on tape was already being researched. In the 1950s a team of very dedicated and very patient men began working on the problem. With much design work, testing and refining the VTR, Video Tape Recorder, was developed. In 1956 they announced their discovery to the press, showed a video tape, then taped the audience and played it back. After the demonstration the audience was totally silent and stunned before erupting into thunderous applause. The recorder was big and bulky, costing US$50 000. It was only used commercially. On 30 November 1956, the first taped television show aired. After that landmark, several companies began working to further the technology. Sony was the first company to move toward introducing a home-use video cassette recorder, or VCR, closely followed by JVC. The Sony system, Betamax, was released in 1975 and used small, compact tapes that recorded up to

an hour each. The JVC tape was slightly different and non-compatible. Eventually the VHS created by JVC gained the most popularity in the consumer market and Betamax disappeared. Sony claims that their product was stolen; they shared their technology with JVC and it was taken, changed and released in a slightly altered but non-compatible format. JVC, Victor Company of Japan, maintains they had already developed their own video cassette and had no interest in Sony's offer.

DVD, which stands for Digital Video Disc or Digital Versatile Disc, was the next generation of optical disc storage technology that rapidly began to replace VHS. DVD holds 4.7 gigabytes of information on one of its two sides, or enough for a 133-minute movie. With two layers on each of its two sides, it will hold up to 17 gigabytes of video, audio or other information. DVD as an industry standard was announced in November 1995 and first appeared in Japan in November 1996, followed by US players in March 1997. The invention of DVD cannot be attributed to one person or one company, but rather a collaboration of all of the technology leaders of the time. In 1998 Sony introduced the first flat screen television. Within five years more than 40 million have been sold worldwide. Our society has changed immensely because of these developments and along with surround-sound home theatre systems and video games, have shaped future entertainment systems.

Opposite: The Sony system, Betamax, was released in 1975 and used small, compact tapes that recorded up to an hour of footage.

1974 Cyclone Tracy Hits Australia

Tragedy struck the small city of Darwin in the Northern Territory of Australia on Christmas Eve in 1974. A tropical cyclone swept through and almost completely demolished the growing city. Though cyclones were common in the area, passing through during the monsoonal wet seasons, none was as devastating as Cyclone Tracy. Darwin's position has always been important to Australia as the gateway to Asia. In the early 1970s, the city became a boomtown, swelling from 15 000 to 48 000 in a matter of years. By 1974 Darwin had grown immensely and many new buildings were constructed, most of them poorly and not suited for the cyclonic weather the city often endured.

On 20 December 1974, a weak tropical low began to form 700 kilometres northeast of Darwin. The storm developed quickly, and by the next day was officially classified as a tropical cyclone and given the name Cyclone Tracy. The storm was well to the north of Australia and weather reports on 22 December assured the inhabitants of Darwin that the storm would not affect the city. It had been many years since a large storm had struck, and no one was concerned about the distant Tracy. The storm was slow and small, only 50 kilometres in diameter and, as forecasted, moved steadily for two days in a southwest path north of Darwin. However, as Cyclone Tracy rounded the western rim of Bathurst Island it abruptly turned 90 degrees. Now heading in an east-southeasterly direction, the storm increased in speed and strength and headed directly for Darwin. As it hit the warm water of the Gulf, it gained even more strength. Warnings were issued but it was Christmas Eve and no one paid attention; few were prepared for the massive destruction.

By late in the afternoon dark clouds hung low over the city, unleashing torrential rain, and the wind began to gust. The storm continued to grow more severe by the hour and though small, it was powerful with winds gusting up to 217 kilometres per hour. Because the storm was slow, the city was under assault for hours. Throughout the night many fled, most in pyjamas or without shoes, driving away in their cars. At 4.00 a.m. on Christmas Day, the eye of the storm passed directly over Darwin. The calm was brief and the winds that followed were even more intense than what

had already been endured. The storm continued to pound the city for three more hours. Darwin was left devastated. The next morning Australia woke to news of the disaster. Forty-nine people had died that night, 16 more at sea, and the number of those injured was staggering. The poorly constructed buildings could not withstand the ravages of the cyclone and 70 per cent were destroyed or badly damaged. All services including power, water, sewage and communications were cut off.

Assistance was rapid and heartfelt, not only from Australia but worldwide. Communities organised help for the refugees—money was donated, and provisions prepared. People who had not been able to leave the city by car were airlifted out and into the waiting arms of volunteers. Within six days the population was reduced to a little more than 10 000. Then the clean-up and rebuilding process began, and with help of the Australian government, Darwin was eventually restored.

Facts and Figures

Size Gales extended to about 40 kilometres from the centre of the cyclone

Diameter of eye About 12 kilometres at Darwin

Maximum wind speed 217 kilometres per hour before the anemometer ceased functioning

Central pressure 950 hectopascals

Storm surge 1.6 metres measured in the harbour; 4 metres estimated at Casuarina Beach

Rainfall 255 millimetres in 12 hours overnight

Death toll 65 people

Injuries 145 serious injuries, over 500 with minor injuries

Houses destroyed About 70 per cent of houses were reduced to rubble and almost all suffered serious structural damage

Total damage costs Up to $800 million

Opposite: Total shock and devastation for the locals of Darwin. Sixty-five people were killed and the number injured was staggering.

1973 The Disco Phenomenon

During the last half of the 1960s the foundations of funk music had been laid by musicians such as James Brown, Sly and the Family Stone and The Ojays. However, it was not until the 1970s that funk music opened the doors to the disco subculture. After rock music's domination of the past 20 years, dance music was reincarnated through the disco. With new instruments such as synthesisers and electronic sounds, music had taken a completely different form, unrecognisable from past records. The female contribution was much more relevant in disco-music than it had ever been in rock music. Several of the early disco singles were sung by women, such as Gloria Gaynor and Grace Jones, establishing a primacy that would endure through the years. ABBA released their song 'Dancing Queen' in 1976. The single went to number one in America and their album broke all advance order records. The band had become so popular that their own movie was released and world tours persisted for almost a decade. The Swedish pop group was the most successful from their native country and second only to the Beatles in total worldwide sales.

In 1977 the film *Saturday Night Fever* officially launched disco fever around the world. Millions of kids stopped dreaming of becoming guitarists and started dreaming of becoming dancers. Soon disco music was becoming a mass-market phenomenon. The movie also launched the Bee Gees into international stardom (once again). The Bee Gees agreed to participate in the creation to the soundtrack for *Saturday Night Fever*, and the album broke multiple records for soundtrack sales. Three Bee Gees hits—'Stayin' Alive', 'How Deep Is Your Love?' and 'Night Fever'—reached number one, launching the most popular age of disco. The album has since sold over 15 million copies worldwide, making it the best-selling soundtrack of all time. The Bee Gees became bigger than ever before and disco was at its peak. After enjoying several years as the leading music genre in Western cultures, disco was rapidly declining in popularity and viability. Music listeners were being drawn to heavy metal and punk music as the 1970s ended. The golden era of disco music essentially ended in 1979, just as Michael Jackson became a solo artist. Jackson went on to release the greatest selling album of all time, *Thriller*, in 1981, using the

disco genre as its backbone. The new form of music used a trivial collage of pop-soul tunes and dance beats, orchestrated by employing state-of-the-art technology such as synthesisers. Though the disco era was relatively short-lived, elements of it can still be heard in today's dance music.

Above: The Jackson 5 led a cultural music shift during the 1970s.
Opposite: In 1977 the film Saturday Night Fever *officially launched disco fever around the world.*

1972 The Space Shuttle

As the Apollo program started to wind down in the late 1960s, NASA began to dream up future programs. The space shuttle was to be the world's first partially reusable space launch system and part of a space station project, designed to shuttle astronauts back and forth from Earth to the station. During these years NASA's plans collided with a small budget and many programs were cancelled. The only program to survive was that of the space shuttle.

In January 1972, the space shuttle program was launched. Each shuttle consisted of four elements including the shuttle itself, two solid-fuel rocket boosters and an external fuel tank which separated 8.5 minutes after lift-off and burnt up in the atmosphere. The project progressed slowly because of budget restraints and the first craft was not completed for four years. The first shuttle was originally called the *Constitution*, but a huge write-in campaign from TV series Star Trek fans led to it being renamed the *Enterprise*. It was used for landing and gliding tests only. The *Columbia*, the first fully functional shuttle, was delivered to the Kennedy Space Center in March 1979 and launched two years later. More shuttles followed. Two shuttles have been lost since the beginning of the program. The *Challenger* exploded during a launch in January 1986 and on 1 February 2003, after a successful mission, the *Columbia* disintegrated during re-entry. In both tragic events, none of the crew survived. Three shuttles remain in operation: the *Atlantis*, *Discovery* and *Endeavour*.

Although the shuttle was initially considered as a money-saving idea, each launch remains very expensive, costing about US$500 million. Much of the cost is due to the measures taken to ensure safety. Each system is individually inspected before the craft is allowed to take off, a process that takes several months. The space shuttle program has overall been very successful. Millions of pounds of cargo, including satellites, have been transported. Scientific experiments and repairs on satellites and observatories have been accomplished. Several hundred people have been transported into space via the space shuttle. There have even been technological spin-offs from the space program, ranging from the artificial heart to jewellery design advances, the ear thermometer to treatment for children with brain tumours. The space shuttle has proven to be the world's most versatile and reliable space-launch system.

Opposite: Astronaut Paul W. Richards, mission specialist, waves at his crew mate during the second STS-102 space walk in March 2001.

1972 Bloody Sunday

After years of violent religious riots in Northern Ireland, the British government introduced a concept of internment without trial on 9 August 1971. In an effort to decrease violence in the country, this concept gave British authorities the right to imprison citizens without due process. Not surprisingly, the policy was not popular. Anger grew, fostering new civil unrest and protests. One such protest was organised in Derry, Ireland, by the Northern Ireland Civil Rights Association. The planned march was not legal as Stormont Parliament had recently banned any protests, fearing they would only cause violence.

Nonetheless, a peaceful march was set for Sunday 30 January 1972. The demonstration would start at the Creggan Estate and end up in Guildhall Square where a rally would be held. On the appointed day a crowd of 10 000 gathered and at 2.50 p.m. the march began. As they marched, the ranks of protesters swelled up to 20 000 and turning onto William Street the crowds were met with a British blockade. All approaches to Guildhall Square were barricaded. The British government, nervous about a possible uprising, had called in troops to keep the situation under control. The British army's 1st Parachute Regiment was there to back up the Royal Green Jackets, as well as other battalions. The well-trained, heavily armed soldiers had set up blockades on several streets. As the marchers reached the blockade, confusion started to move through the crowd. The organisers of the march led most of the demonstrators away from the soldiers, but a few protesters remained, throwing rocks at the soldiers. For their retaliation they received rubber bullets, gas and hosing with a water cannon.

After the main body of protesters turned away, they were met with another blockade. Once again confusion developed and then suddenly, at 4.10 p.m., panic and violence erupted. People began to riot and the soldiers were ordered to make arrests. Over the next half hour troops shot 108 times. Twenty-six unarmed civilians were hit, killing 13 at the time and another dying later. Seven of the dead were younger than 19 years of age.

After the incident the British government appointed Lord Justice Widgery to lead a tribunal and investigate the shootings. The tribunal found the soldiers not guilty of any wrongdoing, stating that they had been fired upon first. Their findings were met by public outrage and the incident served to fuel the cause of the Irish Republican Army, inspiring many new recruits. Bloody Sunday became a call to arms. In response, London worked to directly rule over the area. Northern Ireland, already unstable, erupted in violence and the unrest has continued for decades. Pressured by the families of the victims as well as many other sources, Tony Blair, the British Prime Minister, called for a new inquiry in 1998. The inquiry has continued for five years, and is viewed with hope as a vital step to resolution in Northern Ireland. Both sides want to begin the healing process and hope for resolution.

Chronology of Events

2.00 p.m. 30 January 1972 The Northern Ireland Civil Rights Association march is supposed to officially begin. Delays occur and the march does not begin for a further 50 minutes.

2.50 p.m. The march finally leaves from Central Drive in the Creggan Estate and heads towards the area of Bogside. People continue to join the march throughout the route.

3.25 p.m. The march passes the Bogside Inn and turns up Westland Street before going down William Street. The number of protesters reaches close to 20 000.

3.45 p.m. The marchers follow organisers' instructions and head toward the area where the rally is to be held. However, they are met by a British army blockade and small riots erupt.

3.55 p.m. Hiding in an abandoned building, British soldiers open fire and injure two protesters. They are taken to hospital but one of the injured later dies from his wounds.

4.10 p.m. Soldiers from the Support Company begin to open fire on people in the meeting area, many protesters cannot escape the bullets.

4.40 p.m. The shooting finally ends, leaving 13 people dead and a further 14 seriously injured.

Opposite: An armed soldier attacks a protester on Bloody Sunday when British paratroopers shot dead 13 civilians during a civil rights march in Derry City.

1971 Idi Amin Comes to Power

Idi Amin Dada Oumee, known as the 'Butcher of Africa' ruled Uganda brutally from January 1971 until April 1979. He gained power by a coup and the former president, Milton Obote, fled to Tanzania. Initially, Amin seemed to be a leader with promise. He stated that his intention was to provide a 'caretaker role' until a civilian government could be established. Political prisoners were freed and the Secret Police were disbanded. His public persona was light-hearted, but his brutality soon surfaced. Amin ruled in a military fashion. Killer squads were formed to hunt down and brutally liquidate his opposition, and many were beheaded. The first year he was in power about two-thirds of the army's 9000 soldiers were executed. In August 1972, claiming he was acting upon a 'warning from God' given in a dream, Amin ordered the 50 000 to 70 000 Asian inhabitants in Uganda to leave the country within 90 days. He seized their property and then distributed it to his army. Of course, he also initially benefited from the spoils. The seized businesses were mismanaged and soon failed, resulting in the disruption of the nation's economy. With the heavy burden of Amin's ever-growing army the economy eventually began to collapse.

Shortly after the Asian expulsion, Obote, supported by the Acholi and Lango tribes, endeavoured to regain control of Uganda by a military coup. The attempt failed. Amin responded by bombing Tanzanian towns and wiping out entire villages. In his army, Acholi and Lango officers were purged. The Nile River was clogged with corpses. In Kampala, the Nile Mansions Hotel became the site of Amin's interrogation and torture. Hundreds of thousands were murdered by 1974. Amin fed the heads of his opponents to crocodiles and boasted of eating their flesh. He severed the strained relations with Israel in 1972, and then in 1976 broke ties with Britain. Amin turned to Libya and the Soviet Union as allies. He also attempted to establish ties with the Palestine Liberation Organisation. The hijacking of Air France Flight 139 in 1976 was supported by Amin, and he offered a landing location at Entebbe Airport. Israeli paratroopers launched a successful rescue operation to free the hostages, resulting in Uganda's air force being badly damaged. Embarrassed, Amin ordered more executions, including that of the one hostage left behind—a grandmother who had been released for medical treatment.

By October 1978 an estimated 300 000 people had been murdered but his reign of terror was coming to an end. Internationally, Amin's actions were condemned and no country was willing to stand with him. To bolster Uganda's economy, he decided to take over Tanzania. The backlash from the Tanzanian president and troops ousted Amin. He fled, leaving behind a tattered country with a staggering national debt. With his four wives, numerous mistresses and 20 children, he sought exile in Libya and ultimately ended up in Saudi Arabia where he died in August 2003.

Chronology of Events

9 October 1962 Uganda gains independence after nearly 70 years of British rule.

25 January 1971 Idi Amin seizes power in a military coup and overthrows Milton Obote.

1972 President Idi Amin begins a three-month-long process to expel 50 000 Asians from the country. Many left almost everything they owned behind to be pilfered by Amin's henchmen and handpicked supporters.

18 December 1972 Idi Amin nationalised 41 foreign-owned farms and tea estates, of which 34 were British. This eventually led to the expulsion of all foreign business, the effects of which are still being felt today.

April 1979 Idi Amin is overthrown and Milton Obote once again assumes power.

26 January 1986 After years of civil war in which hundreds of thousands are either killed or are displaced, Yoweri Museveni's National Resistance Army takes power. Under his leadership, Uganda has steadily achieved economic growth, the rebuilding of the shattered infrastructure, a free press and judiciary, and peace in most parts of the country.

August 2003 Idi Amin dies in a hospital in Saudi Arabia, after spending a month on life support. He is 80 years old.

Opposite: Idi Amin, President of Uganda, came to power with a reputation as a man of the people, a genial giant with a ready smile who promised to turn his agriculturally lush nation into a political utopia.

1969 The Internet is Born

The Internet has revolutionised communication and technology worldwide. The developers of the Internet, starting with a few committed researchers, strove to share their ideas and innovations to develop a cooperative venture between academia, government and industry. This joining of minds and resources set the stage for a system that combines the innovations of telegraph, telephone, radio and computer into a technology that has literally changed our society forever.

A glimmer of the concept was conceived in 1961 when a paper was written by Leonard Kleinrock that set forth the packet-switching theory. In the summer of 1962, J.C.R. Licklider wrote a series of memos about a 'Galactic Network', where information could be accessed by anyone, anywhere in the world. A few months later he was made the head of a computer research program for the Defense Advanced Research Projects Agency (DARPA). There, his interest in the concept of networking inspired others.

Five years later the first plan for Advanced Research Projects Agency Network (ARPANET), the original Internet, was laid out. Packet switches were developed in the late 1960s, which proved to be one of the key components in the transfer of information. These switches, called Interface Message Processors (IMP), were installed at the Californian university, UCLA. In 1969 the first host computer was connected. By the end of the year, four host computers were connected. ARPANET worked and the network began to take shape. Development continued steadily and dynamically but usage was limited, designed for scholars and technological scientists. However, as the personal computer developed, applications for a more diverse network became suddenly obvious. Developers adapted the system to meet future demands by using communication, cooperation, flexibility and insight. They developed an 'open architecture' structure that could handle the Internet's potential. Black boxes, or gateways, were used to connect networks. These routers provided a means for the information to travel without retaining any of the information, keeping the system simple. There would be no global control at the operations level.

In 1974 the first public package, named Telenet was made available. Other networks quickly sprung up and by the end of 1989 the network supported 160 000 hosts. ARPANET ceased to exist in 1990, and the system converted to the Internet. When the World Wide Web began in 1991, Internet usage exploded. By 1992 there were more than a million users and surfing the Internet became a common pastime. Soon governments went online, as well as the United Nations, banks and even pizza delivery. The concept started by a small group of researchers has now developed into a global behemoth generating billions of dollars of annual investment.

Chronology of Events

1969 ARPANET, a network with nodes at UCLA, Stanford Research Institute, the UC Santa Barbara, and the University of Utah, is commissioned by the US Department of Defense for research purposes.

1971 Email is developed by Ray Tomlinson to send messages across a distributed network as ARPANET grows to 15 nodes.

1972 The email program for ARPANET is modified and becomes immensely popular. The @ sign is used to specify a string as an email address.

1974 Telenet, the first public packet data service, a commercial version of ARPANET, makes its debut.

1982 The first definitions of the term 'Internet' surfaces. *Time* magazine calls 1982 'The Year of the Computer'.

1986 The National Science Foundation creates NSFNET allowing a large number of institutions, especially universities, to get connected.

1988 Internet Relay Chat (IRC) is introduced by Jarkko Oikarinen. Later Internet chat rooms would be developed using this system.

1991 Tim Berners-Lee invents the World Wide Web.

1993 The first graphical Web browser, Mosaic, is released. Internet traffic explodes at a growth rate of 341 634 per cent annually.

2004 Over one billion people worldwide are linked to the Internet. Personal computer use soars.

Opposite: Cyber cafes now host most of the world's internet use.

1969 Woodstock

Music during the 1960s was dominated by psychedelic rock from artists such as the Doors, Jimmy Hendrix and The Who. The youth at the time were often referred to as hippies who characteristically rejected materialism and authority, protested against the Vietnam War, supported the civil rights movement, dressed unconventionally, and experimented with sex and illicit drugs.

The Woodstock Festival was a defining event for the late 1960s and early 1970s and celebrated peace and the music of the era. Taking place near Woodstock, New York, on 15, 16, and 17 August 1969, it became a symbol of the 1960s American counterculture and a milestone in the history of rock music. Woodstock was devised by Michael Lang, then the manager of a rock band, an executive at Capitol Records, and two venture capitalists, John Roberts and Joel Rosenman. Their original plan was to build a recording studio in Woodstock, a small town in the Catskill Mountains that had become a year-round music resort and artists' colony. It housed campuses for art students and many recording artists such as Bob Dylan and the Band lived in the area. The Woodstock Music and Art Fair was organised to promote the idea of the new recording studio.

The music festival was expected to attract 50 000 to 100 000 people but eventually it was clear that the audience was going to be much larger—over 400 000 people. Traffic jams kilometres long blocked most roads leading to the area as the festival began. It was decided that admission fees would be too hard to monitor with people constantly leaving and returning to the festival, so they were dropped. Crowds were so large that helicopters had to fly in food and medical supplies as blocked traffic routes made access to the farm impossible. Many of the musical acts had to be dropped in by helicopters because of the same problem.

The world's greatest musical talents of the time performed at the massive event, making it a monumental experience. Performers included Creedence Clearwater Revival, Crosby Stills Nash and Young, Joe Cocker, the Grateful Dead, Ravi Shankar and Janis Joplin. Jimi Hendrix was the final act of the festival; he played a solo guitar rendition of 'The Star Spangled Banner'.

Facts and Figures

- It took over six months to prepare the festival.
- Max Yasgur's farm was rented for $50 000 for the festival's three-day duration.
- Over 700 kilograms of food supplies were airlifted in by helicopters.
- Within 14 months of their Woodstock performances, both Janis Joplin and Jimi Hendrix would be dead.
- Over 30 people were arrested during the festival on various drug offences.
- Over 6000 audience members were treated by doctors on the site.
- The average price of drugs such as acid and mescaline was $4. Over 400 people were treated after taking drugs at the concert.
- The festival was a peaceful success and was documented in the motion picture *Woodstock* in 1970.
- An encore performance of the festival was held in 1994, but was not even close in size or effect of the 1969 concert.

List of performers Joan Baez, the Band, Blood Sweat and Tears, the Paul Butterfield Blues Band, Canned Heat, Joe Cocker, Country Joe McDonald and the Fish, Creedence Clearwater Revival, Crosby Stills Nash and Young, the Grateful Dead, Arlo Guthrie, Tim Hardin, the Keef Hartley Band, Richie Havens, Jimi Hendrix, Incredible String Band, Iron Butterfly, Jefferson Airplane, Janis Joplin, Melanie, Mountain, Quill, Santana, John Sebastian, Sha-Na-Na, Ravi Shankar, Sly and the Family Stone, Bert Sommer, Sweetwater, Ten Years After, The Who, Johnny Winter.

Opposite: Over 400 000 people attended the weekend of peace and music.

1969 Man on the Moon

Over half a billion people around the world watched their television sets as Neil Armstrong took his first steps on the Moon. At 10.56 p.m. on 20 July 1969, Armstrong stepped onto the Moon and said, 'That's one small step for man; one giant leap for mankind'. From the time man first dreamed of flying, to the Wright brothers' first flight, man had finally reached out and grasped what once seemed impossible.

Neil Armstrong grew up with a love for flying. Born on 5 August 1930 in Wapakoneta, Ohio, Armstrong was just up the road from where the Wright brothers had lived. He received a degree in aeronautical engineering and a Master's degree in aerospace engineering, then served as a US naval aviator. Later he became a test pilot and was chosen to be a member of the astronaut corps.

Armstrong was part of the back-up crews for several space flights and finally was a crew member in 1966 on board *Gemini 8*. During the highly successful mission he and David Scott performed the first docking in space between two vehicles—a major achievement. *Apollo 11* was America's first attempt to land a man on the Moon. The crew was made up of Neil Armstrong as the commander, Edwin Aldrin and Michael Collins. At 9.32 a.m. on Wednesday 16 July 1969 the three men began their journey when *Apollo 11* was launched from Pad A at the Kennedy Space Center and lifted off on a Saturn V booster rocket. Travelling at the speed of 27 000 kilometres per hour, *Apollo 11* reached orbit in just 11 minutes. It orbited the Earth one and a half times and then fired the Saturn thrusters and shot toward the Moon at nearly 40 000 kilometres per hour.

The 400 000-kilometre journey took only four days and on Sunday 20 July, the astronauts arrived. The lunar module detached from the command module for the final leg of the journey. While Collins circled the Moon, Armstrong and Aldrin started their descent to the lunar surface. The astronauts needed to perform a daring manual landing to avoid a crater and field of boulders. They landed with just 40 seconds to spare before they would have had to turn around. At 4.18 p.m. from the southwestern Sea of Tranquillity, they reported, 'Houston, Tranquillity Base here. The Eagle has landed.' Armstrong was the first man to step

on the Moon's surface and Aldrin joined him 19 minutes later. The two men removed a sheet of stainless steel on the Lunar Module leg to unveil the attached plaque. They read the words to the television audience: 'Here men from the planet Earth first set foot upon the Moon, July 1969 AD. We came in peace for all mankind.' They spent the next two hours and 32 minutes exploring, collecting samples, doing experiments and taking photographs. They then climbed in the lunar module and transferred to the command module, leaving the lunar module behind to orbit the Moon. Two and a half days later, on 24 July, *Columbia* splashed down about 1300 kilometres southwest of Hawaii.

Chronology of Events

9.37 a.m. 16 July 1969 The mission is launched and though hopeful, Neil Armstrong confidentially admits that the lunar landing has a 50 per cent chance of success.

12.18 p.m. 20 July Michael Collins releases the Eagle module from the *Columbia*. It flies towards the Moon.

3.17 p.m. The Eagle lands at Tranquillity Base on the Moon.

9.28 p.m. The astronauts open the Eagle's hatch and stand in the vacuum of space. Armstrong becomes the first human being to step on the Moon.

10.40 p.m. The astronauts plant the US flag on the lunar surface. Around the world over 600 million watch the landing on television.

12.12 a.m. 21 July The astronauts return to the lunar module and at the controls of *Columbia*. Mike Collins continues to orbit the Moon as he waits for Aldrin and Armstrong to return.

12.54 p.m. The Eagle leaves the Sea of Tranquillity.

Midnight 22 July Armstrong, Aldrin and Collins begin their return to Earth.

27 July The astronauts arrive back in Houston.

Opposite: Neil Armstrong was the first man to step on the Moon's surface and Buzz Aldrin joined him 19 minutes later.

1969 Arafat Becomes Leader of the PLO

Yasser Arafat was born in Egypt in 1929. When he was four years old his mother died and his father sent him to live with his married uncle in Jerusalem. Growing up in that area, Arafat developed a passion for the Palestinian cause. When he returned to Egypt to live with his father, it was with deep personal convictions. The young man avoided his studies and instead talked of politics and gathered local children together, forming them into little armies. Arafat went to the University of Cairo to study civil engineering. While there he was elected the president of the Union of Palestinian Students. The group presented a petition to the Egyptian government that read, 'Do not forget the Palestinians'. Their petition was made more forceful by the fact that the message was written in blood. In 1956 a secret organisation, Al-Fatah, was formed by Arafat and other Palestinians. It was an underground guerrilla group that trained units for raids on Israel.

On 27 May 1964 the Palestine National Council met for the first time. The 422 participants represented a wide cross-section of society consisting of students, professionals and labourers. The council then founded the Palestine Liberation Organisation (PLO) to forward their political and military purposes. In 1968 the PLO adopted its national charter, laying out their beliefs and goals. The charter stated that Palestine was the homeland of the Arab Palestinian people and that the Palestinian people have the right to liberate and retrieve this land. Armed struggle was given as the means to obtain their goal. The organisation's ultimate goal was the complete destruction of the state of Israel.

The shocking defeat of the Arab countries in the Six-Day War motivated the Palestinians to look to the guerrilla groups for leadership. Arafat moved from being the head of the Al-Fatah guerrilla group to the leader of the PLO in 1969. Two years later he became the General Commander of the Palestinian forces. One year after Arafat took over the leadership, the growing strength of the Palestinians threatened King Hussein of Jordan. As a result the PLO was thrown out of Jordan in a bloody fight. Arafat has remained the leader of the PLO for over 30 years.

Chronology of Events

24 August 1929 Yasser Arafat is born Mohammed Abdel Rahman Abdel Raouf Arafat Al Qudua Al Husseini in Cairo, Egypt.

1947 The United Nations divides Palestine into Arab and Jewish states, with Jerusalem designated as an international enclave.

1948 Arafat runs arms to Palestine and studies guerrilla tactics.

1949 A truce is declared, but Israel now holds 75 per cent of the former Palestine. Jordan has the West Bank, Egypt holds the Gaza Strip and the Palestinians are left with no land.

1958–59 Arafat founds Al-Fatah with Abu Jihad.

1964 Arab League sponsors the founding of the PLO. The PLO houses a number of Palestinian factions engaging in guerrilla warfare against Israel.

1969 Arafat becomes the chairman of the PLO.

1988 Arafat declares that the PLO renounces terrorism and formally recognises that Israel has a right to exist.

1991 Arafat supports Iraq in the Gulf War, causing political isolation.

1994 Arafat wins the Nobel Peace Prize in conjunction with Rabin and Israeli Foreign Minister Shimon Peres.

1996 Arafat and the newly elected Prime Minister of Israel vow to work towards a peace treaty.

1998 Israeli Prime Minister Netanyahu and Arafat sign a deal promising the transfer of land for peace.

29 March 2002 Israel declares Arafat an enemy and station tanks and soldiers outside his compound.

2003 The USA, Russia, European Union and the United Nations work out a peace plan. The plan includes Palestinian statehood, and a renunciation of violence and terrorism for Israel and the PLO.

Opposite: In 1969 Arafat moved from being the head of the Al-Fatah guerrilla group to the leader of the PLO.

1967 First Heart Transplant

Professor Christiaan Barnard performed the first human heart transplant on 3 December 1967. Mr Louis Washkansky, a middle-aged businessman who suffered from heart failure was near death and agreed to undergo the untried procedure. A heart was located when the family of a young woman who died after being struck by a car agreed to donate her organs. The transplant was a success but unfortunately, due to complications from medication used to keep his body from rejecting the heart, Washkansky died 18 days later with his heart beating strongly to the end.

Christiaan Barnard grew up in the town of Beaufort West in the interior of South Africa, the son of a preacher. While studying medicine at the University of Cape Town he observed his first operation and contemplated leaving the profession as he suffered from intense nausea. He stayed with it and six years later he graduated, completing part of his residency and internship at Groote Schuur Hospital. Eventually he practised family medicine.

When a patient of his delivered a baby with a heart defect and died, Barnard was very disturbed. He began thinking about the possibility of heart surgery and began to research and study, working at night performing research and even surgeries on dogs. Eventually he was invited to work and study in the United States. During this time the heart–lung machine was perfected, making cardiac surgery available. When Barnard returned to South Africa after years of study, he brought a heart and lung machine back with him. The Groote Schuur Hospital was ready to take on his project. A highly skilled surgical team was developed and in 1958 a heart bypass operation was performed. Barnard continued to research and study, working with transplants, building his surgical expertise, and performing the first kidney transplant. The legal side of transplants also had to be handled and clear rules for removing human organs were established.

Finally, in 1967 Bernard told his overseers, 'Everything is ready for a heart transplant. We have the team and we know how to do it.' In November, with a suitable patient, they waited for the organ donor. After midnight on 3 December the procedure began and just before 6.00 a.m. the heart was electrically shocked and began beating. The operation lasted nine hours and Professor Barnard and his team emerged victorious. He called the superintendent of the hospital and said, 'We have just done a heart transplant and thought you should know.' The news of the accomplishment flashed around the world. Professor Bernard became an overnight celebrity, much to his surprise. He said about the operation, 'We really did not see it as a big event. We did not even take photographs of the operation that night.'

After the death of Mr Washkansky, Professor Barnard and his team continued to progress, their second patient living for 18 months after the procedure. Survival time has increased ever since. About transplants, Barnard once said:

For a dying person, a transplant is not a difficult decision. If a lion chases you to a river filled with crocodiles, you will leap into the water convinced you have a chance to swim to the other side. But you would never accept such odds if there were no lion.

Facts and Figures

- In 2003 over 5000 people received heart transplants worldwide and anti-rejection drugs are becoming far more efficient than they were in the 1960s. People who received heart transplants 25 years ago are still living healthy lives with no heart complications, though many have to stay on prescribed medicine for years. Heart transplant survival rates have improved as well, with 85 per cent survival the first year, 77 per cent at three years and roughly 50 per cent at 10 years after transplant surgery.

- Heart failure is the leading cause of death in the developed world and because of this much research has gone into the studies with interesting results. It has been found that heart rejection is more likely to occur when the donor is female, regardless of the sex of the recipient. The average waiting period for a heart transplant is seven months and as many as 40 per cent of patients die while waiting.

- It is estimated that over 50000 people have undergone heart transplants in the past 37 years.

Opposite: South African surgeon Professor Chistiaan Barnard.

Christiaan Barnard

1966 The Miniskirt

The 1960s were a time of social change, much like the carefree 1920s. The postwar Baby Boom had created 70 million teenagers for the 1960s, and these youth swayed the fashion, the fads and the politics of the decade. Young people wanted to take hold of their own lives and rebel from the conservative lifestyles of their parents. Many did this through fashion.

In 1966, girls began to wear skirts far shorter than ever before—the mini was born. Often acknowledged as the creation of Mary Quant, a fashion designer of the time, within a year of its release almost every young girl was wearing the miniskirt. With a standard length of 12 centimetres above the knee, it was even worn during winter. Many young girls were seeking newness and were only too willing to try the daring, shorter dresses. The fashion trend took off because it was so different and emphasised youth—the outfit was very controversial among adults. Minis were simple, neat, clean-cut and young. They were made from cotton gabardines and adventurous materials like PVC.

The mini was not only a symbol of rebellion and youth, it also introduced the full-length pantyhose. As most stockings of the time were knee length, they were not suitable for the mini, whose hemline was far higher than that. When pantyhose or tights were first introduced in the 1960s it liberated women from girdles, roll-ons and suspender belts. A tights revolution had begun as no groomed young lady ever went out bare-legged in the 1960s. Throughout this time skirts were often paired with a matching sweater and matching set of tights for a uniform look. The years 1965 and 1966 also saw the mini coat, perfectly straight and virtually shapeless, and also the pop-inspired dyed furs and PVC designs.

The drastic change in fashion also heralded the creation of new fabrics. During the 1960s synthetic fibres were mixed with natural fibres to improve durability and maintenance. Du Pont and ICI were the giants of synthetic manufacture, producing a wide range of fabrics including nylon. Spandex, Lycra and Spanzelle became popular and were widely used in bras, underwear, swimwear and sportswear. Wigs and fake furs were also very popular as modified acrylics such as Dynel and Teklan became available. Not long after the introduction of the miniskirt was the micro-mini. The hemlines of these tiny skirts averaged 15–17 centimetres above the knee in New York and 18–20 centimetres above the knee in London. Mary Quant is also credited with inventing the micro-mini and hot pants. She shaped the fashion of a decade with her sexy innovations, which are still present in today's fashion.

Above: In 1966, girls began to wear skirts far shorter than ever before—the mini was born. Often acknowledged as the creation of Mary Quant, within a year of its release almost every young girl was wearing the miniskirt. Opposite: With a standard hemline of 12 centimetres above the knee, it was even worn during winter.

1966 Six-Day War in the Middle East

In November 1966 the tension in the Middle East had reached boiling point. A Palestinian terrorist group, Al-Fatah, launched attacks in Israel with the dual purpose of inflicting as much damage as possible and inciting war between Israel and the surrounding Arab nations. Israel retaliated against the attacks, triggering violent Arab protests. The United Nations joined in the condemnation of Israel's acts. Egypt, Israel's neighbour, began to prepare for war. The Egyptian President ordered the UN Emergency Forces, who had acted as a buffer between the two nations since 1957, to withdraw.

Six days later the Egyptians placed a blockade against Israel in the Straits of Tiran. Syria increased their border skirmishes and mobilised their troops and Jordan moved to join the two countries against Israel. The Arab nations were binding together with the goal of utterly destroying their unwanted neighbour. With the surrounding countries organising their troops, Israel began to do the same. Israel was surrounded by three countries—Syria, Jordan and Egypt—and all were preparing to attack. The odds were overwhelming and Israel's populace was terrified, having heard the public declarations from the Arab countries about their impending annihilation. For all these reasons, Israel decided to strike first.

On 5 June 1967, Israel attacked the Egyptian air force. The attack was a surprise and the Egyptians were caught on the ground. Within three hours Egypt no longer had an air force. This move guaranteed Israel's air superiority throughout the remainder of the conflict. The Jordanian troops attacked Israel hours later and the Israelis struck back hard. Within two days not only were Jordan's troops stopped, they were pushed back and a cease-fire was arranged between the two countries by the UN. Israel continued to move rapidly with concentrated strength, breaking through Egyptian lines. Then they attacked the Syrians on the Golan Heights. By 6.30 p.m. on 10 June the war was over, with treaties signed. Israel had not been destroyed; instead they gained the Gaza Strip from Egypt, the West Bank and East Jerusalem from Jordan, and the Golan Heights from Syria. The Arabs suffered a surprising and massive loss.

Chronology of Events

May 1967 Egypt and Jordan sign a defence pact, this raises concerns for Israel who believes that this move increases the danger of war with Arab states.

June 1967 The long-standing conflict between Middle Eastern countries finally breaks into war. Known as the Six-Day War, Egypt, Jordan and Syria go to war with Israel and are defeated. Israel takes control of Sinai, the Golan Heights, the Gaza Strip, East Jerusalem and the West Bank. The defeated countries also lost most of their air force and much of their armed weaponry. Egypt loses 11 000 soldiers, Jordan 6000, Syria 1000 and Israel only 700.

November 1967 The United Nations passes Resolution 242, which calls for Israel to withdraw from the occupied territories in return for independence and guaranteed borders. However, due to the Arabs and Palestinians declaring their intention to continue fighting, Israel refused to give up the newly acquired territories. The long-standing lack of negotiation and compromise leads the war to be known as the War of Attrition.

1973 The Arab–Israeli war is declared. This was not such a victory for the Israelis and eventually a cease-fire was negotiated. Resolution 242 initiated the peace process, which slowly started to come into place in the late 1970s.

Opposite: A soldier watches Arab refugees crossing the Allenby Bridge to Jordan. The bridge was blown up by the Jordanians to prevent Israeli pursuit.

1965 The Bullet Train

Toward the 1960s many thought that rail travel was nearing extinction as faster transportation became available with the development of cars and aeroplanes. The Japanese National Railway did not want to be phased out by such advances so they commissioned a team to begin a feasibility study in May 1956. The trains of the day were steam locomotives, with a top speed of 94 kilometres per hour and it took seven and a half hours to travel between Tokyo and Osaka. As a result of the study, a plan was proposed to build a high-performance train system between the two cities. The rail system, called the Shinkansen, would cut travel time from seven hours to three.

The project went into development on 19 December 1958. Less than four months later, on 20 April 1959, construction began. The project was massive. The track was made of long welded rails, each measuring 1.6 kilometres in length. They were linked together by expansion joints to allow for the contraction and expansion of the metal. The fastenings were double elastic and pre-stressed concrete ties. Standard gauge double track was laid throughout. The curves of the track were gentle, so higher speeds could be maintained by the trains throughout the journey. Amazingly, 80 tunnels were built for the track, 18 of them longer than a kilometre and the longest, the Tanna Tunnel, measuring 7.9 kilometres. The design of the train was intensive and prototypes were tested and retested. The train would be electric and each of the cars was made with devices that eliminated vibration, noise and heat transfer. They were also air tight. This was important because of the many tunnels and passing trains going in the opposite direction. Both trains and tunnels had an unsettling effect when not in a pressurised car. Each train could be composed of up to 16 separate units, with a seating capacity of more than 1200 passengers. The line planned to carry passengers by day, with trains leaving every 30 minutes, and freight by night.

Five and a half years after construction began, Japan's project was completed. The trains started running the full length of the Tokaido Route, 553 kilometres, which connected the two cities. With recorded speeds reaching 217 kilometres per hour, the new train broke speed records and set a new standard for rail travel. At first the trains were making the trip in four hours, but soon were running the route in three hours and 10 minutes. Trains were once again the popular form of transportation. The Shinkansen, the fastest train system in the world, earned the nickname the Bullet Train.

Chronology of Events

1985 The Shinkansen's 100 series is introduced. It includes the first double-decker train and the first Bullet Train with private cabins.

1992 The 300 series is revealed with bodies made of lightweight aluminium alloy that enable them to reach speeds of 270 kilometres an hour. It can cover the distance between Tokyo and Osaka in two and a half hours.

1997 The 500 series begins running Shinkansen's San'yo route. The route has especially good track conditions, allowing the trains to operate at speeds of up to 300 kilometres an hour.

1999 The 700 series is introduced, representing the pinnacle of railway technology. The rides are extremely comfortable as the train glides along at an average of 270 kilometres an hour.

Opposite: With recorded speeds of up to 270 kilometres per hour, the Bullet Train has broken speed records and set a new standard for rail travel.

1965 US Sends Troops to Vietnam

Lyndon Johnson was sworn in as President of the United States on 20 January 1965. On that day he stated, 'We can never again stand aside, prideful in isolation. Terrific dangers and troubles that we once called "foreign" now constantly live among us.' The speech was a prelude to the war to come. The President's National Security Advisor and Defence Secretary had warned him that the US limited military involvement in Vietnam was not working. America had reached a fork in the road and needed to either get out or commit to the conflict. France had waged a painful war in the area earlier and warned America not to get involved as it was futile.

On 4 February 1965 the US National Security Advisor visited South Vietnam and at the same time the Soviet Prime Minister arrived in North Vietnam. The Soviets pressured the North Vietnamese into accepting their aid and soon Soviet military supplies began to pour into North Vietnam. That same week a US military compound at Plieku, in the Central Highlands of South Vietnam, was attacked by Viet Cong guerrillas. US President Johnson approved a bombing campaign in retaliation. Operation Flaming Dart commenced and US navy jets bombed a North Vietnamese army camp near Dong Hoi. At this point America was behind the president and the military involvement in Vietnam. A snowball of aggression was under way. Before the end of February, 6000 Viet Cong massed in the vicinity of Da Nang's American air base and more US troops were needed. The first two battalions of US combat troops, including 15 800 men and 424 helicopters, landed on China Beach on 7 and 8 March. Also in March a sustained air attack was initiated, known as 'Rolling Thunder'.

Though this campaign was only scheduled to last eight weeks it lasted three years. During that period, four times more bombs were dropped than had been detonated in World War II. In April the president authorised additional troops to be deployed to Vietnam. He also authorised American combat troops to conduct offensive patrols in the countryside to root out Viet Cong. This decision was kept secret from the American press and public for two months. The war was no longer popular. Television changed perspectives of war as Americans watched their sons die on the evening news. Protests began and 15 000 students gathered in Washington to proclaim their displeasure. Still, Johnson was pressed to commit more troops. Throughout the year troops continued to pour into the jungle country. Anti-war demonstrations continued to gain momentum as well; on 16 October there were anti-war rallies in 40 American and international cities. The rallies got bigger but the fighting in Vietnam intensified. By the end of the year 184 300 US troops were in the jungle.

Facts and Figures

- Following the end of America's combat role in Vietnam in 1973, the majority of Americans, it appeared, neither wanted to talk or think about their nation's longest and most debilitating war—the only war the United States ever lost. America spent over US$167 billion on the war but it not only weakened the economy, the public faith in government and the competency of its leaders had been lost. The military, especially, was discredited for years.

- Approximately 58 200 Americans lost their lives. This figure does not include the deaths of servicemen outside official combat zones or those killed in 'friendly fire' during training at home. It also does not include those who have died since the war from wound complications or the thousands of Vietnam veterans who have committed suicide. Many have also died of cancers related to their exposure to the dioxin found in Agent Orange and many have children with birth defects related to their exposure.

- South Vietnam itself was left in an economic wreck after the United States completely pulled out in 1975. Having become entirely dependent on American financial aid and the spending of the US soldiers, inflation was up 65 per cent and only 40 per cent of the population had proper employment.

- The environment also suffered with hundreds of kilometres of jungle destroyed by bombings and land mines. Many villages were completely ruined and many people lost their farms. Few in the United States knew whether their sacrifice meant anything at all. Communism had taken over Indochina in the end.

Opposite: A US helicopter arrives near Khe Sanh to pick up the dead and wounded.

1963 Martin Luther King

Michael Luther King was born in Atlanta on 15 January 1929 and six years later his name was changed to Martin, after his father. He enrolled in college in 1944 with no plans to enter the ministry, although his father and grandfather were both pastors. King excelled in his studies and earned his Doctor of Philosophy from Boston University in 1955 and followed in his father's footsteps as a minister. While in college, King became acquainted with the philosophy of Mahatma Gandhi. The doctrine of non-violent social protest intrigued him. In 1959 he travelled to India and met with followers of Gandhi and became convinced that non-violent resistance was the best means for affecting change. After King returned home, he became the pastor of the Dexter Avenue Baptist Church in Montgomery, Alabama. He soon rallied with the black community in a boycott of the city's bus lines which began when an African-American woman, Rosa Parks, was arrested for refusing to give up her seat on the bus for a white woman. His life was threatened many times by racists and those afraid of change and on one occasion his house was bombed while his wife and young children were inside. Prayerfully, King considered the cost and committed himself to the fight. The battle for civil rights was ultimately won and his victory gained national attention.

King quickly became a leader in civil rights. He brought together a group of African-American leaders in 1957 and organised the Southern Christian Leadership Conference. King was elected as president and helped communities organise their own protests against discrimination. During one protest in 1963, violence erupted by the police against the mob, vividly illustrating his plight. Later that same year King was a principal speaker at the historic march in Washington. It was there he delivered a speech that touched the soul of the nation:

…I have a dream that one day this nation will rise up and live out the true meaning of its creed. We hold these truths to be self-evident, that all men are created equal…Let freedom ring. And when this happens, and when we allow freedom to ring—when we let it ring from every village and every hamlet, from every state and every city, we will be able to speed up that day when all of God's children—black men and white men, Jews and Gentiles, Protestants and Catholics—will be able to join hands

and sing in the worlds of the old Negro spiritual: 'Free at last! Free at last! Thank God Almighty, we are free at last.'

King was named Person of the Year for 1963 by *Time* magazine. A few months later he received the 1964 Nobel Peace Prize. King pressed on, eager to address any wrongs. His focus moved to the war in Vietnam and he was joined by a wide array of citizens. He rallied for the poor and planned a massive march on Washington but never got the opportunity. On 4 April 1968 while standing on the balcony of the Lorraine Hotel in Memphis, Tennessee, King was shot and killed by James Earl Ray.

Chronology of Events

1929 Born in Atlanta on 15 January to Alberta Williams King and Martin Luther King Sr.

1953 Martin Luther King Jr marries Coretta Scott. They later have four children.

1955 Elected president of the Montgomery Improvement Association five days after Rosa Parks is arrested for refusing to remove herself from the 'white' section of the bus. Serves in the office until 1956. The Montgomery Bus Boycott also begins at the same time, in December 1955.

1957 King founds the Southern Christian Leadership Conference to expand the non-violent struggle against racism and discrimination in the United States.

1959 King is jailed in Birmingham, Alabama for protesting.

1963 On 28 August Martin Luther King Jr delivers his 'I have a dream' speech. More than 200 000 Americans gather at the Lincoln Memorial in Washington to listen.

1964 King receives the Nobel Peace Prize in December. At the time, he is the third black and the youngest person ever to receive it.

1968 King is shot and killed on 4 April by James Earl Ray, a white drifter and escaped convict. Ray receives a 99-year prison sentence for his crime.

Opposite: On 28 August 1963, Martin Luther King Jr delivers his 'I have a dream' speech. More than 200 000 Americans gathered at the Lincoln Memorial in Washington to hear King's landmark oratory.

1963 John F. Kennedy Assassinated

On 22 November 1963 in Dallas, Texas, President John F. Kennedy became the fourth president of the United States to be assassinated. The event has been surrounded by wild rumours, stories and conspiracy theories.

Just before noon on Friday 22 November 1963 President John F. Kennedy, Jacqueline Kennedy and their party arrived at Love Field Airfield, Dallas. Plans for the day included a motorcade through downtown Dallas, a speech at the Trade Mart and then a flight to Austin for a fundraising dinner and speech. Under sunny skies, the President greeted the crowds from an open limousine. Mrs Kennedy sat on his left and the Texas governor, John Connally, and his wife were in the jump seats. Two Secret Service agents were in the front. Behind the presidential limousine was an open 'follow-up' car with eight Secret Service agents who scanned the crowd for signs of trouble. The motorcade headed for the Trade Mart, moving through residential neighbourhoods and turning onto Main Street, an east-west artery for downtown Dallas. Large crowds gathered to greet the President and First Lady. At the west end of Main Street they turned right on Houston Street, going north for one block, then turned left on Elm Street. Approaching the intersection of Houston and Elm, one of the Secret Service men noted the time on a clock that sat on top of a large, seven-storey orange brick warehouse and office building, the Texas School Book Depository. It was 12.30 p.m. To the left was an open, landscaped area.

Just after making the turn, shots went off in rapid succession and the President fell into Mrs Kennedy's lap. The Secret Service acted as soon as they heard the gunfire, moving to the President's limousine and the direction from which the shots came. The agent in the front of the President's limousine noted the President was down and quickly instructed the driver, 'Let's get out of here; we are hit.' The limousine sped ahead with an agent shielding the President and Mrs Kennedy. At high speed they raced toward Parkland Memorial Hospital, six kilometres away. At the hospital, a team of physicians who had been alerted to the President's arrival began to work. Although the doctors strived, at 1.00 p.m. President Kennedy was pronounced dead.

Vice President Johnson, under close guard, travelled to the presidential plane from the hospital. Mrs Kennedy boarded shortly after, accompanying her husband's body. Two hours after the assassination, Lee Harvey Oswald was taken into custody. With overwhelming evidence, the police moved quickly to charge him in the murder though he was never brought to trial. Just two days later, while being transferred to the Dallas county jail, Oswald was shot by a local night club owner, Jack Ruby. Questions continue as to whether he acted alone or as part of a conspiracy.

Chronology of Events

1917 John F. Kennedy is born on 29 May.

1946 John decides to enter politics. Coming from a strongly political family this was the most natural thing for him to do. Later the same year he is named by the United States Chamber of Commerce as one of the nation's outstanding men of the year.

1953 John marries Jacqueline Lee Bouvier on 12 September. Their daughter, Caroline, is born in 1957. Their son, John Fitzgerald, is born on 25 November 1960. Only 17 days later, Kennedy is elected President.

1962 Kennedy introduces his most important legislative success, the passage of the Trade Expansion Act. It gives the President broad powers, including authority to cut or eliminate tariffs. The act is designed to help the United States compete or trade with the European Economic Community (EEC) on equal terms. Then in October, Kennedy faces the most serious international crisis of his administration. Aerial photographs proved that Soviet missile bases were being built in Cuba. Declaring this build-up a threat to the nations of the Western Hemisphere, Kennedy warns that any attack by Cuba would be regarded as an attack by the Soviets and the United States would retaliate against the Soviet Union.

1963 On 22 November JFK is shot in Dallas, Texas, the fourth United States President to be assassinated.

Opposite: First lady Jacqueline Kennedy stands between her brothers-in-law Robert and Edward (Ted) Kennedy at the graveside.

1961 First Man in Space

On 12 April 1961 the first manned satellite was launched from the Baikonur cosmodrome in Kazakhstan, in the Soviet Union. When the engines fired on *Vostok I* at 9.07 a.m., Senior Lieutenant Yuri Alekseyevich Gagarin was launched into space. Returning to Earth safely 108 minutes later, the project was deemed a success. The Soviet Union had made history by launching the first man into space. With the help of the best minds of the time, aggressive research and development, and the resources of the country the Soviet Union strived to be the first in space. They had already succeeded in launching the first space satellite, *Sputnik I*, in October 1957. The Space Race between the United States of America and the Soviet Union had begun.

Less than three years later the successful *Vostok I* was launched. Yuri Gagarin was well chosen for the job. Born on 9 March 1934 in Klushino, a small village 160 kilometres west of Moscow, he grew up with a desire to become a pilot. After hearing of *Sputnik I*, he knew he needed to be a part of the space program. His request to be considered for the cosmonaut program was accepted. With his wife Valya and daughter he moved to Star Town, which was built especially for the training. Gagarin spent two years at the highly secret training facility.

After the lift-off, two minutes into the flight, four boosters strapped to the *Vostok I* separated and fell away as designed. As zero gravity was reached, a doll that Gagarin had brought along as a gravity indicator began floating. Although Gagarin was technically the pilot of the ship, he actually had no control. A computer sent radio signals that triggered the different phases of the flight. However, there was a key in a sealed envelope so that Gagarin could take control of the craft in the case of an emergency. A braking rocket was fired 44 minutes into the flight to slow the spacecraft, enabling it to fall back into the atmosphere. At 78 minutes a retrorocket was fired to separate the instrument module from the capsule. Because of a wire bundle, the separation did not occur and the service module stayed attached to the Shank re-entry module. Both pieces began gyrating wildly, almost seriously injuring Gagarin, before the wires burned through. Once free, the Shank module performed as planned and successfully re-entered the

Earth's atmosphere. One hundred and eight minutes after take-off, Gagarin ejected from the capsule then separated from his ejection seat and descended by parachute. Gagarin and the craft, which also descended via parachute, landed in the Saratove region of the Soviet Union. Yuri Gagarin, in the Soviet-built *Vostok I*, had orbited Earth one time in space at a speed exceeding 27 000 kilometres an hour. When honoured with a triumphant walk through the Red Square in front of a crowd of hundreds of thousands, he was more nervous than he had been for the flight.

Chronology of Events

October 1957 Russia succeeds in launching the first space satellite, the *Sputnik I*. The Space Race between the United States of America and the Soviet Union begins.

January 1961 US President John F. Kennedy sets the ambitious goal of landing an American on the Moon and to have him return safely by the end of the decade.

April 1961 The Soviets launch the first human being into space, Yuri Gagarin. He makes a single orbit of Earth in *Vostok 1*.

May 1961 The United States launches astronaut Alan Shepard into space, but does not gain enough velocity to orbit.

June 1963 The Soviets break history with a space flight lasting almost five days and Russian Valentina Tereshkova becomes the first woman to enter space.

October 1964 The *Voskhod 1* carries three Soviet cosmonauts, the first multi-person space crew flies into orbit for a day-long mission.

September 1966 On *Gemini 11*, Pete Conrad and Dick Gordon reach a record altitude of 1370 kilometres.

November 1966 American Buzz Aldrin makes a record five hours of spacewalks.

Opposite: Yuri Gagarin, in the Soviet-built Vostok I, *orbited Earth one time in space at a speed exceeding 27 000 kilometres per hour.*

1960 The Space Race

For America, the 1960s begin on an anxious note. Many in the United States feared the nation was lagging dangerously behind the Soviet Union in development of intercontinental ballistic missiles (ICBMs) and also space exploration. On 12 April 1961, the Soviets launched 27-year-old fighter pilot Yuri Gagarin on the world's first piloted space mission. In his spacecraft *Vostok 1*, launched atop a converted R7 missile, Gagarin made a single orbit of the Earth, returning 108 minutes after lift-off. For the young US President John F. Kennedy, Gagarin's flight came as a serious disappointment. In Kennedy's mind, competition with the Soviets in space had become vital to US international prestige. Speaking in 1961 about the prospect of sending astronauts to the Moon, Kennedy said, 'No single space project in this period will be more impressive to mankind, or more important for the long-range exploration of space. And none will be so difficult or expensive to accomplish.'

On 5 May, a former navy test-pilot named Alan Shepard became the first American in space, but did not achieve enough speed to orbit. Less than three weeks after Shepard's flight, speaking before a joint session of Congress, Kennedy made an announcement that would have seemed unthinkable just years before: 'I believe this nation should commit itself to achieving the goal, before this decade is out, of landing a man on the moon and returning him safely to the Earth.' The Space Race had begun.

The Space Race grew out of the Cold War between the United States and the Soviet Union, the most powerful nations after World War II. For half a century, the two superpowers competed for supremacy in a global struggle of democratic society against totalitarian communism. Both countries wanted to win to prove their scientific superiority and to show their military strength. Space was a crucial arena for this rivalry. Before a watchful world, each side sought to demonstrate its superiority through impressive feats in rocketry and spaceflight for over a decade. At the end of the Cold War, the United States and Russia agreed to build a space station and pursue other joint ventures in space. A contest that began in fear and enmity has become a partnership.

Chronology of Events

1957 The Soviet Union launches the first artificial Earth satellite, the *Sputnik*, meaning 'traveller'.

1958 The United States launches its first satellite; *Explorer I*. NASA (National Aeronautics and Space Administration) is formed as a federal agency devoted to exploring space.

1959 The Soviet Union launches *Luna 2*; it is the first space probe to reach the Moon.

1961 Yuri Gagarin, a cosmonaut from the Soviet Union, is the first person in space, and the first to orbit the Earth. Later, Alan Shepard is the first American astronaut in space.

1962 John Glenn becomes the first American to orbit the Earth.

1963 The Soviets claim another first as Valentina Tershkova becomes the first woman in space.

1968 The United States launches *Apollo 8*. It is the first manned space mission to orbit the Moon.

1969 US Astronauts Neil Armstrong, Edwin 'Buzz' Aldrin and Michael Collins make it to the Moon. Armstrong is the first man to walk on the Moon, closely followed by Buzz Aldrin. By reaching the Moon first, the United States won the Space Race. Soviet and American leaders knew that being the first country to land on the Moon would be an extremely important media event. The world watched each country's progress with great interest. Scientists and government leaders in both countries were under intense pressure to meet tough deadlines.

Opposite: Astronaut Buzz Aldrin, lunar module pilot, descends the steps of the Lunar Module ladder as he prepares to walk on the Moon on 20 July 1969.

1960 The Pill

The introduction of oral contraceptives revolutionised birth control and was a major event for women worldwide. The journey to developing 'the pill' began in 1937, when investigators demonstrated that the female hormone progesterone could halt ovulation in rabbits. Subsequent research in other species replicated this phenomenon—that is, if no egg is released from the ovary, then fertilisation and pregnancy cannot occur. While this advance was significant in the first steps to development, several problems remained. Specifically, synthesising progesterone in the laboratory was both difficult and expensive. Furthermore, natural progesterone could not be given orally because it is destroyed in the digestive system when ingested in its natural form. During the following years, American chemist Russell Marker succeeded in producing progesterone from the roots of wild Mexican yams. This resulted in the production of synthetic progestin. The other hormone controlling ovulation, oestrogen, works in conjunction with progestin to prevent fertilisation and implantation. After many years of testing and researching, it was concluded that two synthetic estrogens, mestranol and ethynyl estradiol, could both be taken orally.

Of course, 'the pill' could not be approved without large-scale testing being conducted, a trial which many women were afraid of taking part in. However, this testing during the mid-1950s was successful. In 1960, the US Food and Drug Administration approved the first oral contraceptives for marketing. Ortho Pharmaceutical introduced its first birth control pill in 1963. Response to the development was overwhelmingly positive and the first commercially available oral contraceptive named Enovid, produced by GD Searle and Company, took $24 million in net profits from sales in 1964.

By 1965, the pill became the nation's leading method of contraception. Scientists continued pill research, hoping to eliminate some of the side effects, which included nausea, water retention, weight gain and menstrual pain. Researchers also discovered that progesterone would be effective in treating women suffering from gynaecological disorders, especially painful menstruation. While early pill formulations contained up to 100 to 150 micrograms of oestrogen, later studies confirmed that less hormone could be used to prevent conception. In the 1960s and 1970s pills were introduced with decreasing oestrogen and progestin levels. In 1973, the first progestin-only pill was introduced, which contained 350 micrograms of norethindrone with no oestrogen component. The rest of the decade saw a huge demand for what is an extremely effective form of birth control. It remains the most popular contraceptive method in the world.

Chronology of Events

1937 It is discovered that the hormone progesterone can stop rabbits from ovulating.

1949 Scientists at the University of Pennsylvania achieve the production of synthetic progestin.

1950s Large-scale testing of the contraceptive pill is undertaken and deemed successful.

1960 The US Food and Drug Administration approves the first oral contraceptives for marketing.

1965 The pill becomes America's leading method of contraception.

1973 The first progestin-only pill is developed, which contains 350 micrograms of norethindrone with no oestrogen component.

1982–83 The first multi-phasic pill formulations, called bi-phasic and tri-phasic, are developed. In these formulations, the level of progestin changes during the monthly reproductive cycles.

1988 Several potential non-contraceptive health benefits of pill use are recognised, including a decreased incidence of ovarian cancer, endometrial cancer, pelvic inflammatory disease, ovarian cysts, benign breast disease, iron deficiency anaemia and dysmenorrhea.

Opposite: Production of the birth control pill at a factory in High Wycombe, Buckinghamshire.

1955 The Birth of Rock'n'roll

With the birth of rock'n'roll, popular culture was changed completely. Before the 'rebellious' sounds of Bill Haley and the Comets, Buddy Holly or Elvis Presley, the music scene was far more conventional—as was the lifestyle. Activities such as unwed sexual relations, motorcycle rides and certain types of dancing were socially prohibited. Middle-class white society prospered, self-satisfied yet suspicious of its neighbours—particularly its black neighbours. Rhythm and blues music dominated the American south and targeted a black audience in the late 1940s. The catchy tunes and suggestive lyrics were thought improper, until white entertainers began to cover rhythm and blues songs. During the 1950s the term rock'n'roll was actually a synonym for black R&B (rhythm and blues) music.

Rock'n'roll was first released by small, independent record companies and promoted by radio disc jockeys like Alan Freed, who used the term rock'n'roll to help attract white audiences unfamiliar with black music. Indeed, the appeal of rock'n'roll to white, middle-class teenagers was immediate and caught the major record companies by surprise. The new genre was a combination of rhythm and blues, known as jump blues, the gospel-influenced vocal-group style known as doo wop, the piano-blues style known as boogie-woogie (or barrelhouse), and the country-music style known as honky tonk. The post-war prosperity experienced in most Western societies also contributed to the popularity of rock'n'roll. Suddenly, teenagers had more money and leisure time and marketers began to target their susceptibility. Movies such as *The Wild One, Rebel Without a Cause* and *Blackboard Jungle* were made for a teenage audience and promoted the non-compliance of rock music. The most successful rock'n'roll artists wrote and performed songs about love, sexuality, identity crises, personal freedom, and other issues that were of particular interest to teenagers. Technological impacts were also a major influence.

In 1951 the colour television was introduced to American families, car radios became commonplace and portable transistor radios were very popular. Musically, technology also opened new doors with the invention of the electric guitar and electric bass guitar as well as amplifiers. The group Bill Haley and the Comets had the first big rock'n'roll hit with the song 'Rock Around the Clock' in 1955 and many others would follow. However, the golden age of rock'n'roll only lasted five years, from 1955 to 1959. It is exemplified by the recordings of Chuck Berry, Elvis Presley, Little Richard and Buddy Holly. By the early 1960s, the popular music industry was assembling professional songwriters, hired studio musicians, and teenage crooners to mass produce songs that imitated the late-1950s style of rock'n'roll.

Chronology of Events

21 March 1952 The rock'n'roll frenzy officially begins when a riot breaks out at Alan Freed's concert event, the Moondog Coronation Ball.

September 1952 *American Bandstand* is broadcast for the first time. It is originally called *Bob Horn's Bandstand*.

1954 The term rock'n'roll is first used at a concert promoted by Alan Freed known as the Rock'n'Roll Jubilee. Freed tries to copyright the term but is denied.

July 1955 The first rock'n'roll song ('Rock Around the Clock' by Bill Haley and the Comets) makes it to number one on the charts. It stays there for eight weeks.

April 1956 'Heartbreak Hotel' reaches number one. It is the first hit for Elvis Presley. Hollywood realises the popularity of rock'n'roll and releases music related to movies: *Don't Knock the Rock; The Girl Can't Help It; Rock Around the Clock; Shake, Rattle and Rock!; Rock Pretty Baby;* and *Love Me Tender.*

1957 Buddy Holly gains international attention with his hit 'That'll be the Day'.

Opposite: Hugely influential singer, songwriter and guitarist Chuck Berry on stage at the Birmingham Odeon in England.

1954 The Transistor Radio

When radios had first been introduced the receivers were big, bulky affairs filled with tubes. They were not only large and hard to accommodate they were also expensive and on average limited to one per home. That changed in 1954 when transistor technology made the 'Pocket Radio' possible. The TR-1, manufactured by Regency, measured a remarkable 8 by 12 centimetres and cost a quarter of the price of previous radios. It was available in a wide variety of colours in a cutting-edge style. Initially only 100 000 models of the radio were sold but the sales proved to be the spark in the revolution of technology. Several years before the release of the TR-1, Bell Telephone Laboratories had invented the transistor. At a public press conference on Wednesday 29 June 1948, Bell announced the new technology which led to the transistor radio. When first developed, patents were filed and the information was disclosed to the military. The inventors—Shockley, Bardeen and Brattain—eventually were awarded the Noble Prize in Physics in 1956 in recognition of their accomplishment.

The application seemed very narrow at first, limited to the military and hearing aids. The original point-contact transistor was superseded by the junction transistor, which was easier to manufacture. These new transistors allowed for expansion of application. A company that manufactured the new transistor chips, Texas Instruments, had a vested interest in the sale of the transistor. They approached several large companies with their idea of a transistor radio but were turned down. Finally, they found a small Indianapolis company that was interested in the venture. Two RCA employees, Joe Weaver and John R. Pies, decided to quit the company and start their own engineering consulting partnership. They called the new company IDEA—Industrial Development Engineering Associates. Later, they decided that their company sounded more like a construction company than the development company they were. They renamed their company after a pack of cigarettes because they liked the name—Regency. By June 1954 the two companies came together to produce the transistor radio. Each radio contained four junction transistors. A 22.5-volt battery was used, which could last 20 hours unlike the tube-radio batteries that only lasted a few hours. The radio would receive AM stations only, as FM was still not widely popular. The profit margin for the radio was very small, even though the price was relatively high for the time. Texas Instruments released a bulletin on 18 October 1954 announcing the innovative radio and they hit the market in November. The TR-1 only sold for a year, but radio was changed forever. This first transistorised product was the turning point in modern electronics that would impact society in many ways.

Facts and Figures

The invention of the transistor radio was not only a progression for technology it also helped shape one of the most distinctive eras of the 20th century. In the 1930s and 1940s, when receivers were powered by glowing tubes, families would gather around a large console or a clunky table-top model to hear music or drama. Undoubtedly these families had the same generational disputes about tuning the radio that later families in one-television households had about program choices.

The introduction of the transistor radio in the 1950s changed all that. These were the original 'personal electronics'. The new possibilities revitalised radio broadcasting and for the first time a separate youth culture was explored. In 1955 and 1956, a number of companies, Japanese and American, were making the new radios. The cheaper imports meant that they were affordable for the average teenager. That meant young people could listen to their own music without adult interference, and that music was rock'n'roll. The first hit rock record, 'Rock Around the Clock' by Bill Haley and the Comets, made it to number one on the charts in 1955, coinciding with the boom in transistors. From that point on, radio stations rushed to serve the new market and the era of rock'n'roll exploded.

Opposite: Suna Palamutcuogollari from Turkey and Kristen Krogirus from Finland proudly display their new transistor radios.

1953 Polio Vaccine Developed

Before the 20th century, the disease known as polio surfaced rarely. Surprisingly, the disease became a concern in the early 1900s because of improved hygiene. In more unhygienic conditions children had been exposed to the virus as infants when their immune systems were prepared to ward off the attack. Most infections were mild with flu-like symptoms, leaving the child immune. However, in later years the results were crippling and at times even fatal, invading the nervous system and causing irreparable damage. With improved hygiene, older children and adults were exposed to this virus for the first time and much greater damage occurred. In a short period of time the disease moved from sporadic to alarming, resulting in a devastating epidemic that swept across the globe in ever-growing waves. The medical field focused on the terrible disease, trying to figure out how to quell the tide. Quarantines, serums and vaccines proved ineffective.

Dr Jonas Salk of the University of Pittsburgh began to work on a vaccine in the 1940s. A vaccine introduces a weakened form of a virus into the body so that antibodies are produced which will ward off the disease. In 1952 Salk backed up his research with his life, first injecting himself and his family with the vaccine. They did not get sick and all produced antibodies. After more volunteers and positive results, he published his findings in March 1953. In the spring of 1954, the largest medical experiment in history took place in a field trial with just under two million children, each given either the vaccine, a placebo, or merely observed. Anxiously, the world watched for the results while many countries were in the midst of severe outbreaks.

On 12 April 1955 the results were published. The world's headlines read, 'Salk's Vaccine Works!' Though not totally effective, there was finally hope against this disease. Production of the vaccine raced ahead and in the rush mistakes were made. A few batches were sent out not completely inactivated. Polio was contracted directly from the vaccine in 79 cases, leading to over 200 infections and 11 deaths. All production and vaccines stopped in America. However, Salk's vaccine was one of the most significant medical breakthroughs of the 20th century.

Albert Sabin took the next great step by developing an oral vaccine in the 1960s, this time using a live vaccine, where an immunity developed that would last a lifetime. Millions around the world were vaccinated and the epidemic was over. Although there are still cases of polio today it is mainly in countries where no vaccines are available.

Chronology of Events

1789 British physician Michael Underwood provides the first clinical description of polio, referring to it as 'debility of the lower extremities'.

1894 The first major polio epidemic reported in the United States occurs in Vermont, consisting of 132 cases, including some adults.

1916 There is a large outbreak of polio in the United States. Though the total number of affected individuals is unknown, over 9000 cases are reported in New York City alone.

1934 There is a major outbreak of polio in Los Angeles. Nearly 2500 polio cases are treated.

1945 World War II ends. Large epidemics of polio in the US occur immediately after the war with an average of more than 20000 cases a year from 1945 to 1949.

1948 Jonas Salk's laboratory is one of four awarded research grants for the polio virus typing project. Other researchers given the grant include Albert Sabin, who would later develop the oral polio vaccine.

1952 There are 58000 cases of polio in the United States.

1954 Massive field trials of the Salk vaccine are sponsored by the National Foundation for Infantile Paralysis.

1955 News of the successful vaccine trials is announced and a nationwide vaccination program is quickly started.

1962 The Salk vaccine is replaced by the Sabin oral vaccine, which is superior in terms of ease of administration and also provides longer-lasting immunisation.

Opposite: Dr Jonas E. Salk vaccinates a young girl for polio.

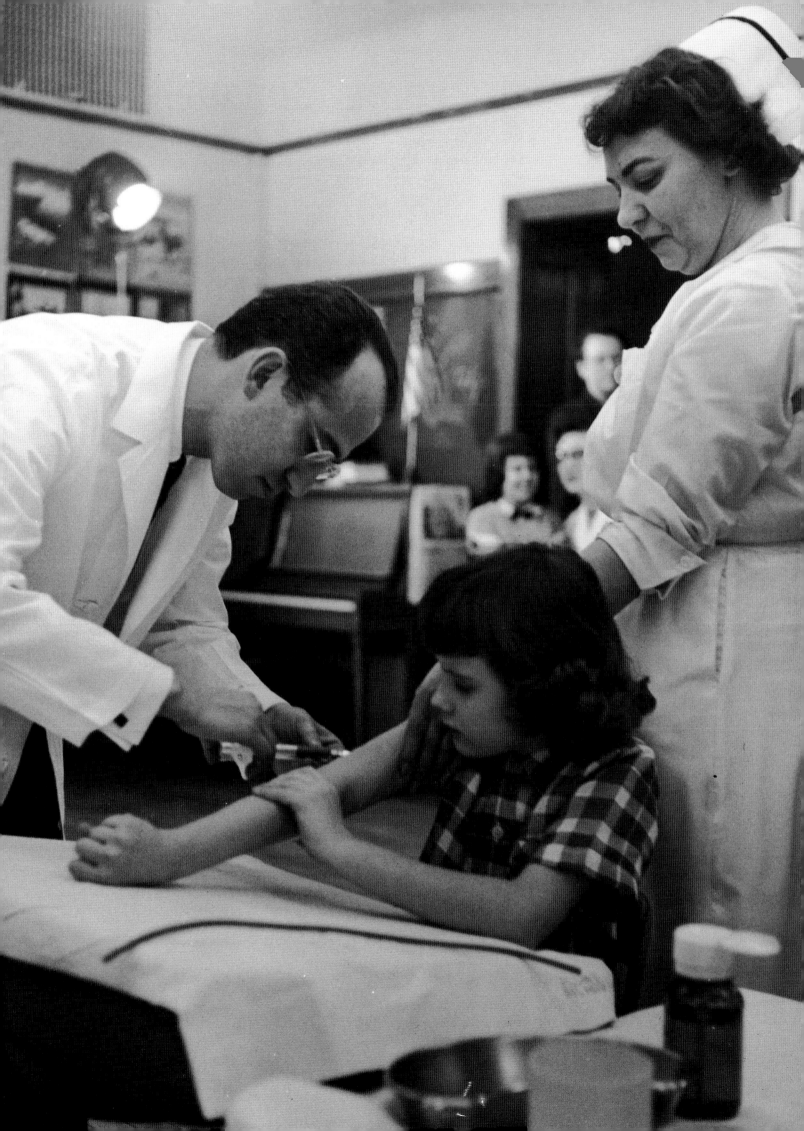

1953 Mount Everest Conquered

On 29 May 1953, at 11.30 a.m. local time Edmund Hillary and Tenzing Norgay stood on top of the world. The two men hugged each other, both relieved and joyful. They were the first people to reach the summit of Mount Everest, at 8850 metres, the world's highest mountain. Aware of the danger, they spent only 15 minutes at the summit. Hillary took pictures of Tenzing waving flags representing Britain, Nepal, India and the United Nations. Knowing they were low on oxygen, they started the long trip down the mountain. Their victory was the culmination of a massive expedition, headed by Colonel John Hunt. Colonel Hunt ran the expedition like a military campaign and laid siege on the mountain. Hunt was a meticulous planner and drew from the experience of previous Everest expeditions. In his words, 'We have climbed on the shoulders of other climbers.' A team of 10 top climbers was assembled and extensively trained. He also established a support base, utilising 350 porters and 20 Sherpas so that the climbers would have what they needed while on the mountain. These factors, along with excellent equipment and good weather set Hillary and Norgay up for success. Located on the border between Nepal and Tibet, Everest stood undisturbed until 1921 when a British expedition was allowed access to the mountain by way of Tibet. Ten other expeditions preceded the 1953 expedition but the top remained unchallenged.

After 1921 access to the mountain shifted with the political tides and by the 1953 expedition, Nepal was the starting point for Hunt's team. From Kathmandu the team set off with several tonnes of equipment. After 17 days of trekking they established base camp on 12 April. On 22 April, Camp VI was set up at the foot of the Lhotse face at almost 7000 metres. Nine camps in all were established. By 21 May the South Column was reached. The date 26 May marked the first summit attempt, but Tom Bourdillon and Charles Evans were forced to turn back due to exhaustion. Two days later Hunt sent out the next pair for the summit bid—Edmund Hillary and Tenzing Norgay, a Nepalese Sherpa who, though he could not read, knew the mountain better than any man. The pair set off and established Camp XI at 8370 metres. After a long, cold night they departed Camp XI at 6.30 a.m. and climbed

steadily until, at 9.00 a.m., they reached the South Summit. From there they continued climbing, now in unknown territory. Hillary stated, 'I continued hacking steps along the ridge and then up a few more to the right, to my great delight I realised we were on top of Mount Everest and that the whole world spread out below us.' Their great success surprised everyone and they gained worldwide attention. There was also much political pressure concerning who reached the top first, since Hillary and Norgay were from two different nations.

Chronology of Events

1852 The Great Trigonometrical Survey of India established that 'Peak XV' in the Himalayas is the highest mountain in the world.

1865 The peak is named after Sir George Everest, a British Surveyor General.

1920 The 13th Dalai Lama opens Tibet to foreigners. Many head to the country to explore the summit.

1924 George Mallory and Andrew Irvine disappear on their way to the summit. Whether they reached the summit remains a mystery.

1953 Sir Edmund Hillary from New Zealand and Tenzing Norgay a Sherpa from India are the first to reach the top of the summit.

1975 Junko Tabei from Japan becomes the first woman to climb Everest.

1999 George Mallory's body is found by a search expedition at 8100 metres. Searchers had hoped to find a camera that might contain photos of Mallory and Irvine on the summit or some other proof that they were the first to the summit, but no evidence is found.

2003 At 70, Japanese climber Yuichiro Miura becomes the oldest person ever to reach Everest's summit, and a 15-year-old Sherpa girl, Ming Kipa, becomes the youngest.

Opposite: Sir Edmund Hillary from New Zealand and Tenzing Norgay are the first to reach the top of the summit.

1953 DNA Proved to be Key to Genetics

In 1953 the age-old question of what determines our physical make-up—our height, hair colour, and even longevity—had finally been answered. DNA, or deoxyribonucleic acid, was slowly understood over a 50-year time span. The process started with a German biochemist in the late 19th century. The German's study of nucleic acids and their make-up resulted in the postulation of two forms, RNA and DNA. But it wasn't until 1943 that DNA was proved to be linked with genetic information. DNA remained elusive and misunderstood. By the early 1950s scientists were sure that DNA was the key to genetics, but did not know how it functioned or what it looked like. Two separate teams determined to unlock the mystery. Francis Crick and James Watson were co-workers at the Cavendish Laboratory at Cambridge. They shared a mutual fascination with DNA and agreed to work together to determine the structure. They believed that by coming up with a three-dimensional model the question of DNA would become clear. Another laboratory at King's College in London, addressed the question.

Rosalind Franklin, a dedicated scientist, approached the mystery from a different angle. She took on the painstaking, detailed task of using X-ray diffraction techniques. By doing so, she was able to work with actual DNA fibres. She studied them and how they reacted to humidity, making great advances in piecing together the structure of DNA. Unfortunately, although Franklin was a brilliant scientist, she was not good at working with others, specifically her overseer, Maurice Wilkins. Tension that had been mounting between the two compounded when he shared her findings, without permission, with the Cambridge team. Shortly thereafter Franklin left King's College and discontinued her work in DNA. Over the next five years she made breakthroughs in the study of virology, but tragically died of cancer in 1958, just 37 years old.

Franklin's work provided crucial pieces to Crick and Watson's puzzle. In March 1953 they published a proposal of the structure of the DNA molecule. They stated that the DNA molecule is made of two chains of nucleotides, in a helix shape. The chains are joined like a ladder, keeping the strands an equal distance from each other. The two strands are mirror images, but flipped so they lay 'head to toe'. In replication, the two strands separate and each builds a new strand, which is an exact replica of the other. In this manner the structure remains unchanged, except for occasional mutations. Their proposal was at first met with scepticism, which is why Watson, Crick and Wilkins were not awarded the Nobel Prize for Physiology/Medicine until 1962. Since that time their work has been deemed the most important biological work of the last 100 years. Their insight into the structure of DNA has opened the door for many breakthroughs in science and technology; with many more still to come.

Chronology of Events

1859 Darwin publishes *The Origin of Species*.

1951 Rosalind Franklin obtains sharp X-ray diffraction photographs of DNA.

1952 Scientists Martha Chase and Alfred Hershey prove that DNA is the molecule of heredity.

1953 Crick and Watson solve the three-dimensional structure of the DNA molecule.

1973 Annie Chang and Stanley Cohen show that a recombinant DNA molecule can be maintained and replicated in *E. coli*.

1977 The first genetic engineering company (Genentech) is founded, using recombinant DNA methods to make medically important drugs.

1989 DNA fingerprinting comes into use in DNA polymorphisms in paternity, immigration and murder cases.

1993 FlavrSavr tomatoes, genetically engineered for longer shelf life, are marketed.

Currently Many of the products we ingest today are genetically modified in some way. Campaigns are currently running urging marketers to label Genetically Modified Food (GMF).

Opposite: Pioneer geneticist biologist James Watson with a molecular model of DNA.

1952 Coronation of Queen Elizabeth II

After the death of her father, Princess Elizabeth stepped up to the role of Queen of England in 1952. Young and vibrant, the 25-year-old queen brought a fresh breeze to the weary British, still recovering from World War II. Both ruling parliament parties, who fought over anything they could, united in their support of the young queen and Elizabeth was ready to take on the responsibility of her role.

She was born on 21 April 1926 in London. Her early education was at home with her younger sister, Margaret. It was not considered a possibility that she would become heir to the throne until Edward unexpectedly abdicated, leaving Elizabeth's father as king in 1936. As she was now first in line for the throne her studies became more extensive and included lessons in constitutional history and law. After her 18th birthday Elizabeth was appointed counsellor during the king's absence, exercising certain functions of the Crown for the first time. Elizabeth began taking a more active part in royal affairs after World War II. Her public engagements grew in number and frequency. In 1947 she went on her first official visit overseas when she accompanied her parents and sister on a tour of South Africa. During the visit, on her 21st birthday, she made an international radio address, proclaiming, 'I declare before you all that my whole life, whether long or short, shall be devoted to your service'. Later in 1947 Elizabeth married Philip Mountbatten, a fourth cousin, at Westminster Abbey, on 20 November. He received the title, the Duke of Edinburgh. Two children, Charles and Anne followed soon after. Ten years later they had two more children, Andrew and Edward.

King George VI's health had begun to decline in the summer of 1951. He died in February of the next year. Elizabeth was in Kenya on vacation and quickly rushed home. Her quick action gave the British people hope in the midst of their grief. She arrived in England as Queen, ascending to the throne as Her Majesty Queen Elizabeth II. Sixteen months later her coronation was held at Westminster Abbey on Tuesday 2 June 1953. In her new position, Philip was a great help. He helped her stay balanced and kept in close touch with the common people, as his upbringing had been relatively simple. He worked to keep their private life separate from their public lives and pushed for reform when he felt outdated demands of the crown should be done away with. Queen Elizabeth has gone on to become the best known and most widely travelled head of state in the world.

Facts and Figures

- Taxpayers' contributions to the monarchy rose by a quarter in 2001, according to figures released by Buckingham Palace.

- Total spending on the civil list rose by 25.3 per cent to £8 153 000 in 2001, from £6 509 000 in 2000, the figures showed. Buckingham Palace said that the increase was funded in part from savings made during the 1990s. The figures have been published as part of an accountability drive within the palace. It is the first time that Buckingham Palace has published a detailed annual report outlining how the Queen spends taxpayers' money.

- Total spending by the Queen as head of state rose by 1 per cent in 2001 to £35.3 million. Detailed breakdown of the accounts shows that 74 per cent of the civil list was spent on 284 full-time staff in the royal household. Total salaries rose from £4 608 000 in 2000 to £6 057 000 in 2001.

- Public spending on the monarchy enabled the Queen to meet 2200 official engagements, entertain 70 000 people at garden parties, state banquets and receptions and send 49 000 items of correspondence.

- The royal catering bill rose from £294 000 to £330 000, although the royal cellars saw spending on wines and beverages fall from £107 000 to £45 000.

- Spending on royal palaces rose to £15.5 million from £15.3 million, including a bill of £3 155 000 for the redevelopment of kitchens at Buckingham Palace. Meanwhile, the Queen's florists were paid £1000 less in 2001 at £24 000.

Opposite: Queen Elizabeth II with Princess Anne and Prince Charles.

1950 The Korean War

Occurring between World War II and the Vietnam War, the Korean War tends to be overlooked. But the conflict was important, as it was one of the first episodes of the Cold War. The war lasted over three years and was between communist North Korea and non-communist South Korea. The growing strife between the two sides erupted in the early hours of 25 June 1950 when 135 000 well-trained North Korean troops crossed the border, symbolised by the 38th parallel, and invaded South Korea. By using Soviet-designed invasion plans—they overran the inferior South Korean army. The United Nations condemned the invasion and called for the withdrawal of the North Koreans. When this did not happen, members of the United Nations were called upon to aid South Korea. Just two days after the invasion, American troops were authorised to assist and within the week 15 other nations joined the South Koreans in the battle.

In the first few weeks of the war, the North Koreans pressed their lead and advanced rapidly. They drove the South Korean army and a small American force all the way to the southeast tip of Korea. The date 15 September marked the beginning of a counter-offensive, with the almost impossible landing, executed flawlessly at Inchon. The North Korean army fell back and they were pursued all the way into North Korea. The North Korean capital, Pyongyang, was captured on 19 October and by 24 November victory seemed eminent as the Allies drew close to the Chinese border. But the victory did not happen. The massive Chinese communist army joined forces with the North Koreans on 26 November and began pushing the UN troops south. The force advanced all the way back into South Korea and in January 1951 recaptured the South Korean capital, Seoul. Many months of bloody fighting followed. Eventually the conflict revolved around the original border, the 38th parallel. There the fighting remained and negotiations for a truce ensued in July 1951. UN troops were denied permission to go on the offensive, but were instructed rather to maintain their position, making for a bloody stalemate. For two years small clashes with significant losses continued while the fragile talks went on.

An armistice was finally signed in July 1953 between the United Nations, the United States, China and North Korea. South Korea refused to sign, leaving a tense stand-off. But the fighting was finally over. Because of the intense fighting and terrible conditions, many died in the conflict. More than 50 000 US soldiers died and the casualties for the Chinese and Koreans were each 10 times as high. The two countries of North and South Korea remain separate—and at odds—to this day.

Chronology of Events

25 June 1950 North Korean forces cross the 38th parallel. The United Nations denounces the action and calls for an immediate cease-fire.

29 June 1950 The North Korean army captures the capital of Seoul.

1 July 1950 First US combat troops arrive in Korea.

26–29 July 1950 Hundreds of fleeing civilians reportedly killed by US troops in the village of No Gun Ri.

15 September 1950 The South Korean and American battalions make a successful assault on Inchon, enabling them to break through the Pusan Perimeter and push toward the 38th parallel.

25 October 1950 Chinese forces fight with South Korean troops less than 70 kilometres south of the Yalu River.

1 January 1951 The North Korean and Chinese offensive begins.

3 April 1951 The Eighth Army crosses the 38th parallel.

10 July 1951 Armistice negotiations begin at Kaesong.

January–7 April 1952 There is massive disorder in prison camps on both sides.

7 May 1953 Both sides announce a stalemate over the prisoner of war (POW) issue.

8 June 1953 POW issue settled on the principle of voluntary repatriation.

17 June 1953 Revised demarcation of the 38th parallel is settled.

Opposite: South Korean political prisoners under guard at Pusan.

1950 The Credit Card

Before World War I the concept of the credit card was beginning to take form. Western Union provided some of their valued customers with a deferred payment service. In a short time others, such as hotel chains and oil companies issued cards for their customers. Every three to six months, oil companies would give courtesy cards made of paper to car owners. The cards did not have a revolving credit feature and were to be paid off in full.

In 1949 the credit card industry was about to change. Frank McNamara was going to a business dinner and first went home to change suits. He then went to Major's Cabin Grill at 35 West 33rd Street. After his meal the waiter presented him with his bill. He reached for his wallet and soon realised he had left it in his other suit. His wife quickly came to his rescue, rushing into the restaurant with cash. McNamara was more than just embarrassed about the incident, he was inspired. He talked with his attorney and they both agreed to launch a new company.

In February 1950 McNamara and his partner went out to dinner at Major's Cabin Grill. When the bill came the waiter was presented with a small, cardboard card—the Diners Club Card. This was the first universal credit card, not made available by one company just for their product. Fourteen restaurants in New York City soon accepted this card. Each cardholder would be charged an annual fee and then billed on a quarterly or yearly basis, the account to be paid within 90 days of receipt. Over 200 people were offered the new card, mostly friends and acquaintances.

The cards were a huge success and their business expanded so rapidly that they had to change offices three times to keep up with the demand. By the end of the first year 20 000 people carried the Diners Club Card. A year later the Franklin National Bank in New York City introduced a credit card to their customers. They extended the payment period and attached an interest rate. This opened up an entirely new revenue-making possibility. Other banks quickly began issuing cards. Years later Frank McNamara's Diners Club Card was named one of the 75 greatest management decisions ever made by the American Management Association International. He was also declared one of the 100 most influential Americans of the 20th century by *Life* magazine.

Opposite: Credit specialist Frank McNamara, inventor of the Diners Club Card, the first credit card in America.

1950 Plastic Surgery

Five thousand years ago Egyptians enjoyed the services of plastic surgeons. They were not the lift-and-tuck variety now associated with plastic surgery, but rather the management of facial trauma. They laid the roots of what is now a thriving profession. This ancient profession moved forward very slowly during the following centuries. Just 1200 years ago surgeons performing reconstructive work practiced in India. In the last 200 years the profession has moved ahead rapidly. Most of the development came to pass primarily due to war. As weapons advanced, surgery to repair the extensive damage also advanced. Doctors rose to the challenge and repaired soldier's damaged bodies, and at the same time gained integrity for their profession. After World War I, plastic surgery established its own branch of medicine. Guidelines and a specific training regime were developed and standardised. During World War I plastic surgery took more steps forward as surgeons laboured to repair the extensive wartime injuries. The profession also spread in popularity from North America to Europe.

By the 1950s plastic surgery was fully recognised by the medical community. As procedures advanced, a wider variety of services became available. Two areas of the profession developed. The first was reconstructive surgery, performed on abnormal or damaged structures of the body and designed to improve function. There also may be a benefit in appearance as a result. Cosmetic surgery, primarily aimed at improving appearance, could also aid in function. Obviously, the two areas overlapped in many instances.

Silicone, a new substance in the early 1960s, proved useful in treating skin imperfections, and by 1962 breast implants were introduced. Instantly popular, breast enhancement suffered a setback in the 1980s and early 1990s when concerns about safety were raised. The silicone was replaced with safer implants filled with saline. The demand for cosmetic surgery has increased dramatically. In the 1990s cosmetic surgery increased by 175 per cent. The most common procedure performed is lipoplasty or liposuction. The second most popular procedure is breast augmentation, which increased in popularity by 413 per cent during the same decade. Lifts, tucks and wrinkle reduction has also become common.

What was at first a procedure for a select few is now advertised on the radio and on the sides of buses. For many, the plastic surgeon has become a viable alternative to the gym, and people regard plastic surgery as a normal solution rather than as an exotic or extreme remedy.

Chronology of Events

1940s Many plastic surgeons served their country during World War II and expanded plastic surgery procedures through treating wounded soldiers. As they sought to repair wounds and disfigurements of soldiers and civilians, new techniques were created and included better facial restorations, improved artificial limbs (known as prostheses), and more successful skin grafts.

1950s With board certification and its own scientific journal, plastic surgery was fully integrated into the medical establishment by 1950. Reconstructive or cosmetic surgery made it possible for individuals who once had severe defects to re-enter society feeling more secure and accepted.

1960s Plastic surgery became even more prominent in the minds of the American public as the scope of procedures performed by surgeons increased. Silicone was utilised in breast implant devices, unveiled in 1962.

1970s Plastic surgeons began moving to the forefront of the medical profession. All parts of the human body, it seemed, could benefit from the skill of a plastic surgeon. Plastic surgery operations doubled since the 1960s.

1980s Plastic surgeries began to operate more like regular businesses for the good of the patient. Studies indicated that patients wanted information to take home and read, so surgeries began producing a host of brochures on the specialty and individual plastic surgery procedures.

1990s By 1990 more than 5000 board-certified plastic surgeons were active in the United States.

Opposite: A young woman in recovery after plastic surgery to enhance the size of her breasts.

1949 China Becomes Communist

China was isolated for 2000 years, often remaining unchanged by historical events that influenced other countries. In the late 1800s, however, outside influence started filtering into the country. Soon change began and Western influences infiltrated the country. Dynasties fell and China was left with little unity and less vision. Two rival parties developed early after the turn of the century, the Nationalist and the Communist. The two united briefly to combine their strength and bring down the Chinese warlords, but quickly split once that was accomplished. The Nationalist party was stronger and dominated the government of China in the 1930s.

In 1931 the Japanese invaded mainland China, occupying many of its richest provinces, then took over Manchuria just a year later. Japan launched a full-scale invasion in 1937. The Nationalists did try to expel the Japanese but instead they wrote off northeastern China. The Communists, though not in power, were willing to put up more of a fight. In 1945 Japan was defeated and driven out of China, but not by the Chinese. With the pressure off from the outside, fighting started again within China. A civil war broke out between the Nationalist and the Communists. The majority of the population, peasants, sided with the Communists, who had displayed more concern for them than the Nationalists ever had. For four years the country fought itself. At the end, the Nationalists were expelled from the Chinese mainland.

The Communist party, led by Mao Tse Tung, proclaimed China the People's Republic on 1 October 1949. The new government faced huge obstacles. China's economy was very bad. Eight years of war with the Japanese and four years of civil war had taxed the country terribly. Strict governmental controls were instituted. The Chinese peasants were given the land they had long desired. Women were given expanded rights in work and marriage. The society was promised freedom from poverty, inequality, corruption and foreign domination. Tragically, millions starved to death as China's zealous race to move forward pressed them into over-extending their resources. China also needed to be unified, so the government was centralised. Aggressive action was taken against communist opponents. Mao claimed to have 800 000 executed, but Western historians say the actual number was several times more. Communism now ruled in China. The capital was moved to Beiping and renamed it as Beijing. The Soviet Union was the first to recognise the new government, followed in quick succession by the rest of the communist countries, and then later by non-communist countries. The United States did not recognise Communist China until 1979.

Chronology of Events

1931 The Communists establish 15 rural bases and set up as a rival to the Nationalist government.

1934 Nationalist leader Chiang forces the Communists to evacuate their bases. The 'Long March' begins.

1935 Mao Tse Tung becomes the leader of the Chinese Communist party.

January 1949 Mao Tse Tung pushes the Nationalists to southern China.

1 October 1949 After the takeover, Mao proclaims the People's Republic of China.

December 1949 Chiang Kai Shek and his followers flee to Taiwan.

1949–52 The Communists establish firm control in China.

1953 China begins its first Five-Year Plan. It is a plan of economic development. Chinese industry grows at a rate of 15 per cent per year.

1958 China introduces its second Five-Year Plan. It is given the name the 'Great Leap Forward'.

1959–61 China's economy is ruined by the Great Leap Forward and they suffer a depression.

1966–70 Universities are closed in China.

1970 The Communists begin to regain control of the country.

Opposite: Chinese communist leader Mao Tse Tung addresses a meeting calling for even greater effort against the Japanese.

1948 First McDonald's Restaurant

In 1940 two brothers, Dick and Mac McDonald, opened a drive-in restaurant in San Bernardino, California. The restaurant featured carhops and barbecue food, and though relatively successful, they closed their doors in 1948. The two had noticed changes in the culture since the war and wanted to try something totally new. Families were looking for value and fast service. In a short time their restaurant reopened as the first McDonald's. The new restaurant was designed with value and speed in mind. The menu was simplified, with only the most popular items. High quality food was served at low prices. Burgers cost 15 cents, cheeseburgers were 19 cents, and there were 20-cent malts and 10-cent French fries. The food was self-serve and drive-in, served on paper—it was an entirely new concept in the food service industry. Business was slow at first, but soon the McDonald's restaurant was thriving.

A few years later a restaurant magazine ran a cover story on the two brothers and their overwhelming success. The brothers decided to franchise and soon were running eight new drive-ins using the same concept. Their success caught the attention of a salesman, Ray Kroc. He sold mixers for milkshakes, and the brothers had bought several. Interested in how things were being run, Kroc went to one of their restaurants. He was stunned. People stood in line waiting for 'fast food'. Three men did nothing but flip burgers, two men made milkshakes and two others cooked fries. Countermen took orders, and people were served in about 15 seconds! Kroc saw the potential in the restaurant. The McDonald brothers had families and were not interested in travelling, so Kroc persuaded them to let him be a franchise agent. The brothers provided the original concept and Kroc brought know-how for expansion.

Kroc bought out the McDonald brothers and established the McDonald's corporation in 1955, and developed a foundation for the vast growth that would occur. He instituted strict standards so that consistent quality, cleanliness, service and value could be expected at each and every McDonald's. A Harvard Business School professor described Kroc as, 'the service sector's equivalent of Henry Ford'. This held true with McDonald's now the world's leading food service organisation. On any given day about 1 per cent of the world's population is served at a McDonald's restaurant.

Chronology of Events

1948 In December, Dick and Mac McDonald open the first McDonald's drive-thru restaurant in San Bernardino, California.

1954 A multimixer salesman named Ray Kroc visits McDonald's and becomes a franchising agent.

1955 Kroc opens his first McDonald's in Illinois, his second in California. Total sales for the company reach US$193000.

1960 McDonald's first jingle sings 'Look for the Golden Arches'. Advertising becomes pivotal, with billboards, radios and sponsorship.

1965 McDonald's Franchise celebrates its 10th anniversary by opening public shares.

1966 Ronald McDonald appears in his first national television campaign. McDonald's is listed on the New York Stock Exchange.

1967 The first international McDonald's restaurants open in Canada and Puerto Rico.

1983 Over 7000 McDonald's restaurants are located in 32 countries around the world.

1992 McDonald's opens its largest ever facility in Beijing, China. It is two storeys high, seats more than 700 and employs 1000 staff. Worldwide sales are over US$21.8 billion a year.

2000 System-wide sales exceed US$40 billion a year and customers exceed 16.5 billion.

Opposite: McDonald's owner Ray Kroc eating a hamburger in front of his first McDonald's restaurant.

1948 State of Israel Founded

The Zionist movement formed and began to pick up speed in the late 1800s. Their goal, which was believed to be from God, was to establish a Jewish state in Palestine. Jewish immigrants began to flock to the Palestine area in large numbers. By the early 1900s friction developed between the Arab and the Jewish populations. At the end of World War I the newly developed League of Nations endeavoured to control the explosive situation. The British government was assigned to the area, the British Mandate for Palestine. In spite of bitter opposition by the Arabs, part of the mandate allowed for Jewish immigration. Tension increased and soon riots broke out. In February 1947 the British government went to the United Nations for help. They could not effectively control the situation any longer. Still weakened by the war, Great Britain did not have the resources to control such a volatile area. The United Nations met in a special session to discuss the situation, approached by a Jewish agency requesting an audience before the council. The United Nations had never worked with any group outside the confines of a government, but still the committee was allowed to speak. They requested that a study be made of the Palestine area, and their request was granted.

During the summer extensive hearings and meetings took place, subcommittees toured the area and interviewed the people. They produced two reports. The majority report called for two independent states to be established in Palestine, one Jewish and one Arab. The minority report proposed the establishment of a confederation of two Jewish and Arab subordinate states. The majority report was accepted. The United Nations General Assembly voted on 29 November 1947 to partition Palestine into one Jewish and one Arab state. On 14 May 1948 the British Mandate ended, British troops pulled out of the area, and Israel declared itself an independent nation. The announcement was read publicly at the Tel Aviv Museum in the evening of 14 May by David Ben-Gurion, the chairman of the Executive of the World Zionist Organisation, later the first Prime Minister of Israel. The Declaration of the Establishment of the State of Israel was signed by members of the National Council, representing the Jewish community in the country and abroad. The United States formally recognised the new country the same evening. Other countries followed a few days later. The declaration went into effect at midnight that same night. The next day five neighbouring Arab states invaded the new state of Israel. This invasion set the pace for the troubled area, assuring conflict and violence.

Chronology of Events

1948 The state of Israel is proclaimed by the Jewish and British troops leave. Fighting breaks out with Arab neighbours ending in 1949. Jerusalem is divided into the western Israeli sector and the eastern Jordanian sector.

1956 Egypt nationalises the Suez Canal and Israel invades Sinai and Gaza; conflicts are resolved after US intervention.

1967 Israel launches a pre-emptive attack on Egypt, Syria and Jordan starting the Six-Day War. Israel is victorious and captures much surrounding land.

1973 Egypt and Syria attack Israeli forces in Sinai and the Golan Heights on the Jewish fast of Yom Kippur. They make initial gains but are soon in retreat after Israeli counter-attacks.

1978 Egypt, Israel and the United States sign the Camp David Accords.

1987 A Palestinian uprising (intifada) against Israeli rule starts in the West Bank and Gaza. More than 20000 people are killed and injured in the fighting.

1991 The Madrid Middle East Peace Conference opens.

1993 Palestine Liberation Organisation (PLO) leader Yasser Arafat and Israeli Prime Minister Yitzhak Rabin sign the Declaration of Principles in Washington.

1994 The Israel–Jordan peace treaty is signed ending a 45-year state of violence.

1997 Israeli soldiers hand over 80 per cent of Hebron, ending 30 years of occupation and formally dividing the volatile town between Arab and Jewish rule.

Opposite: Two members of the Haganah, the Jewish militia, in action on the border between Jaffa and Tel Aviv.

1947 Chuck Yeager Breaks the Sound Barrier

As World War II drew to a close, the interest in how to fly faster gained momentum. Engines of the time were not powerful enough, so new engines were constructed. To go with the new engine a new aircraft was designed. The engine was more of a rocket, with a four-chamber engine fuelled by liquid oxygen. The bright-orange aircraft, designed by Bell Aircraft Corporation, had a high-strength aluminium fuselage, shaped like a bullet with straight, stubby wings. The craft's official name was the XS-1, but became popularly known as the Bell X-1. Standing just more than three metres high and less than 10 metres long, the clean, aerodynamic craft exuded power. Chuck Yeager was the pilot. A World War II pilot with vast experience in testing aircraft, Yeager was meticulous. Reading specifications on every craft he tested, Yeager knew each plane he flew as well as the designers. He was also as wild as his fellow pilots. When he reported for duty on Tuesday morning 14 October 1947 it was with broken ribs after falling off a horse. The hangar for the X-1 was located in the California high desert on a large expanse of a hard, flat lake bed, the home of Muroc Army Air Field. By 6.00 a.m. teams of engineers and technicians began to arrive. This was to be the ninth test flight in the Bell X-1, and today the team was ready to try and crack the sound barrier. No one knew what would happen. Would the plane pass through unnoticed, or be destroyed when it passed through the invisible barrier?

With this in the back of everyone's mind, preparations began for the flight. At 10.00 a.m. the B-29, which carried the X-1, took off. After the B-29 got under way, Yeager began the hardest part of the flight—getting into the plane while it hung suspended under the B-29. After a series of contortionist-like moves, made harder by his broken ribs, Yeager was finally inside the plane. He prepared for the next obstacle, the drop from the B-29, made while moving at 400 kilometres per hour. Once released from the plane, the real mission began. Yeager started all four cylinders and began to climb. Once he got to 10 000 metres he shut off two cylinders. Still, the plane accelerated. At an altitude of 12 000 metres the X-1 levelled off and Yeager fired one of the two shutdown cylinders. The plane's speed continued to climb. The flight was smooth with no violent reaction from the aeroplane and no loss of control. For 18 seconds Yeager flew at Mach 1.06. It was the most significant milestone in flight history since the Wright brothers took to the sky. The sound barrier had been broken.

Chronology of Events

1877 Ernst Mach, an Austrian scientist, uses bullets to record the speed of sound, thereafter known as Mach 1.

1931 The British Supermarine S6B fitted with a Rolls Royce engine becomes the first aircraft to exceed 600 kilometres per hour.

1936 German scientist, Hans Von Ohain enters a patent for his turbo jet engine.

1947 On 14 October, Chuck Yeager becomes the first man to break the sound barrier, in the American Bell X-1.

1948 In September, a new prototype of the De Havilland DH 108 Swallow becomes the first British plane to break the sound barrier.

1953 On 20 November, the American Douglas D558-2 Sky Rocket becomes the first plane to fly at Mach 2—twice the speed of sound.

1964 The official air speed record is held by the Russian E166, which reaches Mach 3—three times the speed of sound.

1976 The SR71 Blackbird becomes the air speed record holder, passing Mach 6—six times the speed of sound.

1997 Richard Noble's team builds the Thrust SSC rocket automobile and with Andy Green at the helm, it breaks the sound barrier on land—moving at 1220 kilometres per hour.

2004 An experimental pilot-less plane breaks the world speed record for an atmospheric engine, briefly flying at 7700 kilometres per hour—seven times the speed of sound.

Opposite: On 14 October 1947, Captain Chuck Yeager became the first man to break the sound barrier, in the American Bell X-1.

1946   The Nuremberg Trials

With the ending of the World War II hostilities, there were still wrongs that needed to be addressed. Crimes against humanity had been committed, and the 'Three Big Powers'—the United States, the Soviet Union and Great Britain—banded together to form the International Military Tribunal, in order to try to punish war criminals. The spacious Nuremberg Palace of Justice was recommended as a venue for the court. With 530 offices, 80 courtrooms, and a large prison it could handle the massive undertaking. The tribunal convened on Friday 20 November 1945, in the principal courtroom. Twenty-one Nazi officials were charged with war crimes.

From November until the end of August, for 218 days of trials, 360 witnesses told their stories, unveiling to the world the horror of the Nazi regime. The testimonies were either by verbal or written statements, and about 200 000 affidavits were taken into consideration. Rudolf Hess, the man who originally helped Hitler write *Mein Kampf* and later became a brigadier general in the SS, gave details of the systematic mass murder that took place at Auschwitz. More than 1000 personnel were involved, tracking and organising the massive amount of information. One judge from each of the three countries, and another from France, presided over the hearings. On 30 September and 1 October 1946 the verdicts were announced. There were three acquittals, 12 sentences to death by hanging, and the rest were sentenced to life imprisonment or lesser terms. On 16 October those sentenced to death were executed. Although there were more trials planned, this was the only international tribunal held. Over the next several years the United States, France, Great Britain and the Soviets conducted individual trials.

Opposite: Nazi leader Hermann Goering (extreme left) and other accused war criminals being guarded by US Military Police during the Nuremberg trials.

1945 United Nations Established

The League of Nations, established during World War I, was designed to promote international cooperation and maintain peace. With the onset of World War II, the League was considered a failure, and the organisation was dissolved. During World War II a new alliance of nations began to take shape. The first steps were taken in the summer of 1941. The Inter-Allied Declaration, an agreement of free peoples to work together in both war and peace, was drawn up in London. One month later, in August, the leaders of the United States and United Kingdom met and produced a document that outlined a set of guidelines for international collaboration. The document, signed while at sea on the HMS *Prince of Wales*, became known as the Atlantic Charter. On 1 January 1942, representatives from 26 countries met in Washington, DC to sign the 'Declaration by the United Nations'. They pledged support for the Atlantic Charter, and agreed to work together in the war effort and not make peace separately. China, Great Britain, the United States and the USSR issued an official statement on 30 October 1943, declaring the need to replace the League of Nations.

One year later, leaders from those same four countries met at a mansion, Dunbarton Oaks, in Washington, DC. There, from 21 September through to 7 October 1944, they began working on the detail of the structure and functioning of a new international organisation. A briefer meeting, the Yalta Conference, took place at Yalta in the Crimea in the USSR on 4–11 February 1945. During the meeting, British Prime Minister Winston Churchill, US President Franklin Delano Roosevelt and Soviet Premier Joseph Stalin decided to ask France and China to join them in sponsoring a founding conference for the United Nations. The founding conference, the United Nations Conference on International Organisation, met in San Francisco. From 25 April until 26 June, representatives from 50 countries worked together to draw up the United Nations Charter. Building from the work done in 1944, they wanted to design an organisation 'to save succeeding generations from the scourge of war'.

The 111-article charter was adopted unanimously on 25 June in the San Francisco Opera House. The next day representatives from all 50 nations signed the charter in the Herbst Theater auditorium of the Veterans War Memorial Building. The charter was ratified by China, France, the Soviet Union, the United Kingdom and the United States—the five permanent members of the Security Council—and by a majority of other signatories on 24 October 1945. The General Assembly met for the first time in Central Hall at Westminster in London on 10 January 1946. Later, the United Nations headquarters moved to New York City. Since its inception, the United Nations has been joined by 100 other nations, and its purpose has broadened to include cultural, economic, humanitarian and social problems.

Chronology of Events

1945 Signing of the Charter of the United Nations and Statute of the International Court of Justice in San Francisco.

1948 Official adoption by the General Assembly of the Universal Declaration of Human Rights.

1960 The General Assembly welcomes 13 African countries and Cyprus. Fidel Castro delivers the longest speech in UN history, four hours and 29 minutes. Later that year, the UN condemns apartheid.

1962 Kuwait becomes the 111th member of the United Nations.

1971 UN General Assembly admits Mainland China and expels Taiwan. By Resolution 2758 (XXVI), the General Assembly decided 'to restore all its rights to the People's Republic of China'.

1974 United Nations recognises the Palestine Liberation Organisation (PLO).

1990 UN Secretary General Javier Perez de Cuellar says he has lost all hope for peace in the Gulf.

1995 The United Nations celebrated its 50th anniversary. The party was the largest gathering of world leaders ever assembled.

Opposite: Political leaders hold the first United Nations conference inside the San Francisco Opera House.

1945 The Bikini is Unveiled

It is hard to imagine that there was once a beach without a bikini-clad woman in sight. But in the early part of the 1900s the swimming suit was a modest affair, covering areas of concern with great abundance. Surprisingly, what shrunk the suit was World War II. Because of war rationing, less fabric was allowed in the making of swim attire. Men on beaches everywhere were overjoyed to see women taking up the call for patriotism, baring midriffs for the first time.

Frenchman Jacques Heim introduced a two-piece bathing suit called the 'Atome' in 1945. Heim described his design as 'the world's smallest bathing suit'. Two months later a French automotive engineer, Louis Reard, who was running his mother's lingerie business, prepared for another unveiling. Not sure what to call his design, he borrowed from current events. The US government had exploded a nuclear device in the Pacific Ocean near several small islands known as the 'Bikini Atoll'. Four days later, on 5 July 1945, the 'Bikini' was introduced in Paris. The new suit was acclaimed by Reard to be 'smaller than the world's smallest bathing suit'. It consisted of 75 centimetres of fabric, and it was claimed that a swimsuit could not be called a bikini unless it could be pulled through a wedding ring. In fact the briefness of his design posed a problem. None of the Parisian models would wear the suit on a runway. Reard overcame his dilemma by hiring Micheline Bernardini, an exotic dancer. She had no hesitancy about being seen in so little. Although she was not exceptionally beautiful, when photos of her in a bikini hit the news stands she became an overnight celebrity, receiving almost 50 000 pieces of fan mail.

The new style was quick to catch on in Europe, and was made popular by Brigitte Bardot, who sported a bikini in the movie, *And God Created Women*. But many European beaches banned the bikini for years. In America, although a few stars like Marilyn Monroe and Jayne Mansfield were seen modelling the new fashion, the bikini would not become popular until the early 1960s. The bikini was even banned from beauty pageants after the Miss World contest in 1951, because it 'posed an unfair advantage to the wearer'. The bikini's popularity finally exploded 15 years later when the song 'Itsy Bitsy Teenie Weenie Yellow Polka Dot Bikini' began to play on the radio and American teenagers began to buy bikinis. In 1962 the first James Bond film, *Dr No*, featured Ursula Andress clad in a bikini and holding a knife. This not only fuelled popularity for the bikini, but set the pace for the future Bond girls. Shortly after, Annette Funicello was often bikini-clad in the *Beach Party* movies.

The bikini was established. More radical designs followed. The mono-kini, only a bottom, and the thong, without a bottom, never gained much popularity, especially in America. Then, in the 1980s and 1990s the one-piece suit reclaimed popularity, and Reard's company closed in 1988. In 1993 the sports bikini, made popular by beach volleyball, brought the bikini back into fashion.

Above and opposite: Many European beaches banned the bikini for years. In America, although a few stars like Marilyn Monroe and Ava Gardner were seen modelling the new fashion, the bikini would not become popular until the early 1960s.

1942
The Battle
of Midway

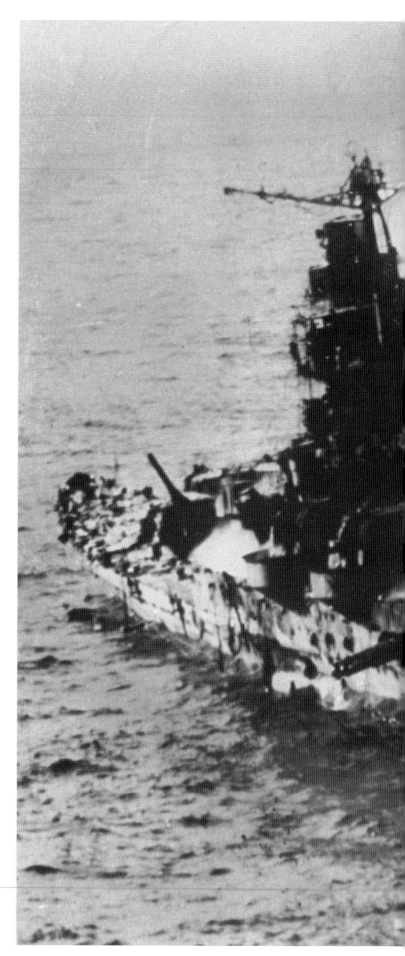

In April 1942 United States fighters bombed the Japanese mainland. They did not inflict much damage, but the Japanese were shaken; the raid was considered an embarrassment. Thus, the decision was made by Japan to launch a large-scale attack on the American fleet. The Japanese fleet was larger and newer, and their planes were extremely effective, particularly the Zero. Their plan called for a small group of ships attacking the Aleutian Islands to the north, to distract and split the American fleet. The main force of the Japanese fleet would attack the tiny but strategic US mid-Pacific base at Midway Atoll, the next day. They also placed a gauntlet of submarines just off the Hawaiian mainland, ready to pounce as the American fleet moved to Midway's assistance. Little would be left of the American force, if the plan worked. Military intelligence had worked on cracking the Japanese codes, and could now effectively understand much of the Japanese communications. Because of this, the American fleet had full knowledge of the Japanese plans, and carefully prepared a counter-attack.

On 3 June the Japanese attack on the Dutch Harbour, a small installation at the tip of Alaska, caused damage, but the ploy did not work to split the American fleet. Also, the Japanese lost a Zero. It crashed intact. This was America's first look inside the Zero, and valuable information was gained on how to defeat the plane. On 4 June the great battle began and raged until 7 July. By the end of the battle four Japanese fleet carriers were lost. America lost one carrier, which had survived several bombings, only to be sunk by a submarine. The base at Midway, though damaged, remained operational. It was later to be a vital component in the American trans-Pacific offensive.

The smoking hulk of the Japanese heavy cruiser Mikuma, *which was destroyed during the decisive Battle of Midway.*

1941
Japan Attacks
Pearl Harbor

America did not want to get involved in World War II, but the aggression and brutality displayed by both Germany and Japan demanded action. America responded by freezing both countries' assets and suspending trade with them. The embargo, and the American naval presence in the Pacific, fuelled Japan's anger.

On 1 December 1941 they decided to attack the United States. With the United States out of their way, Japan could carry out their ambitious plans for expansion. To keep an element of surprise, the Japanese government sent envoys to Washington to begin intensive diplomatic negotiations. With negotiations under way, the Japanese moved six powerful aircraft carriers into striking distance of Hawaii.

The quiet Sunday morning, on 7 December, was shattered shortly before 8.00 a.m. as 181 Japanese planes began their attack on the US naval base and military airfields at Pearl Harbor. The surprise was complete, and the devastation massive. In the first half hour three battleships (the primary targets) were sunk. At 8.30 a.m. the second wave hit. The attack ended just before 10.00 a.m., with 21 American ships sunk or damaged. All the battleships present, eight in total, had been sunk. Over 2400 Americans were killed in the attack. Fortunately, no American aircraft carriers were anchored at the time, and of the ships sunk, all but three were raised and repaired. More importantly, the shock of the attack galvanised the American resolve. The United States was ready to reap revenge and committed to victory. With Germany and Italy declaring war on America three days later, the United States was immersed in a war they had avoided for so long.

The battleships USS West Virginia *(foreground) and* Tennessee *sit low in the water and burn after the Japanese surprise attack on Pearl Harbor.*

1940
The Battle of Britain

Although willing to help, Great Britain had not been able to stop the wave of aggression, and nation after nation fell under the German rampage. With the fall of France in July 1940, Germany, joined by Italy, turned their attention to Great Britain. On 18 June, Winston Churchill, England's prime minister, addressed the nation:

Hitler knows that he will have to break us in this island or lose the war. If we can stand up to him, all Europe may be free and the life of the world may move forward into broad, sunlit uplands. But if we fail, then the whole world, including the United States, including all that we have known and cared for, will sink into the abyss of a new Dark Age made more sinister, and perhaps more protracted, by the lights of perverted science. Let us therefore brace ourselves to our duties, and so bear ourselves that, if the British Empire and its Commonwealth last for a thousand years, men will still say, 'This was their finest hour.'

Germany knew that in order to gain access to the English Channel, the powerful British navy would need to be defeated by air. The German Luftwaffe would first have to neutralise the English RAF. The Germans were far superior in number and were confident of victory. The German air attack began on 10 July 1940, and by August waves of German bombers pounded England relentlessly. The RAF knew that they alone could save their homeland from destruction. With extreme tenacity and undaunted valour they fought for freedom. They were joined by Australians, Canadians, New Zealanders, South Africans, Frenchmen, Poles, Czechs and Americans. England also used radars which, though not perfected, could track German planes. The RAF had the advantage of knowing how large a force was coming and in what direction. With this knowledge, effective counter-strikes were launched. Flight crews worked around the clock to keep the planes in the air and the runways smooth. The Germans continued their attack, dropping more than 50 000 tonnes of bombs on England, but the English would not bend. The date 10 May 1941 marked the final major air assault over London. The tide had turned, and the RAF began the offensive bombing of Germany, marking the turning point in World War II.

British pilots running towards their waiting planes after receiving a general warning from coastal observation stations.

1939 World War II Begins

World War II was an unwanted war of immense proportions. Many nations tried to overlook the insanity that mounted from the German and the Japanese nations, but their hunger for power threatened the entire world. With no other alternative, war ensued. During the 1930s a storm began to brew. Japan began aggression against China, escalating in 1937. Germany, with the power-hungry Hitler as their leader, also began to stir. In March 1938, Germany took over Austria and in September of the same year seized a portion of Czechoslovakia. The rest of Czechoslovakia fell under German rule by March 1939. This aggression was allowed because other nations hoped to avoid war by appeasing Hitler. They were wrong.

In May 1939 Japan began a war, though undeclared on both sides, with the Soviet Union. The fierce battle on the Mongolian planes was decisively won by the Soviets within four months. Japan reorientated their emphasis toward the south—the United States, Britain and the Netherlands. Pressure was building in Europe. Secret pacts were signed and guarantees for assistance made. On 31 August, German SS troops dressed in Polish uniforms staged an attack on a German radio station. This flimsily disguised attempt was used to justify an attack on Poland, Germany claiming that Poland was the aggressor nation.

The next day, on 1 September, German tanks rolled across the Polish border. Using tactics they called 'Blitzkrieg', the Germans moved into Poland with speed and violence. German troops not only shot Polish soldiers, they also shot citizens, many as they were fleeing. Because of the rapid penetration, most of Poland's air force was destroyed while still on the ground. Though Poland had defences, they could not hold up against the German onslaught.

That same morning, at 9.00 a.m., England and France issued an ultimatum to Germany. The next day Germany sank the ocean liner SS *Athena*, killing 112 people, including women and children. Germany was not going to back down. On 3 September 1939, England and France, followed by India, Australia, South Africa and New Zealand declared war on Germany. World War II had begun.

Chronology of Events

The origins of World War II stemmed from the aftermath of World War I. Many countries were not happy with the peace treaties, especially Germany who began to defy them, enticing the Allies to react.

1921 Hitler assumes control of the National Socialist German Workers Party (Nazi Party).

1933 Hitler is appointed Chancellor of Germany and one year later assumes the role of President, claiming the title of Führer. The Enabling Act is passed by the Reichstag (German government) and Hitler is given dictatorial power.

1935 Military conscription is introduced by Hitler. Increasing the army's size immensely, the action violates the Versailles Treaty.

1936 German Troops remilitarise the Rhineland, again violating the Versailles Treaty.

1937 On the other side of the globe, full-scale war erupts between China and Japan.

1938 Germany invades Austria and a union between the countries is proclaimed. German troops also occupy Czech Sudetenland.

1939 German troops take over the remainder of Czechoslovakia, thereby violating another peace treaty, the Munich Agreement.

1 September 1939 Germany invades Poland.

3 September 1939 Britain and France declare war on Germany. World War II begins.

Opposite: 3rd Division troops rush up to the Hornbach Front as the Siegfried Line begins to collapse between Saarbrucken and the Rhine.

1939 Television Debuts at the World's Fair

One event marked the development of modern television moving from concept to reality—the 1939 World's Fair. Sandwiched between great economic uncertainty and World War II, the fair was a welcome diversion from the pressures of the day. With the theme 'Building the World of Tomorrow', the World's Fair was an ideal launching point for a radical new concept—television. The first complete television system, including a picture tube, developed several years earlier, in 1923. This invention was followed by the first electronic television picture being transmitted, four years later. In 1928, WGY-TV in Schenectady, New York, transmitted a 40-minute stage production. Although television companies developed, to the general public television was a virtually unknown concept.

The World's Fair brought the television to the forefront of people's minds. On 30 April 1939, Franklin Delano Roosevelt, the President of the United States, gave the opening speech for the fair. What marked this speech as special was that it was televised. Cameras connected to RCA's mobile television van, the 'telemobile', sent a signal to a transmitter atop the Empire State Building, which was then sent out. The signal was received inside the RCA Pavilion at the fairground and shown on receivers. Other receivers were also installed on the 62nd floor of Radio City in Manhattan, New York. In all, only a few hundred people saw the telecast, but it still was the first televised presidential speech.

The RCA Pavilion had been designed to draw attention. Several televisions were on display, and just inside the exhibit was a special television. The Phantom TRK-12 Teleceiver was built using a new, clear plastic, Lucite, rather than wood, so that people could see the inside workings. This made it obvious that no trickery or sleight of hand was involved. Four designs were offered by RCA, all made with handcrafted wood and very expensive. At $600, a television cost as much as an automobile.

Within the year, six different companies began offering televisions. The concept of television was firmly planted in the imagination. However, with World War II looming,

television did not become widely popular with the general public until 1949, when the 630TS RCA Victor television set sold for $375. With its growing popularity, television technology moved ahead quickly. In 1947 Hollywood produced the first movie made especially for television. In 1953 colour broadcasting began and by 1956 black and white televisions were portable. Perhaps the greatest illustration of how far television progressed from 1939 happened 30 years later when the world watched Neil Armstrong walk on the Moon.

Chronology of Events

1924–25 American Charles Jenkins and John Baird from Scotland each demonstrate the mechanical transmissions of images over wire circuits. Baird becomes the first person to transmit moving silhouette images.

1926 John Baird operates a 30-lines-of-resolution system at 5 frames per second.

1928 The US Federal Radio Commission issues the first television licence (W3XK) to Charles Jenkins.

1929 John Baird opens the first TV studio. However, the image quality is poor.

1930 Charles Jenkins broadcasts the first TV commercial. The BBC begins regular TV transmissions.

1937 CBS begins TV development. The BBC begins high-definition broadcasts in London.

1939 Television was demonstrated at the New York World's Fair and the San Francisco Golden Gate International Exposition. RCA's David Sarnoff uses his company's exhibit at the 1939 World's Fair as a showcase for the 1st Presidential speech on television and to introduce RCA's new line of television receivers, some of which had to be coupled with a radio if you wanted to hear sound.

1967 Most TV broadcasts are in colour.

20 July 1969 The first TV transmission from the Moon—600 million people watch.

Opposite: RCA president David Sarnoff.

1939 Nylon Invented

DuPont was a chemical company with a vision. In the 1930s they funded a group of research scientists to come up with new ideas and new products. The scientists did just that and a string of innovations poured out of their laboratory.

One of the scientists, Dr Wallace Caruthers, began work in 1930 in polymerisation. Caruthers and his team studied chains of molecules called polymers. Their goal was very specific; they wanted to find a replacement for silk so they could compete in the women's hosiery market. Caruthers moved forward and by 1934 was combining chemicals that produced fibres. However the fibres were weak. The forming of fibres, the polymerising process, produced water as a by-product when the individual molecules joined together. This process was called a condensation reaction. The breakthrough came when Caruthers realised that the water that was produced dripped back into the mixture, which prohibited the further formation of molecules. The equipment was modified so that the water was removed from the system. Again the process was tried, this time with great success and a mixture was produced. The mixture could stretch into long fibres when pulled from a beaker with a heated rod. When the fibres were cooled to room temperature they had a silky texture. The thread was strong and elastic and was exactly what they were looking for. Caruthers named it nylon, and it was patented in 1935.

Wisely, Dupont did not register nylon as a trademark, letting the name become synonymous with their product, nylons. Three years later it was introduced to the public at the World's Fair. On 27 October 1938, the vice president of Dupont, Charles Stine, spoke at the fair in a session entitled, 'We Enter the World of Tomorrow'. Very appropriately, the announcement was not made to a group of scientists, but to 3000 women's club members who had gathered for the session. He announced that nylon had been invented, and described the marvellous new nylon stockings. Dupont built the first nylon plant in Delaware and by 1939 nylon stockings hit the market. Women stood in long queues to purchase the wonderful new product. That year alone, 36 million pairs of stockings were sold. Dupont promoted the new fibre, claiming it was as strong as steel and as fine as spider's web. It was also used in surgical sutures, toothbrush bristles and fishing line. Nylon marked the beginning of fibres produced entirely by chemicals—synthetic fibres. This breakthrough launched a 'chain reaction' of developments of a wide variety of fibres with a plethora of uses.

Facts and Figures

- In 1939, DuPont created nylon and revolutionised the fabric market. From the time it went on sale to the general public in May 1940, nylon hosiery was a huge success: women lined up at stores across the country to obtain the precious goods. In 1941 DuPont established a second nylon plant in Martinsville, Virginia, to meet the demand. With the onset of World War II, production was channelled into a host of national defence uses including parachutes and B-29 bomber tyres.

- When beginning production, DuPont was the sole producer of nylon worldwide. Now it accounts for less than 5 per cent of global production and nylon is used for more than just stockings.

- Nylon is currently found in hundreds of applications from carpets to clothing to luggage and automobile parts. In today's sports and swim wear, nylon or other later developed synthetic fibres are used exclusively.

- Nylon changed the way people dressed worldwide and rendered the term 'silk stocking'—once an epithet directed at the wealthy elite—obsolete.

Opposite: A model wearing black nylon net opera length hose permanently attached to high-heeled satin mules.

1937 Amelia Earhart Disappears

One of the most captivating mysteries of the 20th century is the disappearance of the famous female pilot Amelia Earhart. During an around-the-world flight attempt in 1937 Amelia, her co-pilot Fred Noonan and their Lockheed aircraft, *Electra*, vanished near Howland Island in the South Pacific. Hundreds of teams from the United States and the Japanese navy searched for months, looking for any trace of the aircraft, but none has ever been found.

Born in Kansas in 1897, Amelia Mary Earhart saw her first airplane at age 10, but was not impressed by the rusty wire and wooden construction. Years later, while attending a flying exhibition in California, she became intrigued and took her first flight as a passenger. Although the flight was only 10 minutes long, afterwards Earhart decided to dedicate her life to flying. Although it was not considered suitable for women to become pilots, Earhart was not deterred, beginning flying lessons with instructor Anita 'Neta' Snook in 1921 and purchasing her first plane not long after. Several years later, due to family concerns, Earhart sold her plane and moved east with her mother. She became a social worker in the autumn of 1925 in Boston but continued to promote flying, especially for women, frequently writing articles for the *Boston Globe*.

A year later, Captain H.H. Railey invited her on a journey as the first woman to fly across the Atlantic. Amelia agreed and one week later she met the man behind the project, New York Publisher George Putnam. With a remarkable resemblance to Charles Lindbergh, he decided on the spot that she was the woman for the flight. Although her official title was 'commander of the flight', Earhart was only a passenger on the plane. The pilot, Wilmer Stultz, and co-pilot/mechanic, Louis Gordon, did all the work. The team left Newfoundland in a plane named *Friendship* in June 1928 and arrived at Burry Portin in Wales almost 21 hours later. Their flight made worldwide headlines and the team was treated to a huge parade in New York City and a presidential reception at the White House. Although she enjoyed the attention, Amelia was concerned that she received more glory than the people who actually flew the plane merely because she was female.

After the Atlantic flight, Earhart devoted her attention to lecturing, writing and flying. In February 1931 she married George Putnam, but was not ready to settle down. Exactly five years after Charles Lindbergh's solo flight across the Atlantic, Earhart followed suit, becoming the second person and first woman to ever fly solo across the Atlantic. Three years later in January 1935, after 10 pilots had lost their lives in the attempt, she was the first to accomplish a trans-Pacific flight from Hawaii to California, and then on to Washington, DC. Apart from making records with her flights, she was greatly interested in the development of commercial aviation and took an active role in opening the field to women.

She soon began to plan what she titled her 'final big adventure', a flight around the world. Although it would not be the first, her flight path would be the longest, circum-navigating the globe at the Equator. After a false start, she and Fred Noonan began their second attempt, leaving Los Angeles on 21 May 1937. They travelled east through Florida, then on to South America, Africa, Asia and then New Guinea by 29 June. With over 35 000 kilometres behind them and only 12000 remaining, the final part of the journey was entirely over the Pacific Ocean. The pair left New Guinea on 2 July and then, after several radio contacts throughout the day, were never seen again. Costing the US government over $4 million and lasting six weeks, it is the most extensive search to date, recovering not a single clue.

Opposite: Amelia Mary Earhart saw her first aeroplane at age 10, but was not impressed by the rusty wire and wooden construction. Years later, while attending a flying exhibition in California, she became intrigued and took her first flight as a passenger.

1937 The *Hindenburg* Disaster

The *Hindenburg* was the largest airship to ever fly. Longer than the *Titanic* and dwarfing a 747, the craft was built with a rigid aluminium frame covered with a streamlined outer shell of silver fabric coated with a waterproof compound. The airship was able to travel at speeds of up to 135 kilometres an hour and made 10 commercial trans-Atlantic crossings during its existence. The airship was elegantly appointed, with amenities usually found on a cruise ship. The passenger compartment was located inside the hull, and the only break in the smooth outer skin was the control car for the flight crew. The ship moved at an incredible rate, making the Atlantic trip in just two days. The *Hindenburg* was sponsored by the Nazi regime. Overseen by Nazi propagandists, it frequently made flights over Germany, dropping pamphlets. The tail fins were adorned with swastikas. Designers had originally planned to fill the craft with helium rather than hydrogen, because although helium was less buoyant it was non-flammable. However, America was the only producer of helium at the time, and they were nervous about the German's intentions with the ship. The airship had to be filled with the highly flammable hydrogen gas instead. Flights began in 1936 and the *Hindenburg* began making trips from Germany to New York and Rio de Janeiro.

On 3 May 1937 the zeppelin departed Frankfurt bound for New York with 97 people on board. After a smooth trip the ship passed over Boston late in the morning of 6 May. The landing in New Jersey, however, was delayed because of bad weather. Finally, at 7.25 p.m. the *Hindenburg* started its landing. Hundreds watched as the big ship moved to dock. When the ship was 82 metres off the ground, ropes were dropped for the ground crew to tow it into position. Suddenly, a tongue of flame appeared from the back of the airship. Within a few seconds the ship exploded into a huge ball of fire that rose hundreds of metres into the sky. Thirty-seven seconds after the first flame, the ship crashed tail first into the ground. The ship's skeleton was all that was visible through the flames. Passengers jumped out the windows to run to safety. Only 62 managed to escape alive.

The United States and Germany were both eager to quickly resolve the situation, and the investigation of the crash was closed, calling the incident an accident. It was really never determined if the explosion was intentionally sabotaged or if it was a misfortune. Recently the theory of an accident was strengthened by the observation that the chemical used to coat the outside of the hull had the same chemical components as solid rocket fuel. Accident or sabotage, the *Hindenburg* disaster brought the popularity of zeppelins to an end.

Chronology of Events

1910 The most successful airships were created by Ferdinand von Zeppelin. The rigid zeppelin prototype has a highly efficient layout: an essentially cylindrical metal-framed and fabric-covered hull, large tail fins for stability and a streamlined engine, and crew pods hung beneath the hull.

1914–17 Zeppelins are used by the Germans as weapons during WWI. They prove to be very inaccurate, amounting to a few hundred deaths at the most. They are easy targets as well; several are shot down by the British.

1919 The British dirigible R-34 airship lands in New York, completing the first crossing of the Atlantic by an airship and the first non-stop crossing by any aircraft.

1925 The US navy crashes the *Shenandoah* airship; many die. Later all three of the US airships crash, killing over 50 people.

1931 Britain suffers its own airship tragedy when the R101, a fatally flawed machine barely able to lift its own weight, crashes in France with the loss of all on board.

6 May 1937 The *Hindenburg* airship disaster kills 36 people when the airship is engulfed by flames. This causes public faith in airships to evaporate in favour of faster, more cost-efficient aeroplanes.

Currently Blimps are only to be used for advertising and as TV camera platforms at major sporting events.

Opposite: Hundreds watched as the Hindenburg *moved to dock. When the ship was 82 metres off the ground, ropes were dropped for the ground crew to tow it into position. Suddenly, a tongue of flame appeared from the back of the airship. Within a few seconds the ship exploded into a huge ball of fire hundreds of metres high.*

1937 Japan Invades China

During the early 20th century, Japan held the burning ideal that they had a 'divine mission' to lead all of Asia. In the early 1930s they began to move on their desire for expansion and imperialism. Over the next 15 years they brutally attacked the people of China, Korea, the Philippines and other Asian countries, as well as the United States. A bomb set by Japanese secret agents destroyed a Japanese-owned express train on 18 September 1931. The 'Mukden incident,' as it was called, provided the excuse that Japan needed to launch aggression towards China, attacking Chinese troops in Manchuria. Over the next several years Japan slowly increased their hold on China. In July 1937, after 'the China Incident', a skirmish between Japanese and Chinese troops at the Marco Polo Bridge near Peking, Japan launched an all-out war against mainland China.

By August, Japanese planes began to bombard Nanking and Shanghai, concentrating their attacks in the downtown areas where the civilian population was the highest. Japan gave reasons for their attacks, stating they wanted to protect China from inner turmoil. They stated that Japan needed to colonise other lands because their country was over-populated and lacked natural resources, but gave assurances that Japan's takeover would be for the good of China and all of East Asia. As autumn progressed the Japanese troops focused their attack on Nanking, the designated capital of China. In the beginning of the 1930s Nanking had a population of a quarter of a million, but the population had swelled to over a million by 1937 as refugees poured in from the surrounding countryside, where roaming Japanese troops terrorised civilians.

On 11 November, Japanese troops began their advance towards Nanking, moving in from several directions. By early December they had closed in on the city, demanding that Chinese troops surrender. The troops would not surrender and a massive attack was launched. The Chinese military units, overwhelmed and fatigued, did not put up much of a battle. Four days later, on 13 December, Nanking fell to the Japanese army. What followed in the next six weeks is a numbing account of inhuman action. During the Nanking Massacre over 300000 Chinese were brutally murdered, both soldiers and civilians. The long list of atrocities committed included mass execution, raping, looting and burning. The once beautiful city of Nanking was left in smouldering ruins. The Japanese war machine was on the move, aggressively expanding its reach. What was to follow would be World War II.

Chronology of Events

18 September 1931 A bomb explodes under a Japanese-owned express train in Manchuria. The 'Mukden Incident' as it is known, is merely an excuse created by Japanese secret agents for Japanese troops to occupy Manchuria.

July 1937 A skirmish between Japanese and Chinese troops at the Marco Polo Bridge, near Peking, sparks off a full-scale invasion of China.

August 1937 Japanese bombers make the first trans-oceanic raids in history, from Taiwan and Kyushu to Nanking and Shanghai.

December 1937 The Nanking Massacre leaves 300000 Chinese dead. The Chinese capital is sacked by Japanese troops. The US river gunboat *Panay* is bombed and sunk near Nanking.

1939 The outbreak of World War II in Europe. With the fall of France to Nazi Germany in 1940, Japan moves to occupy French Indo-China.

1940 The new temporary capital of China is bombed continuously by Japanese.

7 December Japan bombs Pearl Harbor and invades Siam, Hong Kong, Burma, North Borneo, the Philippines and Pacific Islands. Britain and the United States declare war on Japan.

1945 US planes drop two atomic bombs, one on Hiroshima, the second on Nagasaki. Japanese Emperor Hirohito surrenders and relinquishes his divine status. Japan is placed under US military government. All Japanese military and naval forces are disbanded.

Opposite: Japanese War Minister Hideki Tojo addresses a mass meeting at Korakuen Stadium in Tokyo.

1936 Jesse Owens is a Hero in Germany

James Cleveland Owens was born in 1913 in a small Alabama town, the youngest of 10 children. His health was not helped by the poor living conditions his family endured, and J.C. or 'Jesse' suffered from frequent bouts of pneumonia and bronchial congestion. His life was hard, and by seven Jesse was expected to pick 50 kilograms of cotton a day. The next year his family moved to Cleveland, Ohio. Jesse worked hard. He helped his family out by delivering groceries, loading freight and working in a shoe repair shop. Between jobs he realised that he loved to run. The school's track coach, Charlie Riley, recognised Jesse's raw ability and asked him to run for the track team. Because he was not able to attend after-school practices, the coach offered to train him in the mornings. Jesse's natural athletic ability quickly developed and by the time he was a senior he tied the world record of 9.4 seconds in the 100-yard dash. Colleges and universities competed for Jesse, and Ohio State University was chosen. There, although a gifted athlete, he faced the same fate of other African-American athletes. When travelling with the team, he had to eat at 'black-only' restaurants and stay in 'black-only' motels. He was not given a scholarship and had to continue working to support himself.

At a Big Ten meet on 15 May 1935, Jesse was suffering from back pains until race time, but he persuaded his coach to allow him to compete. He set three world records and tied a fourth. This amazing task was accomplished in just over an hour, one week after Jesse injured himself while training. In 1936 Jesse competed in the Olympic Games held in Berlin, Germany. The Nazi regime was starting to broil and Hitler was determined to prove to the world that the German 'Aryan' people were the dominant race. They openly criticised America for sending the 'Inferior Black Auxiliaries'. Jesse, much to Hitler's chagrin, won the heart of the German citizens. Crowds of 110 000 cheered him on. In all, Jesse Owens triumphed in the 100-metre dash, the 200-metre dash and the long jump. He was also a member of the 4 x 100 metre relay team which won the gold medal. He was the first American in Olympic Track and Field to win four gold medals in a single Olympics, and set records in three of the events. Hitler's myth was demolished by his stellar athletic performance.

When Jesse came back to America, he did not return to a hero's welcome. The segregated standard was still in place, most notably illustrated when Jesse had to ride in a freight elevator to a reception given in his honour. Jesse proved to be a great man off the field as well as on, and believed it was his privilege to 'try to make things better'. Which he did.

Facts and Figures

- Adolf Hitler's racist regime was not supported by the majority of the Germans during the 1936 Olympic Games in Berlin. Hitler viewed African-Americans as inferior and chastised the United States for stooping to send these 'lesser-humans'.

- However, not all Germans were so racist, with many of them supporting Owens, including fellow long-jumper Luz Long. The top German long jumper supported Owens when officials claimed he fouled on his longest jump. Jesse went on to win the event.

- While German officials denounced Owens, an overwhelming majority of the German fans treated him like a hero. In 1984, a street in Berlin was named in his honour.

- His own nation awarded him its highest civilian honour, the Medal of Freedom, in ceremonies at the White House in 1976. President Ford presented the medal, with the 250-member US Montreal Olympic team in attendance. In February 1979 he returned to the White House, where President Carter presented him with the Living Legend Award. On that occasion, the President said, 'A young man who possibly didn't even realise the superb nature of his own capabilities went to the Olympics and performed in a way that I don't believe has ever been equalled since...and since this superb achievement, he has continued in his own dedicated but modest way to inspire others to reach for greatness.'

Opposite: Jesse Owens competing in the long jump event at the 1936 Olympic Games in Berlin.

1936 King Edward VIII Abdicates

On 10 December 1936 at 10.00 a.m., King Edward VIII abdicated the British throne. He was the only British monarch to voluntarily step down from his position, giving it up for love. When Edward, then Prince of Wales, first met American divorcee Wallis Simpson, she did not make much of an impression on him. But over the next few years he fell deeply in love with her, ultimately giving up the throne to marry her.

Less than 11 months before his abdication, the 41-year-old bachelor became king after the death of his father, King George V. The grief of losing his father was compounded by the responsibility that he did not want. Edward was thrust into the public light, his every move judged. He did not gain much support at the beginning of his reign. His first act as king was to order clocks to be set to the correct time, as they always ran half an hour fast. Many took this as a trivial step, and a rejection of his father's work, rather than simply fixing a long-standing problem. Edward wanted to change the monarchy, making it more modern. But this stance only added to his hardship. Many advisers did not trust his insight, and the distrust was returned. Edward started arriving late to appointments or not arriving at all. Paperwork that had always been returned promptly became slow and unreliable.

Edward was distracted as he had fallen in love, tragically with someone he was not allowed to marry and approval was not to be found within his family, the Church of England, or the political establishment. The woman he had fallen for was not only an American, she had already been married twice and her second divorce was pending. There were three options for Edward: he could give her up, keep Wallis and the government would resign, or abdicate the throne. Edward did not want to give her up. He also did not want to hurt the monarchy by marrying her while he was still the king. The possibility of a royal marriage had already caused sensational newspaper headlines around the world and stirred up enormous controversy. He decided to marry her and had little choice but to abdicate.

Surrounded by his three surviving brothers, Edward signed the six copies of the instrument of abdication, just 325 days after his coronation. In a radio address he announced to the world, 'But you must believe me when I tell you that I have found it impossible to carry the heavy burden of responsibility and to discharge my duties as King as I would wish to do without the help and support of the woman I love.' His brother Albert became King George VI, and the title of Duke of Windsor was bestowed upon Edward. He was then exiled from Great Britain. Although a specific time was not set, many thought that the exile would only be for a few years. The exile was permanent, and Edward never returned; the members of the royal family having shunned the couple. On 3 June 1937 the couple was married in France at a small ceremony. They lived in France for the rest of their lives.

Chronology of Events

10 January 1931 Edward meets Wallis Simpson for the first time at a house party. Mrs Simpson is married to her second husband, Ernest, after divorcing her first husband.

January 1932 The Simpsons spend their first weekend at Edward's country retreat.

November 1934 A party is held at Buckingham Palace in honour of the Duke of Kent. Wallis Simpson attends a party but the king, George V, is outraged and refuses to meet her.

20 January 1936 King George V dies and Edward succeeds him as king.

August 1936 Photographs of King Edward and Mrs Simpson together are widely published.

16 November 1936 The king announces he wants to marry Mrs Simpson. Advisers do not approve. The king says he is prepared to abdicate if the government opposes his marriage.

3 December 1936 The people of Britain widely disapprove of the prospect of the couple's marriage. Wallis Simpson leaves for France.

10 December 1936 King Edward VIII signs the instrument of abdication, drawn up by his close friend Sir Walter Monckton.

Opposite: The Duke and Duchess of Windsor on the quayside at Portofino.

1933
The Holocaust Begins

The Holocaust was the systematic annihilation of six million Jews by the Nazi regime during World War II. In 1933 approximately nine million Jews lived in the 21 countries of Europe that would be occupied by Germany during the war. By 1945 two out of every three European Jews had been killed. The European Jews were the primary victims of the Holocaust. But Jews were not the only group singled out for persecution by Hitler's Nazi regime. As many as half a million Gypsies, at least 250 000 mentally or physically disabled persons, and more than three million Soviet prisoners of war also fell victim to Nazi genocide. Jehovah's Witnesses, homosexuals, Social Democrats, communists, partisans, trade unionists, Polish intelligentsia and other undesirables were also victims of the hate and aggression carried out by the Nazis.

Facts and Figures

30 January 1933 Adolf Hitler is appointed Chancellor of Germany.

22 March 1933 Dachau concentration camp opens. The first inmates are 200 communists.

1 April 1933 Jewish shops and businesses are boycotted.

7 April 1933 Laws for the re-establishment of the civil service bar Jews from holding civil service, university and state positions.

10 May 1936 The public burning of books written by Jews, political dissidents and others not approved of by the state.

15 September 1936 Anti-Jewish racial laws are enacted. Jews are no longer considered German citizens. They cannot marry Aryans nor fly the German flag.

26 April 1938 Mandatory registration of all property held by Jews inside the Reich.

9–10 November 1938 Kristallnacht (Night of Broken Glass): 200 synagogues are destroyed, 7500 Jewish shops looted and 30 000 male Jews are sent to concentration camps.

May 1940 A concentration camp is established at Auschwitz. More than 160 000 Polish Jews are confined to the ghetto in Lodz.

November 1940 About 500 000 Polish Jews are confined to the ghetto in Warsaw.

1 March 1941 Himmler orders a camp at Birkenau built.

3 March 1941 Krakow ghetto established.

8 July 1941 Jews in Baltic countries must wear the Star of David.

31 July 1941 Heydrich appointed by Goering to implement the 'Final Solution'.

Opposite: Jewish Holocaust survivors packed into the sweltering hold of a British transport ship after they were forced off their refugee ship.

1929 St Valentine's Day Massacre

During the 1920s, alcohol sales were illegal, prohibition was the law and bootlegging was rampant. Chicago was a land of gangsters and the leader of the mob was Al 'Scarface' Capone. The thorn in his side was George 'Bugs' Moran, operating a rival gang and frequently stealing Capone's shipments of whisky. The two rivals conducted a bloody warfare over money and power. Although never charged with the crime, it is believed that Al Capone ordered Moran killed, and then headed to Miami for an alibi. What took place was the most spectacular hit in gang history. However, Capone's ultimate target, Moran, was not killed and Capone's crime empire would soon crumble under the resulting police and public pressure. From the police investigation, the following was put together.

On the morning of 14 February 1929 at approximately 10.30 a.m., Capone's men drove a stolen police car to the garage in time for the arranged 'delivery' of whisky to Moran's warehouse. Three of the men were dressed as policemen and two in plain clothes. Believing Moran to be on the premises the men entered and told the seven men they found inside that it was a police raid, to put down their weapons and stand against the wall. Once inside, it was obvious that Moran was not in the building, but there was no turning back. Continuing the raid, over 150 bullets were fired by Capone's men; six of the seven men were killed outright. Continuing with the pretence, Capone's five gunmen left with the three uniformed men leading the others out as though they had been arrested. After hearing the shots, neighbours looked out onto the snowy street. What they saw were three men in uniform marching their plain-clothed counterparts out the front door with hands in the air. The men got into the police car and drove away, and the neighbours, glad the police were involved, went back to their business. However, when a dog continued barking someone checked to see what was wrong and discovered the gruesome scene.

The police arrived quickly and found seven well-dressed men riddled with bullets on the floor. One man, Frank Gusenberg, was still alive. He was rushed to hospital where investigators hoped he would regain consciousness and provide a lead. He did wake up; just long enough to say he was not going to talk and then died. The news splashed across the headlines, making the Chicago mob infamous. The police never found the murderers and never charged Capone. Though there were many suspects, none were ever arrested. Because of this incident, Al Capone lost his popularity as a romantic figure in Chicago and his power waned.

Chronology of Events

1899 Alphonse Capone is born into an immigrant family in Brooklyn, New York. Contrary to popular belief his family is not part of the criminal world.

January 1920 The 18th Amendment of the Prohibition Act is introduced, which makes the brewing, distilling and distribution of alcohol illegal. Chicago's criminal underworld begins bootlegging, which proves to be extremely profitable.

1925 Bugs Moran surfaces as the rival gang leader after killing members of Capone's mob.

1926 Tired of the killings, Capone organises a peace conference with rival gangs and all parties agree that there will be no more assassinations.

1928 Capone's close friend and associate Jack McGurn who had two attempts made on his life by Bugs Moran, allegedly sets up a meeting with Capone in the winter of 1928 to plan what would be one of the most notorious gangland killings of all time.

14 February 1929 Seven of Moran's gang members are killed when five members of Capone's gang shoot out the Moran headquarters.

1931 Capone is gaoled for 11 years for violating prohibition laws and tax evasion. Upon his release, he moves to Palm Springs where he lives to be 48.

Opposite: Six racketeers who were executed by a rival gang. The men were lined up facing the wall and shot to death with machine gun.

1925 Hitler Publishes *Mein Kampf*

Mein Kampf, meaning 'My Struggle' was a two-volume publication written by Adolf Hitler. The first volume, *Eine Abrechnung*, 'A Reckoning' was published in 1925, and the second volume, *Die Nationalsozialistische Bewegung*, 'The National-Socialistic Movement' was published a year later. When originally published, *Mein Kampf* was ignored and few outside the Nazi party paid serious heed. No one dreamed that the hate-filled book was the blueprint for a coming nightmare filled with violence and bloodshed.

Hitler was born in 1889 in the small Austrian town of Braunau, by the Bavarian-German border. He was a mediocre student who increased in rebelliousness as he grew. Not lasting in college and not willing to hold down a job, Hitler wandered in the woods, reading and painting. Twice he tried to enrol in the Academy of Fine Arts in Vienna so that he could become a famous artist. He didn't gain admission and as a result became very depressed and lived a vagrant lifestyle on the streets of Vienna.

Unfortunately, this time of his life made a huge impact on him. Hitler fought with distinction in World War I on Germany's Western Front, but after the war ended, he again had no purpose. He attended the German Workers Party meetings, a nationalist group that was anti-Semitic in 1919. Within a short period of time he became the leader, the Führer, of the group. Under his leadership the membership increased dramatically and was renamed the National Socialist German Workers Party (NSDAP), the official name of the Nazi party. In 1923 Hitler attempted a coup against the Berlin government, the Munich Beer Hall putsch. His attempt failed, and he and his chief collaborators were tried for treason and sentenced to a year's imprisonment in Landsberg. During that time he dictated and Rudolf Hess wrote *Mein Kampf*. What started out as a pamphlet called 'Settling Accounts' soon became his missive to Germany. Adept at propaganda, Hitler aimed to reach the populace in his 872-page book. He stated, 'All propaganda must be popular and its intellectual level must be adjusted to the most limited intelligence among those it is addressed to. Consequently, the greater the mass it is intended to reach, the lower its purely intellectual level will have to be.' With that in mind he loaded his book with about 500 proverbs amidst his convoluted autobiography. He also laid out his plans for Germany, stating its destiny was in national socialism and an Aryan race. His ultimate goal was world domination. Hitler was an obscure politician when he published his book, and *Mein Kempf* was equally obscure.

As Hitler rose to power, the book gained popularity. This is due in large part to the book becoming required reading material. First party members and then the general public were pressured to buy it. Many only did so as a means of gaining position or avoiding the attention of the Gestapo. By 1933 Hitler was chancellor of the Third Reich, and *Mein Kempf* was a best-seller. By the end of the war 10 million copies had been sold, though far less had been read. Today *Mein Kampf*, so boldly written and so quickly overlooked, stands as a reminder of the most evil dictator of all time.

Introduction to *Mein Kampf*

On April 1st, 1924, I began to serve my sentence of detention in the Fortress of Landsberg am Lech, following the verdict of the Munich People's Court of that time.

After years of uninterrupted labour it was now possible for the first time to begin a work which many had asked for and which I myself felt would be profitable for the Movement. So I decided to devote two volumes to a description not only of the aims of our Movement but also of its development. There is more to be learned from this than from any purely doctrinaire treatise.

This has also given me the opportunity of describing my own development in so far as such a description is necessary to the understanding of the first as well as the second volume and to destroy the legendary fabrications which the Jewish Press have circulated about me.

In this work I turn not to strangers but to those followers of the Movement whose hearts belong to it and who wish to study it more profoundly. I know that fewer people are won over by the written word than by the spoken word and that every great movement on this earth owes its growth to great speakers and not to great writers.

Opposite: A portrait of Adolf Hitler taken in 1933 on his accession to power in Germany. He is in the uniform of his party, the NSDAP.

1924 Frozen Food Marketed

Clarence Birdseye once said, 'Go around asking a lot of damn-fool questions and taking chances. Only through curiosity can we discover opportunities, and only by gambling can we take advantage of them.' This statement characterised his lifestyle and revealed how he became the inventor of frozen food.

Born in Brooklyn, New York in 1886, Birdseye studied at Amherst College, majoring in biology. He was forced to drop out in 1912 due to a lack of money. He pursued a career as a field naturalist and ended up working for the US government. The next five years were spent on the Peninsular of Labrador in Canada, near the Arctic. While in the frozen north he discovered something that would change the way people prepared and served meals. He noted that when fish were caught and placed on the ice, exposed to the frigid wind and Arctic temperatures, they froze quickly. Later, when this frozen fish was prepared, it tasted fresh. He also realised that food frozen in the dead of winter tasted better than what was frozen in the milder temperatures of spring and fall. With a passion for biology and an inquisitive mind, Birdseye set out to determine why the quick freeze was effective. He soon discovered that when food is frozen quickly only small ice crystals are able to form. The small crystals do not damage the cell walls, unlike the larger ice crystals that form at higher freezing temperatures. Food frozen in this manner has maximum flavour, texture and colour, and maintains its nutritional value.

With this knowledge in hand, and a bit of a gamble in mind, he headed back to New York. Seven dollars was invested and soon he was using an electric fan, buckets of brine and ice cakes to experiment with the process. He tried different foods and different temperatures and soon perfected the freezing process. With his 'Quick Freeze Machine' he packaged fish and other food in waxed cardboard cartons and then quick-froze the contents by pressing the cartons between two flat, refrigerated surfaces. Fresh fish from Fulton Fish Market in New York City was frozen by this process. An entirely new market had been discovered.

With the help of financial backers he opened up the General Seafood Company. Unfortunately this idea was slow to catch on. Freezing had been tried with foods before, but the results were disappointing, so people were slow to give his food a try. He also had a problem with the machines; they were very expensive to build and maintain. He sold his company in 1929 for a bargain price for what would become the General Foods Corporation and Birds Eye. The new company, with Birdseye's help, presented 26 different fruits and vegetables, fish and meat for the 'Springfield Experiment Test Market' in Springfield, Massachusetts, in 1930. Frozen food was introduced to the world. Birdseye was a prolific inventor and had almost 300 patents during his lifetime. He once said, 'Mix your knowledge with imagination and apply both.'

Chronology of Events

The 1930s Clarence Birdseye launches retail sales of frozen food products in Springfield, Massachusetts.

The 1940s Annual frozen food production rises from slightly over 3 billion kilograms to 5 billion kilograms.

The 1950s Frozen food sales exceed the $1 billion mark. By the middle of the 1950s, 64 per cent of all retail stores have frozen food sections. The introduction of pre-cooked or prepared frozen foods opens up an entirely new field for industry growth.

The 1960s The microwave oven is introduced, making frozen foods easy to defrost and opening a new market. Frozen food sales soar when astronauts, upon return from landing on the Moon, eat prepared frozen entrees and side dishes.

The 1980s Fast-food items are frozen for retail, including hamburgers, french fries, milkshakes and breakfasts. Microwave items increase in popularity.

The 1990s With almost 60 per cent of married women working or looking for work, as compared with 46 per cent in 1973, the Home Meal Replacement (HMR) trend dominates consumers' buying habits.

Opposite: Frozen food changed the way housewives filled the family larder in the 1940s.

1924 Air-conditioning Invented

Willis Haviland Carrier changed the world with his invention of the air-conditioner. He was born in Angola, New York, in November 1876 and was raised on a farm on the New York shore of Lake Erie. Although he was awarded a scholarship in 1895 to attend Cornell University, he still had to work odd jobs in order to meet his expenses. When he graduated from college in 1901 it was with a Master's Degree in electrical engineering. Within the year he got a job at a top engineering company at the time, the Buffalo Forge Company. His pay was $10 a week, for helping design heating systems to dry lumber and coffee.

One night in 1902, while waiting in a Pittsburgh train station, an idea occurred to Carrier. Drawing from the principles used in heating, he applied them to cooling. He formulated an idea and quickly sketched a model on a napkin, so not to forget. He realised that by passing cold liquid refrigerant through coils at low pressure, and then blowing warm air from a room over the coils, the air would cool. The cool air could be sent back into a room, effectively cooling the room. By utilising a second fan, a series of coils, a condenser and an expansion valve, along with other gizmos the coolant could be recycled, making the cooling process continuous. He quickly came up with a working model.

That same year the new system was installed at a Brooklyn printing plant, much to the owner's joy. Previously, changes in temperature caused instability in the printing process, making four-colour printing almost impossible. With the cooling system in place printing progressed smoothly. Carrier applied for a patent, which was granted in 1906. In 1915 Carrier took a big step. After leaving the company he had worked with for so long, he and six friends invested their savings and formed the Carrier Engineering Company, based in New Jersey. His company pioneered many new designs and the manufacture of refrigeration machines.

It was not until 1924 that the cooling concept was used for people. Three Carrier 'chillers' were installed in the J.L. Hudson Department Store in Detroit. The cooling was a sensation and shoppers flocked to the comfort of the store. Quickly more orders came from stores and theatres. Business owners placed their orders also, realising that workers would produce more in the summer months if kept comfortable. The Carrier Company introduced their first residential unit in 1928—the 'Weathermaker'. Although Carrier was not the first to develop an interior cooling system, his was the safest and most efficient. Air-conditioning had widespread ramifications. The century-long migration from the southern to the northern states stopped, and even reversed as living was made comfortable in warmer areas. Food production and distribution became more varied. Industrial production increased, science and medicine was even affected as environments were able to be sustained at a constant temperature.

Chronology of Events

1882 The first electric power plant opens in New York making it possible for the first time to have an inexpensive source of energy for residential and commercial buildings.

1902 Willis Carrier builds the first air-conditioner to combat humidity inside a printing company. This was the start of managing the inside environment.

1917 The first documented theatre to use refrigeration is the New Empire Theater in Alabama. In that same year, the Central Park Theater in Chicago is built to incorporate the new technology—air-conditioning.

1930 The White House, the Executive Office Building and the Department of Commerce are air-conditioned.

1946 After World War II, the demand for room air-conditioners begins to increase. Thirty thousand room air-conditioners are produced that year.

1953 Room air-conditioner sales exceed one million units with demand still exceeding supply.

1957 The first rotary compressors are introduced, permitting units to be smaller and quieter, weigh less and be more efficient than the reciprocating type.

1969 Neil Armstrong and Buzz Aldrin walk on the Moon in spacesuits with life support and cooling systems using air-conditioning technology.

Opposite: Room air-conditioner sales exceeded one million units in 1953.

1922 Discovery of King Tutankhamen's Tomb

Although the Valley of the Kings was thought to hold no more secrets, in 1917 Howard Carter and his sponsor, Lord Carnarvon, began looking for the tomb of an unknown Egyptian king that Carter was sure existed. Five years of searching turned up little and Lord Carnarvon had to be convinced to let Carter continue his search for one more year. On 4 November 1922, just four days after renewing his search, Carter found a step at the base of the tomb of Ramses VI. Thousands of tourists had walked over the area and archaeologists dug within metres of the discovery. After uncovering more stairs the next day Carter was very excited. He had the stairs covered back up, set trusted workers to stand guard, and cabled Lord Carnarvon: 'At last have made wonderful discovery in Valley; a magnificent tomb with seals intact; re-covered same for your arrival; congratulations.'

Three weeks later with Lord Carnarvon present work begun again on the site. Sixteen stairs were uncovered and a doorway with seals bearing the name of Tutankhamen were exposed. On 25 November the door was removed. Behind it lay a passageway filled with limestone chips. This was cleared by the following afternoon, exposing another doorway. A small breach was made in the doorway and with a candle Carter peered in. After his eyes adjusted he stood speechless. Finally, those with him asked if he could see anything, and he responded, 'Yes, wonderful things'. The next day the door was unsealed and the antechamber entered; it was stacked with golden objects. A sealed doorway flanked by life-size statues of the king was to the right. To the left another sealed door had a hole in it. They crawled through the hole into a room later named the Annexe. The enormity of the find began to settle in on Carter. The Annexe, though in disarray, was also filled with priceless objects. Wisely, before unsealing the other doorway, Carter spent 10 weeks carefully clearing the two rooms.

News of the find travelled fast and people lined the entrance to watch stretchers of objects carried out. Around the world people clamoured for daily updates; fashion and architecture reflected the world's preoccupation with Egypt. On 17 February 1923 a small hole was finally made in the doorway between the two statues. Peering in, they saw a wall of gold. The wall turned out to be shrines of gilded wood with brilliant blue porcelain inlay nearly 5 metres long, 3 metres wide and 2.7 metres tall, almost filling the room. Next to the burial chamber was yet another room, the treasury, filled with burial items. Under the large shrine there were three other shrines, one within another. Beneath the fourth was the king's sarcophagus made of a single block of yellow quartzite. Inside the sarcophagus was a gilded wooden coffin. At this point Carter stopped to preserve what had already been uncovered. A year and a half later the coffin was open to reveal another coffin, and then the final coffin of pure gold. Inside that lay the mummy of King Tutankhamen—with a golden burial mask, the most famous of the 3500 items recovered. It took over 10 years for Carter and others to document the items from the tomb. This was the only royal Egyptian mummy ever discovered untouched. A relatively unimportant king in his time, Tutankhamen's obscurity protected the location of his tomb. Today King Tutankhamen is the most well known of all Egyptian royalty.

The Curse of the Mummy

The curse of the mummy originated when many terrible events occurred after the discovery of King Tut's tomb. Legend has it that anyone who dared to open the tomb would suffer the wrath of the mummy. Lord Carnarvon died shortly after the discovery. In the spring of 1923 a mosquito bit Lord Carnarvon on his cheek. During his morning routine shaving he cut the mosquito bite. It soon became infected and Lord Carnarvon died. At that exact moment, the lights in Cairo mysteriously went out. It is said that Lord Carnarvon's dog howled and dropped dead when Carnarvon died. New findings are showing that bacteria on the wall of the tomb might have been the cause of the curse. The bacteria would release spores into the air allowing it to be inhaled. Could this be what killed Lord Carnarvon?

Opposite: British archaeologist Howard Carter is flanked by assistants as they view the sarcophagus of King Tutankhamen for the first time.

1920 Women's Fashion Revolutionised

The first two decades of the 20th century are often regarded as the most radical and significant period in women's fashions—the fundamental breakaway from tradition. At the turn of the century, women were expected to have wardrobes consisting of tightly laced corsets, long knickers, slips, undergarments, petticoats, gloves and a hat to suit every outfit. Mass-produced clothes were unheard of and hours were spent by dressmakers, seamstresses and embroiderers producing complicated, highly decorated clothes. During the next decade, that was to change.

As the early 1900s proceeded, social changes became more apparent. More women were going to universities and colleges, entering professions and participating in active sports. The fashion of the time followed women's new attitudes and was reflected through more practical and less fussy garments—whalebone corsets were out. Dresses and dress suits were tailored to suit the more active lifestyle of the 'new woman'. The shape of the thighs and legs showed clearly for the first time in 100 years. Technical developments such as the telephone, electric lights and motor transport had meant a drastic change of lifestyle, all of which was bound to affect clothes and introduce a more practical style of dress.

By the early 1920s, clothes were enormously different from the fashions of the late 1800s. Prohibition, the proliferation of jazz, and the development of mass media were the hallmarks of the 1920s. The hedonistic lifestyle of the youth ruled the day and was valued as so many young people were killed during World War I. Changes in fashion included a more carefree style and cosmetics became a major industry. Glamour was now an important fashion trend, due to the influence of the motion picture industry and the famous female movie stars. There was also the emergence of three major women's fashion magazines: *Vogue*, *The Queen* and *Harper's Bazaar*. These magazines provided mass exposure for popular styles and fashions. The Roaring Twenties became a time of huge social change. It was the jazz age of dancing, rebelling and having fun. The era went down in history as a 'fun period' of

the century with daring young fashions and new styles in popular music and dancing. These changes would continue throughout the 1900s making it the century to see the most changes in the history of fashion—from the glamour of the 1920s to the lycra and platform-filled 1970s, and everything in between.

Facts and Figures

- During the early 1920s, almost every 'fashion rule' was broken. Waistlines became loose, unlike the fitted corsets of yesteryear. They eventually dropped to the hips in relaxed, almost baggy styles. By the mid 1920s there was no waistline at all, just 'shift dresses' with straight designs and collars.

- Not only did the waistline disappear, the hemline was taken up dramatically. By 1925 it was popular to have knee-length dresses and skirts—a sacred taboo of the 1800s.

- The zipper appeared in the latter part of the 1920s. It was originally known as a 'locker', and did not receive its current name until 1926. It was not widely used until the late 1930s.

- Cotton and wool were the most common fabrics. Nylon or synthetics had not been invented yet. In the mid-1920s the new material known as rayon was beginning to be used in place of silk.

- The curiosity for exotic arts and culture was fuelled by the discovery of Egyptian King Tutankhamen's tomb in 1922. Egyptian themes appeared in everything from furniture to clothing. Bright fabrics and brilliantly dyed leather were popular.

- In the 1920s, men were still fairly conservative in the fashion stakes. Animal fur became popular later in the decade. Many college boys were wearing the popular raccoon coat.

- The hedonistic and rebellious fashions of the 1920s were quietened by the great stock market crash of 1929. The Great Depression meant that the focus was less on reckless lifestyles and the general tone became far more serious.

Opposite: By the early 1920s, clothes were enormously different from the fashions of the late 1800s.

1920 Gandhi Leads Non-violent Reform

Mohandas Karamchand Gandhi was born in October 1869, in a small town on the west coast of India to a middle-class family. Although his father was involved in government, Gandhi was a very shy student. At 13 he married, as was the custom, a 13-year-old girl, Kasturbai. When Gandhi was 18 he sailed for England to become a barrister. This was frowned upon by his caste, and he was formally excommunicated. During his time in England he was introduced to a wide variety of religious writings and developed an attitude of respect and a burning desire to understand the best in each. When he returned to India he set up practice, which floundered for two years. An opportunity to go to South Africa to represent Dada Abdulla & Co arose and he accepted. This proved to be a decision that would place him in the centre of a political conflict and frame much of his actions and thinking. Very affected by the indignities suffered by fellow Indians living in South Africa, he began to organise his countrymen. What followed was a campaign that would last 20 years, with ultimate victory for the Indians. During his time in South Africa, Gandhi continued to study and pray, moving toward a lifestyle of extreme simplicity. He also developed the Satyagraha—holding to the truth—his ideal for political action, using non-violence. With his rare combination of warmth, love and ability to resist what he considered wrong, he confused his enemies, while winning their admiration.

In 1914 Gandhi returned to India with no possessions and one desire—to serve his fellow Indians. He spent his first year touring India with 'his ears open but his mouth shut'. He then began to help teach the Indian people freedom from fear and challenging them to stand on their own feet. He encouraged a nationwide peaceful protest, which was carried out enthusiastically. As part of a reaction to the protest a British general ordered a massacre of unarmed citizens at Amritsar, putting a wedge between the British and Indians that would not mend. Gandhi attended the Lucknow session of the congress in 1920. There he inspired the politicians to rise up and take action. This provided a major turning point in India's history. From this point on the congress fought for and ultimately won India's independence. Gandhi had touched their souls, and helped them gain their freedom. He won the hearts of India and captured the hearts of people worldwide with his message of love. After returning from a trip to England he said, 'I have been convinced more than ever that human nature is much the same, no matter under what clime it flourished, and that if you approached people with trust and affection you would have tenfold trust and thousand-fold affection returned to you.' With a great ability to love and conviction to see things right, one man changed a nation.

Chronology of Events

2 October 1869 Mohandas Karamchand Gandhi is born at Porbander in Gujarat, India.

1888–90 Gandhi studies law in England.

1893 He goes to South Africa after being employed by a Muslim firm for legal work. He is thrown out of the first-class carriage of the train because he is coloured.

1914 Returning to India at the age of 45, Gandhi attracts worldwide attention by conducting a fast as a form of political protest against the British.

1932 Gandhi begins a 'fast unto death' in protest of British rule in India. He urges boycotts of British goods.

1942 The All-India Congress passes Gandhi's 'Quit India' resolution and Gandhi begins another campaign against the British. He is arrested for the demonstration.

1944 After a decline in his health, Gandhi is released from detention.

1947 India is partitioned and granted independence after 200 years of British rule.

1948 Gandhi is assassinated by Nathuran Godse, a Hindu fanatic, at a prayer meeting. He is 79 years old.

Opposite: Mohandas Karamchand Gandhi, the Indian political leader who led the campaigns of civil disobedience and non-violence in the struggle for Indian independence.

1920 Prohibition

Late in the 19th century in the United States there was a growing concern for the moral fabric of society, mainly generated by the middle class. Chief among their grievances was the condition of the local saloon. Saloons were everywhere. In the competitive market saloons began to offer more than just alcohol; gambling and prostitution were added to draw in customers. Indignation regarding the saloons led to concern about drunkenness, and prohibitionists began to take up the cause. In 1893 the Anti-Saloon League started to gain momentum. Once it joined forces with groups like the Woman's Christian Temperance Union, the movement wielded power. By the end of the 1800s one-third of America lived under a state or local prohibition law. Momentum continued and 5000 prohibitionists marched down Pennsylvania Avenue in 1913, presenting a petition to Congress calling for National Prohibition. The movement even influenced elections, leading to the two-thirds majority in both houses of Congress needed to initiate the 18th Amendment to the Constitution of the United States. This amendment, ratified on 16 January 1919, made malt beverages with an alcohol content greater than 0.5 per cent illegal. It went into effect exactly one year later.

Prohibition did not work well and there were many repercussions. Much of the support given to the movement was withdrawn as people became disillusioned. Breaking the law became commonplace, and bootleggers, speakeasies, gangsters, bathtub gin and payoffs were daily reminders of the corruption Prohibition fostered. The conflict reached deeper than the use or abuse of alcohol. America was in transition in the 1920s, moving from a predominantly rural to urban attitude. Prohibition became a symbol of the dilemma of the day—modern verses traditional principles. Groups formed, committed to repeal Prohibition. The Association Against the Prohibition Amendment (AAPA) was made up of a number of wealthy and prominent Americans. They stated that Prohibition threatened American liberties and was too harsh. They were joined by other organisations like the Women's Organisation for National Prohibition Reform.

The resolve of the conflict came from an unexpected direction—the stock market crash of 1929 and the onset of the Great Depression. The economic disaster made the lure of thousands of jobs in America's brewing industry and revenue from taxation of beer irresistible. Part of Franklin D. Roosevelt's presidential campaign platform, the 'New Deal' called for the repeal of Prohibition. Once elected, Roosevelt pressured Congress into raising the allowable alcohol content to 3.2 per cent, effectively resurrecting the brewing industry and ending Prohibition after 13 years. During the first 24 hours that beer became legal, on 7 April 1933, celebrating Americans consumed more than one million barrels of beer. On 5 December 1933, the 21st Amendment was ratified, officially ending National Prohibition.

Chronology of Events

1917 The Prohibition amendment is introduced, prohibiting the manufacture, sale and transportation of intoxicating beverages throughout the nation.

1919 The Association Against the Prohibition Amendment is formed in Washington, DC. Its backers are wealthy industrialists who fear that the government's loss of beer taxes will cause increased taxation for big industry.

16 January 1920 National Prohibition officially begins. Any beverage containing more than 0.5 per cent of alcohol by volume is considered intoxicating and thus illegal.

1925 In Chicago, mobsters have taken control of many of the city's old breweries, churning out illegal, full-strength beer.

1933 Nine days after taking office, President Roosevelt sends a directive to Congress urging them to support the legalising of beer.

12.01 a.m. 7 April 1933 Beer containing 3.2 per cent alcohol by weight becomes legal for the first time in more than 13 years.

5 December 1933 The Constitution officially repeals National Prohibition.

Opposite: An illegal still formerly used for manufacturing bootleg liquor is put to the test by authorities..

1918 Russian Tsar Nicholas and Family Assassinated

Nicholas Alexandrovich Romanov was crowned in 1896, the last in a 400-year reign of Russian Emperors. Although Nicholas was well educated, his views were narrow and the country was in the midst of great turmoil. Kaiser Wilhelm, Alexandra's first cousin, was relied upon for advice in running the country. Unfortunately, Wilhelm did not have Russia's best interest in mind. In 1904 Russia became involved in a war with Japan. Lasting a year, it caused severe casualties and was extremely costly, taxing the country and causing much unrest. As a result there were widespread peasant revolts, industrial strikes and violence: the Revolution of 1905. Nicholas tried to tighten his hold, but power slipped through his fingers.

In January a peaceful crowd had gathered in front of the Winter Palace to petition the tsar. Troops fired upon the crowd, killing hundreds. The original 'Bloody Sunday' marked the move toward Nicholas's eventual demise. Later that year Nicholas was pressured to allow an indirectly elected national assembly, or Duma. The matter of succession was also a concern to Nicholas. He and Alexandra had five children: Olga, Tatiana, Maria, Anastasia and Alexei. Alexei, their son, had haemophilia, an untreatable and usually deadly disease. Only the royal household knew of his condition. A wandering mystic, Grigori Rasputin, came into the royal family's lives. Alexandra, desperate for her son, sought his help. He seemed to be able help Alexei's internal bleeding. Alexandra was soon dependent upon Rasputin for council and accepting his advice unconditionally.

In 1914 war broke out against Germany and an unprepared Russia incurred huge losses. Nicholas set off for the front to lead the troops, leaving the domestic issues in the hands of Alexandra. With Rasputin pulling her strings, Alexandra's decisions were disastrous. Top leaders resigned from office and were replaced by people of Rasputin's choosing who were shady at best. Eventually, he was murdered by a group of patriot nobles in 1916. The much despised Rasputin was poisoned, shot and thrown into a frozen river and later buried. When the nobles were punished for the murder, public opinion turned against the tsar.

The 'February Revolution' in March 1917 brought Nicholas's abdication of the throne. The family remained at the royal residence until they were moved for their safety to Siberia, in August 1917. They remained in Siberia until the Bolshevik Revolution in November 1918. With the revolutionary forces fearing that Nicholas might be liberated, Nicholas and his family were sentenced to death in a secret meeting. The family and their remaining servants were shot in a cellar on the night of 17 July 1918.

Chronology of Events

1896 Coronation of Nicholas as Tsar of all the Russians.

22 January 1905 'Bloody Sunday.' Marchers are fired on by imperial troops. After internal riots and unrest Nicholas re-establishes his power.

5 September Russia is defeated in the war against Japan.

30 October Tsar proclaims October Manifesto including the establishment of the Duma.

1906 The Duma is created, Russia's first elected parliament.

1907 Russia, England and France form Triple Entente.

1911–13 Series of Balkan wars.

1 August 1914 Germany declares war on Russia.

September 1915 Tsar Nicholas assumes active command of military operations.

16 March 1917 Abdication of Nicholas II and formation of the provisional government.

May 1918 Civil war between the Red Army and White Russians, or anti-communists, who were aided by Britain, France and the United States.

16 July 1918 Tsar Nicholas and his family are executed at Ekaterinburg.

Opposite: Tsar Nicholas II of Russia with his wife, Alexandra Feodorovna, and their five children. All perished at Ekaterinburg in July 1918.

1914 Outbreak of World War I

World War I, which started in 1914, was at first known as the 'European War'. The events leading up to August 1914 were the outcome of years of protracted troubles in Europe. But the 'trigger' was the assassination of Archduke Franz Ferdinand, heir to the throne of the powerful Austro-Hungarian empire, and his wife Sophie. The assassination set off a chain of incidents that led directly to a war, the course of which would shape the rest of the 20th century.

The royal couple were visiting the Bosnian town of Sarajevo on the anniversary of the Battle of Kosovo (1389). The nationalist Black Hand gang planned to ambush them. A bomb was thrown at their car, but it went off under the vehicle. Franz Ferdinand and his wife were unharmed, unlike unlucky passers-by, who the Archduke decided to visit in hospital. On the way, his driver took a wrong turn. By chance, they were spotted by Gavrilo Princip, a young member of the Black Hand. Realising his opportunity, he fired two fateful shots into the vehicle.

Austrian agents quickly pursued the gang and almost immediately Austria planned to attack Serbia, and absorb it into its empire. Germany was Austria's ally at the time and, believing that Russia would not stand by Serbia, offered Austria unconditional support. However, the Austrians opted to present the Serbs with a list of demands. This delay made things awkward for the Russians who made it clear that if war broke out, Serbia would have their support.

France, fearful of letting down its ally, Russia, now entered the fray. On 27 July Serbia responded to Austria's ultimatum, accepting only eight out of the ten Austrian demands. The next day Austria declared war on Serbia. Russia mobilised its forces but did not declare war on Austria. Then on 31 July, Germany mobilised and demanded that Russia cease all military preparations. Receiving no response from the Russians, on 1 August 1914 Germany declared war on Russia. This signalled that a peaceful resolution of the situation was near impossible.

By 3 August war had also been declared on France, the French having refused to comply with Germany's demands regarding the forts along its eastern frontier. When German forces entered Belgium on 4 August, Britain was forced to act. The German attack had broken the treaty guaranteeing Belgian neutrality. Britain declared its own ultimatum: if German forces didn't quit Belgium, Germany would face war with Britain. By midnight no reply had been received and Britain declared war on Germany. Japan sided with Britain almost from the outset, while Turkey sided with the Central Powers (Germany and Austria). By December 1914 the war had spread across Europe, despite the prediction by many that it would be 'over by Christmas'. Over the course of the war, numerous other countries entered the hostilities. When the United States got involved in the conflict in 1917, what was then called the Great War gradually became known as the 'World War'.

Chronology of Events

1908 Russia begins building up its army. A revolution changes the government in Turkey.

1908–09 In the Balkan Crisis Russia says it cannot agree to the plan for Bosnia-Herzegovina coming under Austrian rule but Austria goes ahead with the annexation. Germany backs the Dual Alliance; France and Britain, Russia's allies, are not prepared to go to war over the issue. Russia backs down. Bosnia-Herzegovina remains within the Austrian empire.

1909 With long-standing tensions between Britain and France, Britain and Russia, and Russia and Japan, talk of a war is already widespread.

1911 A German gunboat enters the Moroccan port of Agadir. The French are told it is to protect German interests. Not wanting to miss out in North Africa, Italy attacks Libya, part of the Turkish empire.

1912 The small states of the Balkan peninsula decide to drive the Turks out of their region. In the First Balkan War, the Turks are swiftly defeated.

1913 The Treaty of London is signed in an attempt to resolve the Balkan crisis peacefully. However, by the end of the year, the situation in the Balkans is very unstable. Austria once more threatens to attack Serbia.

1914 Archduke Franz Ferdinand of the Austro-Hungarian empire visits Bosnia with his wife Sophie.

Opposite: Gassed Australian soldiers at an overcrowded aid post near Villers-Bretonneux in May 1918.

1913 The Traffic Light

Long before automobiles became our chief form of transportation, traffic in big cities was heavy and dangerous. Pedestrians, horse and buggies and wagons made police officers a necessity at some intersections. Their full-time job was to direct traffic. A traffic lantern was tried out, installed at the intersection of George and Bridge streets, near London's House of Commons in the late 1800s. This lantern, invented by J.P. Knight, had red and green signals and revolved as the operator controlled a lever. However, it exploded after a few months, injuring the policeman operating it and ending the experiment. The need for a traffic system increased with the advent of the automobile and many had ideas of how to fix the problem.

In 1910 Earnest Sirrine, of Chicago, Illinois developed a traffic system using the non-illuminated words 'stop' and 'proceed'. Two years later in Utah, Lester Wire invented an electric traffic light with red and green lights. A year later, James Hoge combined the two ideas and made a traffic light that had illuminated words 'stop' and 'move'. In 1913 these traffic lights were installed by the American Traffic Signal Company in Cleveland, Ohio. Other versions of the invention popped up all over England and America. A Detroit police officer, William Potts, used railroad lights and about $37 worth of wire and electrical controls, making the first overhanging four-way traffic light. It was installed in 1920 on the corner of Woodward and Michigan Avenue and was manually controlled.

The man credited with developing the technology of the modern traffic signal is Garrett Morgan. His system was an early example of what is known today as Intelligent Transportation Systems. Garrett was a son of former slaves and had not been educated beyond elementary school. After moving from his native Kentucky to Ohio he began to make his fortune. A successful businessman and inventor, Garrett witnessed an accident with a horse-drawn carriage and a car. The accident impressed upon Morgan that something needed to be done to improve traffic safety. He developed the Morgan traffic signal, receiving the US patent on 20 November 1923. He sold his rights for the traffic signal to the General Electric Corporation for $40 000. The Morgan traffic signal was a T-shaped pole that had three positions: stop, go, and an all-directional stop

position. The third position allowed pedestrians to cross streets safely by stopping all other forms of traffic. His design was inexpensive to produce. This signal was used throughout North America until finally replaced by the red, yellow and green light system we use today. Shortly before his death, Morgan was awarded a citation for his traffic signal by the US government.

Chronology of Events

1868 The first traffic lights were installed outside the Houses of Parliament in London. They resembled railway signals of the time, with semaphore arms and red and green gas lamps for night use.

1910 Earnest Sirrine of Chicago, Illinois, patented the first automatic street traffic system. Sirrine's system used the non-illuminated words 'stop' and 'proceed'.

1912 Lester Wire of Salt Lake City, Utah, invented an electric traffic light in 1912 that used red and green lights.

1913 James Hoge patented manually controlled traffic lights, which were installed in Cleveland, Ohio, a year later by the American Traffic Signal Company. Hoge's electric-powered lights used the illuminated words 'stop' and 'move'.

1917 William Ghiglieri of San Francisco, California, patented perhaps the first automatic traffic signal using coloured lights (red and green) in 1917. Ghiglieri's traffic signal had the option of being either manual or automatic.

1920 Around 1920, William Potts a Detroit policeman, invented several automatic electric traffic light systems including an overhanging four-way, red, green and yellow light system. This system was the first to use a yellow light.

1952 The first 'Don't Walk' automatic signs were installed in New York City.

Opposite: A policeman wearing a set of portable traffic lights for effective traffic control.

1913 Stainless Steel Invented

Harry Brearley was born in Sheffield, England, in 1881, the son of a steel melter. At 12 years of age, Brearley left school to start work as a bottle-washer in a chemical laboratory. During the next several years, by private study and night school, he became an expert in the analysis of steel and its production. When he was 26 years old he was put in charge of the Brown–Firth Research Laboratory in Sheffield, which was financed by the two leading steel companies of Sheffield.

In 1912 Brearley was asked to look into a problem a small arms manufacturer was having with the internal diameter of rifle barrels. Due to erosion from combustion, moisture and gases produced during discharge, the guns quickly became less efficient. Brearley made a number of different melts, or samples, by using a crucible process—melting the metals at high temperatures. He tried various combinations of metal to develop a steel alloy that would resist rusting. Previously, others had tried adding chromium to steel, but at low amounts it actually increased the amount of erosion. Brearley noticed that the process did not follow a linear pattern, so he tried a higher percentage of chromium. On 13 August 1913 he tried a mixture containing 0.24 per cent carbon and 12.8 per cent chromium. The first true stainless steel was formed. When he tested the sample he found that it was very resistant to etching (a way of measuring the resilience of the steel using acid). Brearley quickly saw possibilities for application, and set out to market it. He called the metal 'rustless steel' but manufacturers were not so excited. Undaunted, he kept moving ahead and stainless steel soon began to gain popularity.

Elwood Haynes, of Indiana, came up with the same idea at the same time. An amateur scientist and school teacher, he had a small metallurgy shop set up at his home. The two men found out about each other when they applied for patents at the same time. Having seen examples of people fighting over patents, they did not want to end up bankrupt and bitter. Rather than fight they decided to pool their applications and worked together. This decision benefited both. Other types of stainless steel were soon invented. The lightweight, corrosion-free stainless steel quickly became vital in multiple ways, including food preparation, medical instruments and, of course, construction.

Facts and Figures

- Stainless steel is a family of iron-based alloys that must contain at least 10.5 per cent chromium (Cr). The presence of chromium creates an invisible surface film that resists oxidation and makes the material 'passive' or corrosion resistant (i.e. 'stainless'). This family can be simply and logically grouped into five branches. Each of the branches has specific properties and a basic grade or 'type'. In addition, further alloy modifications can be made to 'tailor' the chemical composition to meet the needs of different corrosion conditions, temperature ranges, strength requirements, or to improve weldability, machinability, work hardening and formability. Stainless steel is used in many everyday applications in the home, industry, hospitals, food processing, farming and aerospace. There are currently over 150 different stainless steel grades, but only about 15 or so are commonly used.

- The non-corrosive and rust-resistant properties of stainless steel have made it essential in the preparation, delivery and storage of food. Stainless steel is a standard in modern restaurant kitchens since it can be easily cleaned and dried. Its surface resists oxidation at high temperatures, making the sterilisation of medical instruments possible. Its light weight and durability allowed the development of streamlining in transportation. The sleek design of new trains, planes and automobiles allowed for less wind resistance, sparking a new design movement. Everything from toasters to vacuum cleaners now use stainless steel. The alloy paved the way for modern technology and continues to influence our lives every day.

Opposite: Stainless steel scraps are placed in a furnace for testing.

1912 The *Titanic*

During its time, the *Titanic* was the largest moving object that had ever been built. It was lavishly appointed and rivalled the finest hotel. On 10 April 1912 the SS *Titanic* of the White Star Line set sail from Southampton, England, on her maiden voyage bound for New York. In possibly the most memorable disaster of the 20th century, the ship never reached port and the voyage ended in tragedy with less than a third of those on board living to tell the story. The *Titanic* was more than 264 metres long and 53 metres high from keel to the top of the funnels. Not wanting to clutter the deck or worry passengers unnecessarily, only 20 lifeboats were installed, far less than originally planned. Labelled unsinkable, the *Titanic* was built with a double-plated keel, 16 watertight compartments and watertight doors. It was designed to withstand up to four of the compartments flooding without sinking.

By the fourth day of the voyage, 14 April, the *Titanic* was well into its journey across the North Atlantic. The firm belief that the *Titanic* was unsinkable clouded the crew's judgment. At 11.40 p.m. the lookouts shouted, 'Iceberg right ahead!' The first officer turned the ship, trying to avoid the 22-metre high iceberg just over 100 metres away. A head-on collision was avoided, but the side of the hull scraped along the iceberg for the first 90 metres, causing widespread damage that could not be contained. After examining the damage it was evident that the ship would sink. The captain ordered a CQD (Come Quick, Danger) distress signal to be sent out. Lifeboats were uncovered and people ordered to go to the deck in life jackets. With the ship's band playing on the deck, the lifeboats began loading, women and children first. Many boats were lowered only partially full, people believing the ship would not sink.

However, at 2.20 a.m. on 15 April, the *Titanic* slipped under the ocean. Of the 2200 passengers, only 700 made it into lifeboats although there was room for 400 more. Most of those in the water died of hypothermia in the almost freezing sea. Help did not come quickly. There was a ship less than 30 kilometres from the *Titanic*, but their radio operator had retired for the evening and the *Titanic's* distress signals were never heard. Ninety-two kilometres away the *Carpathia* heard *Titanic's* cry for help and took action. Travelling as fast as they dared through the icy waters, they arrived one hour and 20 minutes after the *Titanic* went under and at 4.10 a.m. began picking up survivors. The *Titanic*, built as a testimony of achievement, instead became a sober memorial to the fragile nature of humankind. As a result of this tragedy many measures to promote safety at sea were established, including laws ensuring there are enough lifeboats to carry everyone on board. Today the memory of the *Titanic* lives on.

Chronology of Events

10 April 1912 The *Titanic* begins her maiden voyage. Estimated total number of passengers on board: 2227.

11.40 p.m. Lookouts see an iceberg dead ahead. After several seconds *Titanic* begins to veer to port, but the iceberg strikes the starboard bow side and brushes along the side of the ship.

12.00 a.m. It is calculated the ship can stay afloat from one to two-and-a-half hours only. *Titanic's* bow begins to sink. Captain Smith orders a CQD distress call for assistance to be sent out over the ship's wireless.

12.05 a.m. 15 April Orders are given to uncover the lifeboats and to get the passengers and crew ready on deck. There is only enough room in the lifeboats for 1178 passengers if every boat is filled.

1.20 a.m. Many of the lifeboats are only half filled and begin to move away from the *Titanic*. Most passengers refuse to believe the ship is sinking.

2.20 a.m. Slowly the remainder of the ship fills with water and again tilts its stern high into the air before slowly sinking into the sea.

4.10 a.m. The first lifeboat is picked up by the *Carpathia*. Ice floats all about the disaster area amid the debris from the *Titanic*.

Opposite: The luxury liner SS Titanic *in dock at Southampton, England, prior to her fateful maiden voyage.*

S.S. TITANIC.

1911 The Chinese Revolution

For over 2000 years China was ruled by emperors. By the end of the 1800s cracks were beginning to show in the empire and the Boxer Uprising broke out at the turn of the century, causing turbulence and unrest. Although the Empress Dowager realised that changes needed to be made and began to do so, the unrest had turned into an uprising. By the time she died in 1908 the old systems that had held China together for so long were beyond repair. The Chinese political system was crumbling. Across China people turned their eyes towards the government. They wanted change, and secret revolutionary groups began to form. Small revolts began to break out. On 10 October, one such revolt sparked the mutiny of troops in Wuchang, the 'Double Ten' rising. This incident ignited revolts across the nation. The 1911 Chinese Revolution had begun.

The leader of the revolution, Sun Yat-Sen, centred his ideals on 'Three Principles of the People'—nationalism, democracy and people's livelihood. Ahead of his time, he wanted a popularly elected republic form of government for China, something that had not existed in Asia. Fifteen of the 24 Chinese provinces declared independence from the Qing Empire by mid-November. Yuan Shih-k'ai, the strongest regional military leader, was appointed as president of the republic and on 15 November he assumed the office of Imperial Premier. The next day he announced his cabinet. Yuan quickly moved to gain control of key government positions, removing or murdering any opposing leadership.

Sun returned from oversees at the end of December, where he had been raising money to support the revolution. On 1 January 1912, Sun was made the provisional president of the new Chinese republic. This did not sit well with Yuan. Yuan demanded that China be governed under a Beijing government, headed by him. Sun graciously stepped down, wisely avoiding a civil war ripping apart the young republic. The last Chinese Emperor, the child Henry Pu Yi, abdicated on 12 February 1912, ending the ancient empire. Yuan was sworn in as the provisional president of the Republic of China on 10 March in Beijing. The fall of the emperor did not end China's troubles. Yuan did not carry out his many promises. A self-centred ruler, his main aspirations revolved around obtaining more power.

Although the government had changed, the class system was little affected and living conditions remained stagnant. Yuan did not stay in power for very long, but he set the pace for the stormy leadership that would plague China for many, many years.

Chronology of Events

1890s Many unhappy Chinese begin forming secret societies. They opposed Western and Christian influences in China. One of the groups is called the Boxers.

1900 The Boxer Rebellion takes place but is squashed by eight different countries.

1905 Many revolutionary groups organise the United League. Sun Yat-Sen becomes their leader.

14 October 1911 Revolution in China begins. The revolutionary movement spreads rapidly through west and southern China.

December 1911 The Republic of China is established with Sun Yat-Sen as temporary president.

12 February 1912 Six-year-old Henry Pu Yi, Manchu emperor, gives up the throne of China.

1913 The Nationalist Party attempts a revolt against Yuan, but fails. Yuan became a dictator and takes steps to establish himself as emperor.

1916 Yuan dies. Power shifts to the war lords in northern China.

1917 Sun Yat-Sen sets up a rival government.

1922 The republic is declared a failure as civil war is rampant throughout the country.

1925 Sun Yat-Sen dies. Chiang Kai Shek becomes the new leader of the nationalists.

Opposite: A prisoner is made ready for execution during the revolution in China.

1911 Structure of the Atom Discovered

The atom was known to exist, but how it was formed and what was inside remained a mystery until Professor Ernest Rutherford opened the door to our understanding. The leading nuclear physicist of our century and one of the most illustrious scientists of all time, Rutherford was an explorer of the vast universe within the atom. At the Manchester Literary and Philosophical Society, on 7 March 1911, Professor Rutherford read his paper entitled, 'The Scattering of the Alpha and Beta Rays and the Structure of the Atom' before the Manchester Literary and Philosophical Society. In the paper, he set forth what he believed was the structure of the atom, a miniature solar system with a nucleus at the centre, a millionth the total size of the atom. He added that the small nucleus contained 99.9 per cent of the mass and was positively charged, balancing the negative electric charge of the electrons that orbit it. What he established in 1911 is valid today. Professor Rutherford had won the Nobel Prize for Chemistry in 1908 for his work, and continued on pioneering further work in the field after his landmark discovery in 1911. Warm and outgoing, many outstanding scientists began their careers under his tutelage.

A forward thinker, Dr Rutherford was disciplined in experimentation, building his ideas on laboratory results. He said his willingness to experiment and ability to find unorthodox solutions came from his upbringing in New Zealand: 'We don't have the money, so we have to think.' Ernest Rutherford was born in rural New Zealand, the fourth of 12 children, on 30 August 1871. He grew up surrounded by skillful, hardworking people. He did very well in school and won several scholarships, which enabled him to continue with his education. After getting his masters degree, and failing for a third time at securing a job as a school teacher, his options were limited. He decided to work towards another scholarship. He did not win the scholarship, but came second. Then he had a break. The winner of the scholarship did not accept it; it was now Rutherford's. With the scholarship he was able to join the research team of J.J. Thompson, the man who discovered the electron. Thompson recognised Rutherford's abilities and encouraged him in the field of nuclear physics. Many of the scientific terms used in the field today were coined by Dr Rutherford: alpha, beta and gamma rays, proton, neutron, half-life, and daughter atoms. Like other pioneers, he opened vast territories to exploration. Our understanding of nature was altered by his study, and the steps he began have changed the world we live in.

The Breakthrough

Rutherford's find came from a very strange experience. Everyone at that time imagined the atom as a 'plum pudding'—that is, it was considered to be roughly the same consistency throughout, with negatively charged electrons scattered about in it like raisins in a pudding. As part of an experiment with X-rays in 1909, Rutherford was shooting a beam of alpha particles (or alpha rays, emitted by the radioactive element radium) at a sheet of gold foil only one-3000th of an inch thick, and tracing the particles' paths. Most of the particles went right through the foil, which would be expected if the atoms in the gold were like a plum pudding. But every now and then, a particle bounced back as though it had hit something solid. After tracing many particles and examining the patterns, Rutherford deduced that the atom must have nearly all its mass, and positive charge, in a central nucleus about 10 000 times smaller than the atom itself. All of the negative charge was held in the electrons, which must orbit the dense nucleus like planets around the Sun.

Opposite: An atom smasher generating an ion beam that is carried below the floor to the target.

1911 South Pole Reached

Born in 1972, Norwegian native Roald Amundsen had a lifelong passion for Arctic exploration. He spent several years exploring the North Pole region, but once learning of Peary's success in reaching the North Pole, his northern interest quickly faded. Amundsen set his sights on the South Pole. Secret preparations began for a South Pole expedition, and only a handful of trusted men were aware of his intentions. On 9 August 1910 Amundsen sailed from Norway. Though provisions for two years in the Arctic and 97 Greenland dogs were on board the *Fram*, none of the crew knew of his plans. They were not told until three hours before sailing on the final leg of the journey. Then Amundsen laid out his plan and asked if they would join him in the historic journey. Many disapproved of this secrecy. It took the *Fram* four months to reach the Ross Ice Shelf, and the Bay of Whales was chosen as a winter head-quarters. The area was the closest starting point to the South Pole and its abundant wildlife provided fresh meat for the men. A base camp, named Framheim, was established three kilometres inland. A flurry of activity followed as the men raced to stock not only the base camp but also three depots, the last within 750 kilometres of the Pole.

When the sun finally set for the long winter, on 21 April, the men began their winter sojourn. Wisely, Amundsen structured the time with specific meal times, work sched-ules and tasks, and the winter passed quickly. Even though the sun began to peak over the horizon by 24 August, two months passed before the weather cleared enough for a Pole bid. During the first attempt, the group was forced back after several days due to extremely cold weather. The second attempt would be more carefully planned and five men finally departed on 20 October. Amundsen and four others departed with four sleds, each pulled by 13 dogs. By 11 November they saw the peaks of mountains. Amundsen named them Queen Maud's Range, after the Queen of Norway. After negotiating the mountains their final chal-lenge was 'The Devil's Ballroom'—a nasty plateau covered with a thin crust of snow hiding many dangerous crevasses. On 8 December they surpassed Shackleton's record, just 150 kilometres from the Pole.

Finally, at 3.00 p.m. on Friday 14 December 1911, they reached the South Pole. Together, the men planted the Norwegian flag. They returned to Framheim successful, on 25 January 1912. Their journey lasted 99 days, and covered 2976 kilometres. Amundsen's planning had been masterful. Tragically, 39 days after their success, explorer Robert Scott and his party reached the South Pole. Not yet aware of Amundsen's success, they were surprised to find a tent and the Norwegian flag. It broke their hearts. Already tired and low on food, the five men died on their return trip, just 17 kilometres from food and shelter. Amundsen continued his exploration of Arctic regions after his South Pole victory. He disappeared without a trace in 1928 while participating in a rescue operation.

Chronology of Events

1902 In November Robert Scott, Edward Wilson and Ernest Shackleton depart for the South Pole. Leaving McMurdo Sound heading south across the Ross Ice Shelf, two months later they find themselves at 82° South suffering from snow blindness and scurvy. Forced to return home, they nonetheless cover 4960 kilometres.

October 1908 Explorers Ernest Shackleton, Frank Wild, Eric Marshall and Jameson Adams attempt to reach the South Pole. Within 30 days they have surpassed Scott's effort in 1903. Reaching within 155 kilometres, the group is severely ill and undernourished requiring them to abandon their attempt on the pole.

January 1909 Edgeworth David, Douglas Mawson and Alistair McKay reach the South Pole.

November 1911 The first Japanese Antarctic Expedition sails south led by Lieutenant Nobu Shirase and lands at the Bay of Whales.

14 December 1911 Norwegian Roald Amundsen and four team members reach the South Pole. Letters are left for Scott, a Norwegian flag planted and then they return to the Bay of Whales.

18 January 1912 Robert Scott, Edward Wilson, Edgar Evans and Lawrence Oates reach the South Pole.

Opposite: Norwegian native Roald Amundsen had a lifelong passion for Arctic exploration.

1909 Peary Reaches North Pole

Robert Peary graduated from Bowdoin College in 1877 and a few years later entered the US Navy Corps of Civil Engineers as a lieutenant. He worked to survey Nicaragua, endeavouring to find a canal route. His proposal was well received, but the canal later ended up being built through Panama. During his time in Nicaragua he met and hired Matthew Henson, a highly skilled man who would become Peary's most trusted associate in later adventures. In 1988 Peary married Josephine Diebitsch, who shared his love for exploration. While accompanying Robert in Greenland, Josephine delivered their first child, the farthest north any white child had ever been born. Peary led four expeditions to northern Greenland and proved that Greenland was an island rather than a continent. He also showed that Greenland was not the place to begin from to reach the North Pole.

While in Greenland, however, the idea of reaching the North Pole began to gel in Peary's heart. Although 756 people had died in the attempt to reach the Pole, Peary and Henson prepared to succeed. Peary's motto became 'I shall find a way or make one', and is the hallmark of what transpired. They spent 18 years working towards their goal. Henson proved to be vital in the task, his expertise and insight adding valuable support. Not daunted by setbacks, the two consistently moved ahead, building on their experiences and their failures. They worked closely with the Inuit, learning how they survived and travelled. Peary planned the expedition with military precision and calculated movement. He loaded the *Roosevelt* with an entire village of Inuit and hundreds of dogs. The ship, an icebreaker, was designed for arctic travel. They travelled through the northern waters until they reached Ellesmere Island and there they waited until the winter ice surrounded them. Peary put everyone to work preparing the needed supplies, dispelling the tedium of the long wait. Sleds were made as well as fur coats and dog harnesses fashioned from walrus hides.

On 1 March 1909, 24 men and more than 130 dogs set off on the long trek north. Peary had five teams set up. Each took turns 'pioneering' the route, breaking trails and making a base camp for the others that followed. In this leapfrog fashion they made their way north. As their supplies were used up, one team at a time was sent back while the others moved on. Finally they were within 200 kilometres of the Pole. Peary, Henson and four Inuits with light loads and the best dogs dashed toward the Pole. The weather was favourable and they were able to travel 40 kilometres a day.

On 6 April they reached the North Pole. They stayed through the next day, rechecking their coordinates to make sure they were at the right place, and then started their long trip back. They raced toward safety, acutely aware of their precarious position, hundreds of kilometres in the midst of the Arctic Ocean. The weather held and they made it back safely. Five months after their success they were finally able to send this message to the world: 'Stars and Stripes nailed to the North Pole–Peary'.

Chronology of Events

1897 Salomon A. Andrée from Sweden tries balloon flight over the North Pole; party perishes.

1903–06 Roald Amundsen from Norway traverses the Northwest Passage and fixes the approximate location of the North Pole.

1908 American Frederic A. Cook claims he reached the North Pole but later his story is discredited.

1909 Robert E. Peary reaches the North Pole.

1926 Roald Amundsen, Lincoln Ellsworth and Umberto Nobile are the first to fly over the North Pole, travelling in an airship.

1928 George Hubert Wilkins from Australia is the first to fly over the North Pole in an aeroplane.

1951 Charles Blair (US) makes the first solo flight over the North Pole.

Opposite: Robert E. Peary with his sled dogs after returning from the North Pole expedition on 5 September 1909.

1906 San Francisco Earthquake

In the pre-dawn hours of Wednesday 18 April 1906, San Francisco slept, unaware that one of the largest earthquakes in history was about to occur. At 5.12 a.m. a foreshock was felt throughout the San Francisco area. For about 20 seconds things were still—then the great earthquake erupted. The terrible shaking rolled the earth like waves on the sea. Buildings shook and chimneys toppled. The quake lasted for a total of 57 seconds and measured 8.3 on the Richter scale. The shock of the earthquake ran from Coos Bay, Oregon, down the west coast to Los Angeles, and as far east as central Nevada. Two of the world's largest tectonic plates, the North American and the Pacific, had snapped past each other. The ground was ripped open for more than 432 kilometres along the San Andreas rift and the shock wave moved through the ground at more than 11 200 kilometres per hour. Along the fault line buildings were destroyed and trees uprooted.

San Francisco, just 48 kilometres south of the epicentre, was hard hit. In the city the destruction had just begun. During the quake many gas connections were broken, electric wires crossed, chimneys and stoves overturned, and lanterns tipped over. Over 50 fires broke out across the city, and while most were quickly extinguished, some raged out of control. The underground pipes that carried the city's water from reservoirs 30 kilometres away had been badly damaged, and 180 million litres of water leaked into the ground leaving the firemen precious little water to work with. By 7.00 a.m. thousands of people were crowding the streets. The army began to arrive to maintain control in the panic-stricken streets, with orders to shoot to kill any looters. At 8.14 that morning a major aftershock once again shook the city. Many of the damaged buildings collapsed.

Throughout the day there were 27 separate quakes. By nightfall, more than a quarter of the city's inhabitants were homeless and the fires continued to burn. By Thursday most of the fires were under control, but some were not extinguished until Saturday. A fire in the Mission district was finally stopped by 3000 volunteers and a few firemen who fought the blaze with brooms and knapsacks. It finally rained on the Saturday night.

The downtown area was completely ruined. Early estimates of the death toll and damage to the city did not accurately reflect the grim numbers. About 3000 people died in the four days. More than 490 city blocks—1145 hectares—were lost, including 250 000 homes, 80 churches and 30 schools. The damage tally came to almost half a billion dollars—a massive amount in 1906. The only thing not shaken was the citizens' resolve. Just five days after the earthquake the governor told a newspaper reporter, 'The work of rebuilding San Francisco has commenced, and I expect to see the great metropolis replaced on a much grander scale than ever before.' It was time to rebuild.

Facts and Figures

- The earthquake shock was felt from Coos Bay, Oregon, to Los Angeles, and as far east as central Nevada. The region of destructive effect extended from the southern part of Fresno County to Eureka, about 650 kilometres, and for a distance of 40 to 50 kilometres on either side of the fault zone. Of course, all structures standing on or crossing the rift were destroyed or badly damaged.

- After the San Francisco earthquake of 1906, many building requirements were changed in the area. The city was completely redesigned and many precautions were put in place. However, one of the most world-changing effects of the quake was the discovery of earthquake faults, or fractures in the rocks of the Earth's crust. This discovery was made by American seismologist Harry Fielding Reid in 1911. Before his work, it had long been assumed that faults were created by earthquakes. Reid realised that the opposite was true: pressures within a fault, as two plates come together, cause quakes.

- Due to the instability of the San Andreas Fault, many seismologists have theorised for years that a massive quake is due again in the San Francisco area. One such quake occurred in 1989, during the height of evening rush hour and as baseball fans packed Candlestick Park during the World Series. This quake measured 7.1 on the Richter scale. Seventy deaths were reported, and many areas of the city, particularly the Marina district, were hit hard.

Opposite: San Francisco, just 48 kilometres south of the epicentre, was hit hard. In the city, the destruction had just begun.

1905 Einstein's Special Theory of Relativity

Albert Einstein shook the foundations of physics in 1905 by introducing his Special Theory of Relativity. Newton, the developer of modern physics, had defined the behaviour of the entire cosmos by using mathematics, but 26-year-old Einstein contested Newton and redefined physics. By the time he was 10 Einstein was reading all he could about science. In 1894 his family moved to Italy, but Albert stayed in Munich to finish his high school degree in electrical engineering. Failing his exams, he moved to Milan to rejoin his family. He graduated from high school in 1897 at the age of 17. Albert enrolled in the Federal Polytechnic in Zurich. The next year, in 1899, he met and fell in love with a fellow classmate, Mileva Maric. He graduated from the school in 1901 and received a teaching diploma for physics and mathematics. Unfortunately, while his classmates secured posts, Einstein continued job hunting. His flat feet and varicose veins kept him out of the army.

After a few stints at temporary teaching posts with no long-term prospects, he accepted a job working as a technical assistant in the Swiss Patent Office in 1902 and in January 1903 Albert and Mileva were married. Their first son, Hans Albert, was born in 1904. While working at the patent office, Albert started to write theoretical physics publications. His 1905 thesis, 'On a new determination of molecular dimensions', earned him a doctor's degree. The year 1905 was later called by historians the *annus mirabilis*, the miracle year. Einstein produced an unprecedented amount of new material.

One of the papers, submitted on 30 June, was called, 'On the electrodynamics of moving bodies'. In this paper he proposed what is now commonly called the Special Theory of Relativity. He wrote the paper in an attempt to reconcile the laws of the electromagnetic field with the laws of mechanics. No part of what he set forth was uniquely new, but his melding of the concepts was revolutionary. The two parts of his theory state that the laws of physics and speed of light are consistent no matter what frame of reference. He later added that mass and energy were equivalent and that the mass of electrons increase as the velocity of the electrons approaches the velocity of light. By the end of 1905 he elegantly framed his theory: $E=mc^2$. An innovative thinker, Einstein had an innate understanding of physics, saw the problems therein, and set out to solve them. In doing so he opened a new era in physical understanding.

Chronology of Events

1879 Albert Einstein is born in Germany.

1905 Einstein's Special Theory of Relativity is born. At age 26, he applies his theory to mass and energy and formulates the equation $E=mc^2$. He publishes four papers: 'Brownian motion', 'the photoelectric effect', 'finding the size of molecules', and 'relativity'.

1907 Einstein begins applying the laws of gravity to his Special Theory of Relativity.

1913 Einstein works on his new Theory of Gravity.

1914 Einstein becomes director of the Kaiser Wilhelm Institute in Berlin and professor of theoretical physics at the University of Berlin.

1915 Einstein completes the General Theory of Relativity.

1919 A solar eclipse proves that Einstein's General Theory of Relativity works.

1922 Einstein is awarded the Nobel Prize in Physics for 1921.

1932 Einstein is 53 and at the height of his fame. Identified as a Jew, he begins to feel the heat of Nazi Germany.

1933 Albert and his second wife Elsa set sail for the United States. They settle in Princeton, New Jersey, where he assumes a post at the Institute for Advanced Study.

1940 Einstein becomes an American citizen but retains Swiss citizenship.

1955 Einstein dies of heart failure on 16 April.

Opposite: At the beginning of World War II, Einstein wrote his famous letter to President Franklin D. Roosevelt warning him of the possibility of Germany building an atomic bomb and urging nuclear research.

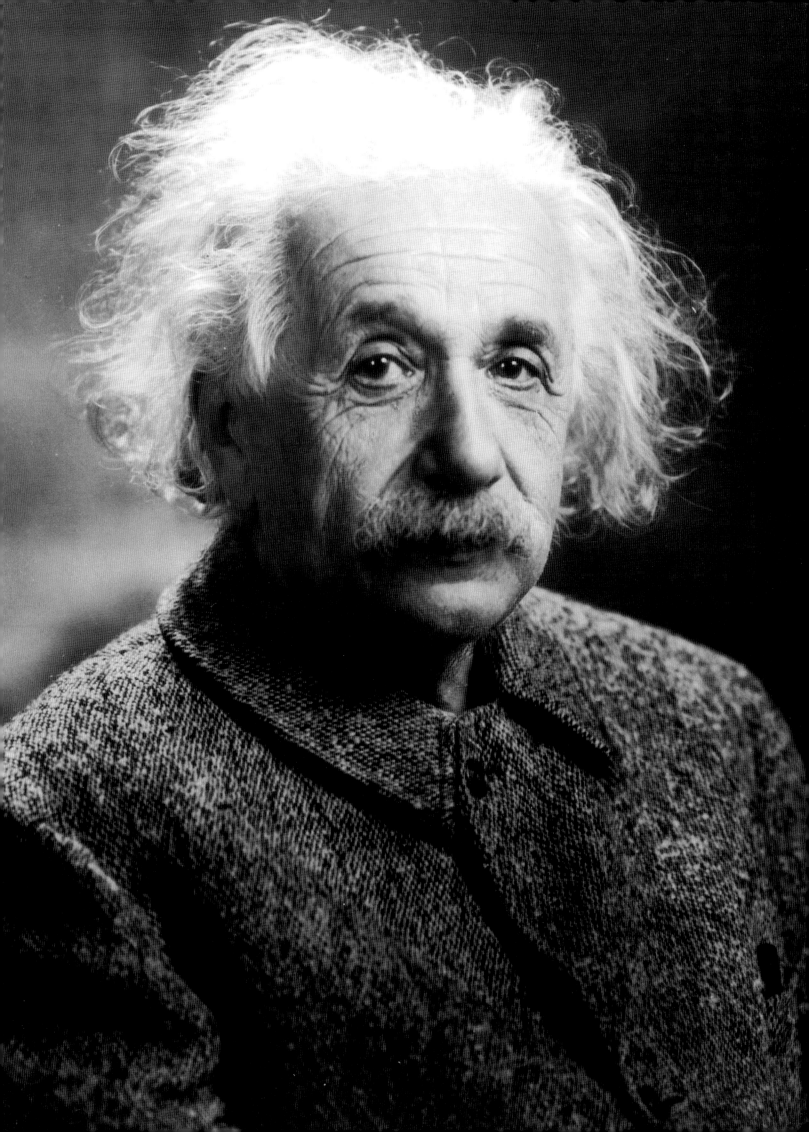

1903 Wright Brothers Introduce Flight

Flight has always captured man's imagination and for centuries many scientists and engineers worked to unlock the secret of flight, with little advancement. However, by the late 1800s flying had become more than a fantasy. Two unlikely figures emerged, a couple of brothers who ran a bicycle shop in Dayton, Ohio, managed to unlock the doors that no one else could. Orville and Wilbur Wright were ultimately successful due to clear thinking and hard work. They researched tirelessly; in 1899 they wrote to the Smithsonian Institute for information on flight experiments and began corresponding with researchers in the field. They read books and studied notes, experiments, successes, failures—and birds. Though lacking a scientific background, they had an ability to weed out useless information and recognise the potentially useful.

By 1900, they were ready to put their research to test. A 25-kilogram biplane glider with a 5-metre wingspan was brought to the coast of Kitty Hawk, North Carolina. They chose Kitty Hawk because of the abundant wind, soft sand, hills to launch off and remote location as publicity was not wanted. They were successful in their testing and moved to build the next glider. In 1901 the brothers again went to the coast for testing. This time they were disappointed. Wilbur wrote:

When we left Kitty Hawk at the end of 1901, we doubted that we would ever resume our experiments. When we looked at the time and money which we had expended, and considered the progress made and the distance yet to go, we considered our experiments a failure. At this time I made the prediction that men would sometime fly, but that it would not be within our lifetime.

Instead of quitting, they conquered. By systematically testing individual components and with the help of a wind tunnel, they were able to solve problems in calculations and made great advancements. Their elegant 1902 glider solved the basic problems of flight: lift and control. They were now ready to add propulsion. Months were spent studying propeller design, again using a wind tunnel. A special four-cylinder engine was designed and built in their shop. They went back to Kitty Hawk confident of success.

On 17 December 1903, the Wright brothers made the first successful powered, piloted flight. Soaring at an altitude of three metres, *The Flyer* covered a distance of 36 metres in a flight that lasted 12 seconds. Not only did they develop an aeroplane, they also had to learn how to fly it. With their breakthrough, innovations in flight raced ahead. In 1904 *The Flyer II* was airborne for more than five minutes. By 1907 a helicopter got off the ground for a few seconds and in 1936 the first practical helicopter was introduced. Commercial trans-Atlantic flights began in the 1930s, and in 1949, by way of midair refuels, Captain James Gallagher and his crew flew *Lucky Lady II* non-stop around the world.

Chronology of Events

1903 Orville Wright's first flight on 17 December lasted just 12 seconds and covered a distance of about 36 metres, a measurement shorter than the wingspan of many modern airliners.

1911 An airmail service makes its debut with irregular trips between cities in England.

1914–18 During World War I planes were used in pivotal bombing missions and aerial combat encounters between 'flying aces'. Commercial aviation begins in January 1914.

1947 Chuck Yeager exceeds the speed of sound, creating a sonic boom and remaining in control as the plane's speed neared Mach 1, something many thought was impossible.

1952 The jet engine debuts in commercial aviation and six years later, Pan Am inaugurates the Boeing 707 jet service, cutting flight durations in half.

1976 The Concorde embarks on its first commercial flight from Paris to London to New York, crossing the Atlantic in three hours and enabling passengers from Europe to beat the time difference and land in New York before their local departure time.

1987 Records break as it is announced that one billion passengers are now flying annually.

Opposite: The Flyer *at Kitty Hawk in 1903.*

1903 The First Silent Movie

The first silent movie, *The Great Train Robbery*, filmed in 1903, was directed and photographed by Edwin S. Porter. A forward thinker who worked for several years with Thomas Edison, Porter was called 'The father of American story film'. The cast included Gilbert 'Broncho Billy' Anderson, Justus Barnes, Walter Cameron and George Anderson—no actors of note, because there was no media to advertise them. With a running time of about 12 minutes, the movie consisted of just 14 scenes.

Based on a story by Scott Marble, it was a western filmed at Edison's New York studio, Essex County Park in New Jersey. Obviously, by today's standards the film was rough, but it was a milestone, changing the picture industry. The movie was also very innovative for its time, initiating many precedents. For example, there was camera movement, pan shots and location shooting. The editing was cutting edge for 1903. It was the first time a body (dummy) was thrown off a moving train and the first time someone was forced to dance while being shot at on film. This first action film included fights, blasts, chase scenes—and the bad guys receiving their dues in the end. The last scene in the movie was a shot, literally. A gun pointed at the camera was fired. This last shot was added to the film, designed to startle the audience—and it worked. Many of the audiences, never having seen a movie before, ran screaming from the theatre, believing they were seeing an actual hold-up. The description given by Edison's studio read:

This sensational and highly tragic subject will certainly make a decided hit, whenever shown. In every respect we consider it absolutely the superior of any moving picture ever made. It has been posed and acted in faithful duplication of the genuine hold-ups, made famous by various outlaw bands in the far West, and only recently in the East has been shocked by several crimes of the frontier order, which in fact will increase the popular interest in this great headline attraction.

The one-reel film travelled around the country and proved to be very popular. It made enough money to encourage the development of studios to meet the demand to the new form of entertainment. *The Great Train Robbery* was the first in a long line of westerns, and created an entirely new source of entertainment that would soon dominate the later half of the century.

Chronology of Events

1870s Movement of a horse is the first action photography on glass plates.

1882 Frenchman Etienne-Jules Marey designs a camera to record 12 separate images on a single strip of film. In 1888 he designs the first flexible film.

1889 Eastman Kodak introduces a celluloid flexible film base.

Late 1880s Edison commissions William Dickson to build a film camera. Dickson develops the Kinetograph which couples recorded images with phonographic sound.

1895 Louis and Auguste Lumiere present the first film projector, the Cinematographe.

1903 The world's first silent movie, *The Great Train Robbery*, premieres.

1904 Frenchman Eugene Lauste records sound onto a piece of photographic film.

1907–13 Various film and sound inventions include the Vivaphone, Synchroscope, the Cameraphone and the Cinephone.

October 1927 *The Jazz Singer*, featuring Al Jolson, is released by Warner Bros. Not an immediate hit in New York, it gains long-lasting fame when it moves into America's heartland. It is rebooked in 1928 in New York and grosses US$100000 a week.

May 1927 Fox Film Corporation works with a new AT&T development—sound on film. Fox uses this system to produce newsreels which would play prior to feature films at theatres. The first big publicity coup is the flight of Charles Lindbergh across the Atlantic.

Opposite: A scene from the silent film The Great Train Robbery, *directed by Edwin S. Porter.*

1902 Women Granted Equal Rights

After centuries of injustice, New Zealand was the first country to give its women the right to vote. Not far behind was Australia, when in 1902 women were allowed to vote for federal government. Finland led all Europe in May 1906. Soon women everywhere were allowed these basic civil rights, marking the end of a long, 20-year suffrage campaign. New Zealand, with a population of half a million, had shown the way to the rest of the Western world.

The biggest contributing factor for Finnish women gaining the right to vote came from the universal lack of rights. Finland was a prosperous, agricultural-based country with a growing culture and excellent education, but it was not an independent state. They were under Russian rule. Surprisingly, the heart of the conflict was not with the Russian empire but with Sweden. Much of Finland's governmental structure had been set up by Sweden, which was Finland's overlord before Russia. The time had come to break down the strict class divisions. Men and women fought together for the right to voice their opinions. As the movement became organised Russia became nervous. Instead of melding into a Russian state, Finland was becoming more of its own country.

Pressure was applied to quell the uprisings and a full-blown social revolution began. Everything was called into question. The right to vote, the class system, and political representation were all held up for examination. It was not a battle of women against men but the majority of the population suffering under a class-based political system, fighting the elite few. Working-class men and women joined together to obtain the reforms. There were a few small women's suffrage groups comprised mainly of the middle and upper class, however the large national movement was not based on gender but, rather, the obtaining of universal and equal voting rights by all. Opponents endeavoured to break the movement from within by dividing the reformers. Questions were raised and suspicions fostered. The fight for rights had formed alliances that crossed the lines of classes. The women's suffrage groups from the upper classes were used as a wedge, and the resistance began to stall.

Eventually the cause did move ahead, pushed forward by Russia. Internal turmoil within the Russian empire forced more of a focus at home, loosening the grip on Finland. Finland breathed freely and the political lines did not seem to matter, everyone wanted reform and independence. A new constitution was drawn up, instituting a parliament elected by all. The document was sent to Russia and the Emperor, rather than fostering another battle, agreed to give them what they wanted. Finland's bold step forward in woman's rights resulted from striving together to reach a worthwhile goal—everyone won.

Chronology of Events

1872 Susan B. Anthony is the first US woman to register to vote; subsequently she becomes the first to make a ballot, for which she is arrested.

1893 New Zealand is the first country in the world in which women gain the right to vote.

1902 Australian women get the right to vote in all federal elections. Vida Goldstein runs for the senate, becoming the first woman in the British empire to run for a national office.

1906–07 Finland becomes the first European nation to give women the vote, and 19 women are elected to the new 200-person Finnish parliament.

1917 After the Russian Revolution Soviet women get the vote.

1920 With the passage of the 19th Amendment to the US Constitution, American women get the vote.

1928 Women aged 21 to 29 in Britain are able to vote for the first time, as women's suffrage is reduced from age 30 to 21.

1946 Women vote and stand for election to the House of Representatives for the first time in Japan. Of the 79 women running for office, 39 are elected.

Opposite: Miss Alice Paul, an American suffragette, broke up a Guildhall meeting by shouting 'Vote for women' through a skylight.

1901 Queen Victoria Dies

At the time of Queen Victoria's death it was said that the sun never set on the British empire. During her almost 64-year reign, Great Britain enjoyed a time of industrial growth and relative peace. At 82 years of age, on 22 January 1901, Victoria died at Osborne House on the Isle of Wight, with her eldest son at her side.

Victoria was born on 24 May 1819, the only child of the Duke of Kent and Princess Victoria of Saxe-Coburg-Gotha. Her father died when she was eight months old, and Victoria grew up in seclusion at Kensington Palace. After her Uncle William IV died, Victoria took the throne, becoming queen on 20 June 1837. Just 18 years old, she was small, but carried herself well. Her voice had a silvery quality that remained her entire life. Three years later she fell in love with and married Prince Albert of Saxe-Coburg, her cousin. Albert was a steadying figure for Victoria and the two loved each other dearly. Together they produced nine children—four sons and five daughters. As Victoria became a mother, Albert took on more of the role of overseer of the country. Osborne House became their family retreat in 1845 and was a refuge from the rigid formality of London, a place their family could call home.

Albert died of typhoid fever in 1861 while at Windsor Castle and Victoria withdrew from public life as she mourned her husband. For more than a decade she was seldom seen, and her popularity declined. Finally, in the late 1870s, she began to return to public life and regained her popularity. In 1887 Queen Victoria's golden and diamond jubilee were national celebrations. Many Britons had spent their entire lives under Victoria's reign, and she remained popular until her death. The kingdom enjoyed unusual peace during this time.

Before Victoria died she was known as 'the grandmother of Europe'. She was the longest reigning monarch and she had 37 great-grandchildren at the time of her death. Victoria's reign was a paradox. She had no interest in social issues, but the 1880s were a time of reform. She resisted change, but mechanical and technological advances reshaped Europe. She wanted political power, but ultimately set the standard of a ceremonial monarchy. And, although she did not particularly care for children, she had nine who were perhaps her greatest legacy.

At 82 years old, Queen Victoria died leaving her son, the Prince of Wales, to be King Edward VII. Victoria was buried on 4 February 1901 beside her beloved Prince Albert. Although she had spent the years since her husband's death wearing black, she requested a white funeral. The Royal Mausoleum at Frogmore, in Windsor, was to be the final resting place for Victoria and Albert. Inscribed above the door are Victoria's words: 'Farewell best beloved, here at last I shall rest with thee, with thee in Christ I shall rise again.'

Facts and Figures

- Queen Victoria's reign until 1901 dominated the rest of the 20th century through the many changes that were made during her sovereignty.

- These changes included the move to a more constitutional monarchy during the 1840s and 1850s as well as massive industrial transformations. A people's charter was published on 1 May 1838 which constituted six demands: a demand for universal manhood suffrage; secret ballot; annual parliamentary elections; equal electoral districts; the abolition of the property qualification for MPs; and the payment of MPs (which would allow working-class representatives to sit in parliament). The charter was continually rejected, but the people persisted for decades until eventually by 1999 all but the annual election of MPs are accepted parts of the British constitution.

- During Victoria's reign, the revolution in industrial practices continued to change British life. With it came increased urbanisation and a burgeoning communications network. The industrial expansion also brought wealth—and ultimately peace—in the 19th century. Britain became a champion of free trade across her massive empire. Both industrialisation and trade were glorified in the Great Exhibitions; however by the turn of the century, Britain's industrial advantage was being challenged successfully by other nations such as the USA and Germany.

- During Queen Victoria's reign, Britain was one of the most powerful and wealthy countries in the world, providing perfect foundations for the empire's move into the turbulent 20th century.

Opposite: Queen Victoria's reign dominated the rest of the century through the many changes that were made during her sovereignty.

Index